Intoxication in Mythology

Intoxication in Mythology

*A Worldwide Dictionary of Gods,
Rites, Intoxicants and Places*

Ernest L. Abel

McFarland & Company, Inc., Publishers
Jefferson, North Carolina, and London

LIBRARY OF CONGRESS ONLINE CATALOG

Abel, Ernest L., 1943–
    Intoxication in mythology : a worldwide dictionary of gods, rites, intoxicants and places / Ernest L. Abel.
        p.   cm.
    Includes bibliographical references and index.

    ISBN-13: 978-0-7864-2477-1
    ISBN-10: 0-7864-2477-X
    (softcover : 50# alkaline paper) ∞

    1. Mythology—Dictionaries.   2. Alcoholic beverages—Religious aspects—Dictionaries.   I. Title.
    BL303 .A24   2006
    394.1'4—dc22   2006026548

British Library cataloguing data are available

Cover image ©2006 Digital Vision

Manufactured in the United States of America

McFarland & Company, Inc., Publishers
    Box 611, Jefferson, North Carolina 28640
    www.mcfarlandpub.com

To my personal intoxicants: my wife, Barbara;
my mother, Rose, and my father, Jack;
my children, Jason and Leah, Rebecca and David;
and my grandchildren: Jack, Elliot, and Emily

Table of Contents

Preface

Stories about intoxicating elixirs that imbue wisdom, alter the course of history, liberate the soul, or confer immortality are common in world mythology. The ancient people of India believed that *amrta*, their divine elixir, was created when the gods of good and evil liberated it from the primordial ocean and then fought with one another for its control. *Ambrosia*, the intoxicating drink of the Greek gods, is etymologically related to *amrta;* both terms literally mean "nondeath," immortality. Norse myths tell of a super being named Kvasir, from whose blood an intoxicating "mead of inspiration," which conferred ineffable wisdom, was created.

Stories from other parts of the world contend that intoxicants contain the earthly embodiment of a divinity or spirit. Aztec myths describe intoxication from peyote, datura, or morning glory seeds, the god within those plants "taking possession of" or "coming out in" their users.

The ancient Greeks likewise believed that when they became drunk on wine, they imbibed the spirit of their wine god, Dionysus, who then took "possession" of them. For many Greeks, possession by Dionysus was more than simply intoxication, an altered state of consciousness in which their minds were able to forget their daily cares for a time. For some people it was a liberation of an entirely different dimension. When a god like Dionysus took possession of these people, possession meant ecstasy, a freeing of the soul from its material body, enabling it to commune with that god.

Communion with the spiritual world by way of wine and other intoxicants occurs in other world mythologies as well. In Dionysus' case, that communion held out the possibility of life after death. This was because Dionysus was also an agricultural deity who died and was reborn each year. For those who participated in his "Mysteries"—one of several religious cults promising immortality through resurrection—his wine-induced ecstasy enabled their souls not only to commune with his

1

immortal spirit, but also to become one with him. In this state of "enthusiasm," they believed they could attain his ineffable wisdom and their own immortality through the salvation he represented. Myths about Dionysus are especially noteworthy for this archetypal theme of soul fusion and spiritual immortality.

There is in fact no society in the world where some kind of consciousness altering substance hasn't been used. Except for a few groups, like the Arctic Inuit, who inhabit places where the plant sources for these substances can't grow, it has been that way forever. Some experts on the subject of intoxicants, most notably Dr. Andrew T. Weil, contend that we have an "innate, normal drive" to alter our consciousness periodically that is analogous to our other basic physical needs. For most people, this "drive" may simply be a yen for novelty. But for some, an altered consciousness was (and still is) the prelude to communing with the gods who they believed created and ruled the world; hence the universality of intoxicants in world mythology. Writing in the prestigious journal *American Scholar*, Mary Bernard asks rhetorically what is the more likely scenario: (a) Humans spontaneously came up with the idea of a disembodied soul which, when liberated from the restrictions of time and space, was able to travel to another realm of existence where it could experience eternal bliss in the presence of supernatural beings and commune with them; or (b) humans accidentally discovered intoxicating plants that made them euphoric and by coincidence, also produced these ideas?

World mythology, the prehistorical record of mankind's innermost thoughts, is solidly on the side of the second possibility. Ancient myths are always about beginnings; they are sacred traditional narratives describing how things came into being in primordial time. They tell, among other things, how the world and its inhabitants were created; they explain the origins of life and death; the changing of the seasons; the nature of the gods that rule the world; the beginnings of culture; and what happens to people after they die. Thematic similarities in these myths imply either an original story, an Ur-myth, which through geographical spreading gave rise to different variations, or to some common human experience. Most scholars of myth believe the latter is more probable.

This dictionary provides numerous points of entry into the world's mythologies in which intoxicants have an important role in accounting for why the world is the way it is. While scholars continue to argue over the distinguishing features of myth as opposed to legend and folklore, this reference work makes no such distinctions; the common element uniting these stories is that they are traditional, anonymous stories that explain the origins of a particular intoxicant or how that intoxicant was involved in creating a particular culture. Surprisingly, these myths have not been previously collected in one book. Instead, they exist in various texts, discussed in the narrow context of a particular set of cultural myths, or occasionally when a plant with intoxicating effects is mentioned.

In many instances, these myths are very elaborate and contain additional themes that do not involve intoxicants. Those have been rewritten here to exclude the other parts of the story so as to maintain the focus on the main theme of intoxication. In instances where there were several variants of the same myth, the different versions have been included if pertinent to the overarching theme. In each case I have endeavored to remain loyal to the source material.

Selection Criteria: There are a great many plants with intoxicating properties that are listed in excellent books such as Richard Schultes' *Plants of the Gods*, but which have not been included in this book. For inclusion, the intoxicant had to have been mentioned in a myth. Secondly, to be included, an intoxicant had to have a connection with the supernatural; either it is considered a gift from the gods, contains their spirits, or liberates the soul so that it can commune with the supernatural. This excluded substances such as qat, betel nuts or coffee. Likewise, elements of stories about plants such as mandrake that have been used to influence romantic attraction have not been included. These "aphrodisiacs" may also cause an intoxication called love, but those who use them have no expectation or perception of communing with the supernatural world. For the same reasons neither intoxicants derived from animals nor synthetic intoxicants are included.

Organization: The entries in this dictionary are arranged alphabetically without regard to category (e.g., gods, intoxicants, places, rites). With the exception of explanatory terms, entries are followed by the identity of the culture from which the myth came and the name of the intoxicant featured in the myth. Entries for intoxicants contain information about plant sources and pharmacological effects. Sources for each entry appear at the end of that entry. Cross-references to related entries, explanatory terms, and concepts are indicated in **bold**.

Two appendices at the end of the book contain a grouping of the entries by way of general category (Appendix 1) and by geography (Appendix 2). A list of the sources used in compiling this book follows the appendices.

The Dictionary

Acan. Mayan god of intoxicating drinks, especially a fermented honey called **balche**. The name means "bellowing," and refers to the loud noises and foolish behavior caused by balche. (Thompson, 311)

Acetes *see* **Dionysus.**

Acolhua. A Mayan **pulque** god about whom nothing is known other than his name. (Anderson and Dibble, 2:51; I. Nicholson, 167; Bancroft, 3:418)

Admetus. In Greek mythology, the man whose death was postponed when the **Fates** became drunk.

As punishment for offending Zeus, Apollo was forced to work as a slave to Admetus, the king of Perae, for a year. Instead of taking advantage of Apollo's situation, Admetus treated him as a guest. Sometime later, when Admetus became mortally wounded from a snake bite on his wedding night, Apollo intervened with the Fates on Admetus's behalf by getting them drunk and persuading them to delay taking his life if he could find someone to die in his stead. The only one willing to do so was Admetus' devoted wife, Alcestis, who took poison and died in his stead. By chance, Heracles, Admetus' friend, came to visit on the day of Alcestis' death. When told what had happened, Heracles descended to the Underworld and after defeating Thanatos, the god of death, brought her back to Admetus.

Although not the main theme of the story, it indicates that even the Fates are not immune to intoxication, and that the course of destiny can be altered by it. (Gantz, 195, 396–397)

Adonis *see* **Aphrodite, Myrrha.**

Adrastia *see* **Amalthea.**

Aegeus. In Greek mythology, the king of Athens who was told by the oracle at Delphi that he would have a son who would become a great hero, but warned him not to drink any wine ("do not undo the wineskin's mouth") until he got back home, or his son would cause his death. On his way back to Athens, Aegeus stopped at the palace of King Pittheus of Troezen and told him the oracle's prediction. Pittheus saw this as an opportunity to gain power for him and plied Aegeus with wine and then, while he was asleep, ordered his daughter, Aethra, to sleep with the intoxicated guest. However, that same night Poseidon, the god of the Sea, also slept with Aethra, and Poseidon was Theseus' real father (Theseus could not have become a hero had the drunken Aegeus been his father since he would have been effeminate, owing to the Greek belief that drunkenness during sexual relations resulted in the conception of girls).

Totally unaware of Poseidon's visitation, when Aegeus left Troezen, he told Aethra that if she gave birth to a boy, she should raise him without telling him who his father was. When the boy was grown enough to move a large rock that he showed her, she was to send him to Athens with the sandals and sword he would find hidden underneath the rock, so that he would know who he was.

When Theseus came to Athens to find Aegeus, the city was paying a tribute of seven men and seven women every nine years to King Minos of Crete, who in turn fed them to the Minotaur, a half-man, half-bull creature that lived in a labyrinth. Theseus volunteered to go to Crete as one of the men, hoping to put an end to the tribute. As he left, he promised to fly a white sail on his ship as a signal of his success, but if he failed, the returning ships were to fly the traditional black sails. Aided by Minos' daughter, **Ariadne**, Theseus killed the Minotaur and escaped from the labyrinth. On his way back, however, he forgot to change sails. Seeing the black sail, Aegeus was stricken with grief, and committed suicide by throwing himself into the sea, thereby fulfilling the oracle's warning of what would happen to him if he drank wine before returning to Athens. (Grimal, 17)

Aegir (also known as Gymir or Hler). In Norse mythology, a giant (as opposed to a god), who ruled the seas and was renown for his brewing.

Although nearly all the giants were the mortal enemies of the gods, Aegir was one the few who lived peacefully among them. However, being a giant, he could be irritable in their presence. When the **Aesir** gods, **Thor** and Tyr, asked him to brew them enough ale for their **divine banquet**, Aegir was obligated to comply, but was resentful. As a way of avoiding the request, he feigned agreement but said he didn't have a **cauldron** big enough to brew that much beer. Thor didn't know what to do until Tyr said his father, the giant Hymir, had one that was big enough.

When Thor asked Hymir for his cauldron, he didn't want to give it to him, but obligated by hospitality, couldn't refuse them outright, so he challenged them, saying that Thor could have it if he could smash a certain drinking mug that he, Hymir, had made. Thor threw the mug at a pillar expecting it to break easily, but the mug was **magic** and instead the pillar broke. Wanting to help her son, Tyr's mother told Thor he could overcome the mug's magic by throwing it at Hymir's head.

When the mug subsequently smashed, Hymir had to keep his promise. Thor then brought the cauldron to Aegir, who was now obligated to brew ale every winter for the gods at what became known as "Aegir's Drinking Party"(Aegir's dual association with the ocean and brewing is thought to have originated from the earlier Indo-European myth of the **Churning of the Ocean** in a large cauldron). (Glendenning, 91–111; McLeish, 11; Orchard, 1; Lindow, 191–3)

Aesir. One of the two groups of gods in Norse mythology, from whose spit the **mead of inspiration and poetry** was eventually created.

The Aesir were sky gods and were warriors led by Odin, the "All Father" who created mankind, and subsequently by **Thor**, his son and successor. The other group of gods, the Vanir, were earth gods associated with agricultural activities.

While the Aesir and Vanir lived together peacefully they initially were constantly warring with one another. Since neither group could permanently gain the upper hand, they concluded a truce in which they exchanged hostages and sealed the truce by spitting into a cauldron (the Norse counterpart to the "divine marriage" in Greek mythology where the fertility of the universe comes from the union of the male sky gods and female earth gods). In Norse mythology, wisdom in the form of **Kvasir** was one of the results of the union between the sky and earth gods. Kvasir was a being of such wisdom that he could answer any question that emerged. Shortly thereafter, he was murdered by two dwarves who drained his blood into a cauldron, mixed it with honey, and brewed it into a "mead of inspiration" that had the power to inspire anyone who drank it with wisdom and enabled him to create extraordinary poetry. (Fee and Leeming, 17–18)

Aethra *see* **Aegeus.**

Afagddu (also known as **Avagdu** or **Morfran**). In Celtic mythology, the misshapen son of **Ceridwen**, for whom she concocted a brew that would make him exceedingly wise to compensate for his appearance. However, the first drops of the brew spilled onto **Gwion Bach**, whom she had put in charge of maintaining the fire below her cauldron and, instead, he became the wisest man in the world. In Wales, Afagddu is a synonym for Hell. (Ford, 162; Rhys, 546)

Agathos Daimon. In Greek mythology, the "good daimon" to whom wine was sacrificed for a happy life. Sometimes identified with **Dionysus** in his earliest incarnation as **Zagreus**.

Daimons were divine spirits occupying the middle ground between the gods and humans. The daimons were not worshiped, but were equated with the spirit that brought good fortune. Agathos Daimon, who was depicted as a young boy holding a horn of plenty and a bowl, was associated with the proper consumption of wine. Often the first drink of wine or a small libation of unmixed wine was offered to them after the meal. In Boetia, an area in central Greece, offerings were made to them before a new vintage was opened. Those who honored their demons in this way lived happy lives; those who did not, lived in melancholy. (Elderkin, 427–430; Robertson, 227)

Agave. In Greek mythology, the mother of **Pentheus**, the king of Thebes, who killed her son after **Dionysus** made her insane because she refused to recognize his divinity. In her maddened condition, she noticed her son secretly watching the mysteries of the god's rites. Hallucinated into imagining Pentheus was a lion, she, along with other women driven similarly insane, savagely attacked him and tore his limbs from his body. When she finally came to her senses, Dionysus appeared to her and told her that he had punished her for her disbelief, and then exiled her from Thebes. (Gantz, 481–483)

Agni. In Hindu mythology, the god of fire, sun and lightning. Although born in the heavens, Agni's spirit resided among humans on earth and he was their most devoted divine ally. When priests rendered their **soma** sacrifice to the gods, they offered it to Agni, who carried it for them in the smoke that rose from it, to the other gods and especially **Indra**, his twin brother. In this way, Agni brought the human spirit into contact with the divine through soma. (Mahony, 122–124)

Ahura Mazda *see* **Haoma.**

Aittah Slahsa. In Bolivian Mataco Indian mythology, the "good spirit" that energizes plants and produces the fermentation that animates their algaroba beer. (Karsten, 1931, 125–127)

Aittah Tavakai. In Bolivian Mataco Indian mythology, the "evil spirit" that animates distilled liquors, which unlike their beer, incites aggression. (Karsten, 1935, 126)

Aitvaras. Lithuanian god of fermentation. (Greimas, 44)

Alcohol. From the Arab al-kohl. *Al* in Arabic means "the," *kohl* means "powder" or "essence." In Cleopatra's day, women heated antimony sulphate until it vaporized, then cooled it to make it condense into a powdery black distillate or essence that they applied to their eyelids as modern Western women do with eye shadow. Centuries later Arab chemists discovered that other substances could also be heated and cooled to more concentrated distillates, and likewise referred to such substances as kohl, i.e., essences.

The isolation of alcohol came in the wake of alchemy which became widespread in Europe during the 13th century. One of alchemy's most diligent obsessions was the isolation of the "spirit" or elixir of life. In the 14th century, alchemist Arnold of Villanova, who learned about distillation from the Arabs in Spain, became the first European to isolate alcohol from wine. Arnold called the distillate *aqua vitae*, the water of life. Subsequently it acquired other names like *aqua ardens*, "strong waters." In Germany, alchemists called it brandewin, "burnt wine." The Swiss alchemist, Theophrastus Phillippus Aureolus Bombastus von Hohenheim Paracelsus (1493–1541), was the first to call the distillate "alcohol." Paracelsus was familiar with the Arab process of distilling antimony sulphate, and simply used the Arab term for this distillate as well, since he regarded alcohol as the "essence" or "spirit" of wine.

When chemists found that the alcohol made from wine was chemically similar to the alcohol made from wood and other materials, they chose alcohol as a collective name for these chemicals. Each member of the group of alcohols was then given a specific name. The intoxicating form of alcohol is called ethyl alcohol or ethanol.

Alcohol results from the fermentation of fruits or grains. These vegetative substances contain sugars that are acted on by yeast which converts them into alcohol.

Alcohol's effects are legion. Entheogenic effects include hallucinations, a sense of floating, inebriation, and euphoria. Overindulgence can result in depression, irritability, incoordination, mental confusion, aggressiveness, delirium, death from respiratory failure, and dependence, along with many other conditions.

Because of their psychological as well as their nutritive effects (calories), alcoholic drinks are regarded as sacred gifts from the gods which come from the spirits that inhabit or inspire the growth of the plants from which these drinks are made. When the spiritual forces in these plants are personified by a deity, the beverages made from them are regarded as the "blood" or "milk" of that god or goddess. (Abel, 1987, 1ff)

Ale of Goibniu *see* **Goibniu.**

Alkaloid. A class of organic compounds in plants that contain nitrogen. These substances are found in many psychoactive plants and affect the brain because they have chemical structures that are similar to the **neurotransmitters** that nerves use to communicate with one another. Among the most potent psychoactive alkaloids are those found in the potato family of plants, known as Solanaceae, which were allegedly used in "witches' brews" that induced flying. These included **belladonna, datura, henbane**, and mandrake. The three main psychoactive alkaloids in these plants are atropine, scopolamine, and hyoscyamine, all of them having in common interfering with the neurotransmitter, acetylcholine. (Rudgley, 8)

Allegory. A story that contains a broader abstract idea than the seemingly literal plot. Allegories often contain several levels of meaning. For example, the gods in myths are often regarded as allegorical personifications of natural forces; the constant battle between the gods and demons or giants for possession of a magical elixir represents the ageless conflict between good and evil and the idea that ownership of the elixir confers dominance. The abduction of **Persephone** and her reunion with her mother **Demeter** allegorically represents the cyclical change of seasons, but in the **Eleusian mysteries** it represents the even deeper allegorical meaning of survival of the soul after death. (Price and Kearns, 19–20)

Alofi. In East Futuna, in Polynesian mythology, a culture hero who went into a trance and was transported in a spirit boat to the gods. The gods gave him a **kava** root which he planted in the earth when he returned. (Lebot et al., 125)

Alonkok. In Pygmy cosmology, the Great Mother goddess from whose mushroom body the earth came into being when it split down the middle. The upper half of her body became the heavens, while the lower half became the earth. (Samorini, 23)

Alrek *see* **Geirhild.**

Altered State of Consciousness. A qualitatively different level of awareness in which there is a perception of another realm of existence. The difference between dreaming and waking consciousness represents one state of altered consciousness. In this altered state of consciousness perceptions are still recognizable as variations of the waking world. In trance induced altered states, there is a feeling of exceptional sensations, thoughts, feelings and a sense of a supernatural or sacred realm unlike any previously encountered in the waking world. This altered state of consciousness has been induced in many ways, such as rhythmic music, dancing, and especially ingestion of intoxicating substances. These substances are often considered sacred because in producing the altered state of consciousness, they bring the user under the influence of, or into the sacred realm of, a supernatural power. (Goodman, 6, 41)

Alwiss. In Norse mythology, a dwarf whose name means, "he who knows all." Like the dwarves who kill **Kvasir** and brew the **mead of inspiration** from his blood, Alwiss was possessed of a special knowledge, including the names of all the alcoholic beverages consumed by various races of beings and the ingredients used to make them.

Alwiss lived in the underground and only emerged during the dark because the light could turn him into stone. He fell in love with **Thor**'s daughter, but Thor didn't want him for a son-in-law. To prevent the marriage, Thor told Alwiss he would give his consent if Alwiss was able to answer all the questions he put to him. When Alwiss agreed, Thor kept asking him so many questions that Alwiss lost track of time. When dawn broke, he was caught unawares and turned into stone. (Lindow, 56–57)

Amalthea. In Greek mythology, a goat whose fermented milk was mixed with honey and nourished Zeus when he was an infant, or alternatively, the goat whose horns provided the infant Zeus with **ambrosia** and **nectar** (the food and drink of the gods); ambrosia flowed from one of her horns, nectar from the other.

When Zeus was born, his mother Rhea entrusted him to the care of two nymphs, Adrastia and Ida, the daughters of Melisseus, on mount Dicte on the island of Crete, to keep Cronos her husband from killing him. The nymphs kept him in a hammock which they hung from a tree so that Cronos wouldn't find him in heaven, earth or in the sea, while another group of spirits, the Curetes (forerunners of the **Maenads**) engaged in orgiastic dancing to drown out his crying. The nymphs fed the infant Zeus honey mixed with milk (which would have produced mead if fermented) from Amalthea's udders. In gratitude, Zeus later transformed Amalthea into the constellation, Capricorn. Amalthea's counterpart in Norse mythology is **Heidrun**, a goat that fed on branches from the world tree, **Yggdrasil**, whose sap contained mead. (Grimal, 35–36)

Amanita Muscaria (fly agaric). A mushroom with intoxicating properties that figures prominently in many Indo-European myths. Its primary psychoactive compounds are muscimole and ibotenic acid; its primary psychoactive effects are euphoria and colorful visions. Amanita is widely believed to have been introduced into India by Aryans from Siberia, and has often been identified as the **soma** of the Rig Veda, one of the oldest of India's ancient religious texts.

Amanita grows in forests typically under birch and fir trees. It can sometimes be 8 to 9 inches in height. It has an oval cap that measures 3 to 8 inches across. There are several varieties of Amanita. In Siberia and other parts of Asia, Europe, and northwest America, the cap is reddish with white warts; farther to the south, the cap is yellowish-orange, with yellowish warts. The stem is usually thick and white and metaphorically likened to a pillar; the gills are usually cream colored.

Amanita mushrooms are eaten raw, sun dried, toasted, or soaked in water and taken as an extract. Since the active ingredients are not metabolized very much and pass into the urine unchanged, in some cultures, the urine of those who have eaten mushrooms is drunk as a way of achieving the same experience without having to find more mushrooms. Urine from reindeer who have become intoxicated from eating these mushrooms is likewise drunk for the same reason. In some instances urine from someone or from an animal that has eaten mushrooms is preferred because it is regarded as more potent or as a way of prolonging the intoxication by continually imbibing it in this form instead of searching for more mushrooms.

Psychoactive effects usually begin about 15 to 20 minutes after ingestion and may last for several hours. The initial effect is lethargy and a half sleepiness characterized by colored visions. A common experience is a sense that objects have become bigger or smaller. This is followed by a sense of euphoria and exhilaration, lasting three to four hours in which individuals feel as if they can perform extraordinary physical activities. (Rudgley, 102–113; Schultes and Hofmann, 17, 29, 34, 70, 81–85)

Amasanga. In Quicha (Ecuador) South American Indian mythology, the god of thunder and lightning and the spirit of **datura**.

After the sun emerged out of the cosmic waters and created day and night and east and west, and brought order to human life, Amasanga and Nungui (the female datura spirit) emerged, each with their own discreet color manifestations. Amasanga the datura spirit enabled humans to visit that world through his entheogenic visions. (Whitten, 847)

Ambrosia. In Greek mythology, a celestial material, exclusively the possession of the Olympian deities. In very rare occasions it was given to mortals like Heracles, and Semele, **Dionysus'** mother, when they were assumed into Olympus. Literally, the term means "immortality," (from the Greek *a* "not" and *mbrotos*, "mortal"). Once ingested, it alchemized the blood into a special fluid coursing through the veins called ichor, which was what actually produced immortality.

Ambrosia also conferred many other divine effects, such as instant maturation. After his mother Leto, who was seduced by Zeus, gave birth to the sun god Apollo, on the Island of Delos, instead of suckling him herself, she fed him nectar and ambrosia. This immediately transformed him into an adult, and he began to speak, demanded a lyre and bow, and announced his intention to create an oracle.

Ambrosia also conferred eternal youth and beauty: In Homer's *Iliad*, the sea-nymph, Thetis, preserved the dead body of Patroclus in ambrosia and nectar to keep it from rotting, while Athena gave ambrosia to Penelope in the *Odyssey* to beautify her, although in this instance, it did not make Penelope immortal.

Ambrosia and nectar are generally regarded as the heavenly counterpart of grape wine in most myths, but may originally have been two different types of fermented honey. In ancient Greece, people believed honey had special healing powers. The invention of fermented honey (mead) was attributed to **Aristaeus** and was used as an **entheogen** until wine was created (See **Amethyst**). Some scholars, e.g., Robert Graves (1966), however, contended ambrosia was **amanita muscaria**, the fly agaric.

One of the best-known myths about ambrosia concerns its theft by Tantalus, the son of Zeus, from the Olympians. As punishment, he was condemned to stand chin deep in water with all kinds of sweet smelling fruit just above him. However, whenever he tried to drink, the water instantly drained away and when he tried to eat, the fruit suddenly rose beyond his reach, giving rise to the word "tantalize."

Ambrosia is also the name of a nymph devoted to **Dionysus** who accompanied him on his journey from Asia Minor to Greece. During Dionysus' fight with **Lycurgus**, she turned into a vine and held Lycurgus so that he could not escape.

Ambrosia was also the name of an annual autumn festival celebrated by the **centaurs** in honor of Dionysus, in which presumably the half-man half-horse creatures became very drunk. In India's mythology, its counterpart is **soma**; in Persian mythology, **haoma**, in Scandinavian mythology, the **mead of inspiration**, in Celtic mythology, **Goibiniu's** ale (Wright, 2–6).

    Magic elixirs are common in many mythologies. The oldest occurs in the Mesopotamian **Gilgamesh** epic, where the hero finds and then has it stolen from him by a snake. While often it is the drink of immortality, in various mythologies, it instead confers wisdom, usually in the form of the ability to create poetry (Price and Kearns, 22–23). See also: **Goibiniu.**

Ambrosia Cycle. The collection of Indo-European myths describing the creation of a **magic** elixir, its theft, and its subsequent recovery. In India, the elixir was lost in the cosmic ocean and recovered during the **Churning of the Ocean.** In Scandinavia, it was created from the blood of **Kvasir**, lost, and then recovered by **Odin.** In Ireland, it was created by **Ceridwen** and lost when it accidentally spilled on **Gwion Bach,** and then recovered through the birth of **Taliesin.** In many myths, the creation of the elixir involves an immense **cauldron.** Once produced, it often resulted in a battle between rival factions for its possession. For example, in the India myth of the Churning of the Ocean, the demon **Asuras** battle the **Deva** gods. In Scandinavian mythology, the giants battle the gods for the **mead of inspiration.** Another common motif in the cycle involves the elixir's theft and its recovery through flight, a metaphor for spirit travel. (Dumezil, 1924, 1ff; Oosten, 52–71; Worthen, 39–69)

Amen. In Irish mythology, the magic **cauldron** used by **Ceridwen** to brew a **magic** elixir that inspired divine wisdom in anyone who drank it or on whom it spilled. (Sykes, 9)

Amethyst. In Greek mythology, the luckless beautiful girl who was the object of a curse by **Dionysus.**

    The usually playful Dionysus became irate one day because of an insult from another god. Since he couldn't avenge himself on his tormentor, he took his anger out on a mortal, declaring that the next human he would encounter on earth would be attacked and eaten by a tiger. The luckless human was Amethyst on her way to worship at the goddess Artemis's shrine. As the tiger lunged toward her, Amethyst called out to Artemis, the goddess of virgins, for help. To prevent Amethyst from being mauled and eaten, Artemis turned her into a six-sided white stone. When Dionysus saw what had happened, he regretted his cruelty and poured grape juice over the stone as a sign of his remorse, turning it violet. Just as the stone protected Amethyst from being devoured, the stone into which she was transformed was believed to protect whoever wore it from drunkenness, one of Dionysus' destructive powers.

Etymologically, amethyst comes from the Greek *a*, meaning "not," and *methuein*, to be drunken, which in turn is derived from the Greek *methu*, an intoxicating drink. The root goes back to Indo European *medhu*, "honey," which also became the word for honey in Sanskirt, and gave rise to the word *mel* in Latin. Mead is a type of wine made from honey.

Because of its alleged **magic** power to prevent drunkenness, amethyst was a very popular gem used in amulets up to the Middle Ages, for women who worried about a drunken husband beating them. By extension, amethyst amulets were also worn by lovers who feared becoming overly passionate through the intoxication of love. The amethyst amulets worn for this purpose were spelled amatist—the "lover's stone" (from the Latin *amor*). Today, the term for drugs that act like sobering-up pills is "amethystics." (Abel, 1987, 20–22)

Ampelos. In Greek mythology, the youthful companion of **Dionysus** who was turned into the eponymous grapevine when he died.

When Dionysus was still a youth in Phyrgia and had not yet become the god of wine, he became friends with another youth named Ampelos. However, their friendship was destined to be short lived because the **Fates** had decreed that anyone as beautiful as Ampelos had to die young. One day while Dionysus was away, Ampelos was fatally wounded by a bull. When Dionysus saw his dead friend, he was unable to console himself and poured **ambrosia** into his mortal friend's wounds. The ambrosia transformed Ampelos' body into a grapevine that produced fruit that was the earthly counterpart of Olympian ambrosia, for the comfort of humans. The myth is preserved today in our word "ampelography," the science of vine identification. (Nonnos, 11.240; 12.142–160; 270–271)

Amphictyon. In Greek mythology, the king who taught the Athenians to mix wine with water to reduce its power. Amphictyon was the second son of Deucalion, the Greek **Noah**, who survived the flood and along with his wife, Pyrrha, repopulated the earth.

After **Dionysus** came to Athens and taught **Icarius** how to make wine, Iccarius was killed by his neighbors who were not used to its effects. At the time, Amphictyon was king of Athens, and when Dionysus came to the city, he graciously entertained his divine guest. In return, Dionysus taught Amphictyon to mix wine with water to reduce its undiluted power; Amphictyon in turn taught the Athenians to mix wine and water, and established the cult of Dionysus Orthos (literally, Dionysus upright—being able to stand on one's feet when drinking wine in contrast to those who drank wine unmixed and fell down regularly). The term, however, also was taken to mean "ithyphallic," an allusion to the fertility attributed to the wine god. (Robertson, 217, 226, 245)

Amphictyonis. In Greek mythology, a little known goddess of wine, friendship, and good relationships between neighbors. Sometimes considered an epithet of Demeter (Graves, 1992, 38.8)

Amrta. In Vedic and Hindu mythology, the sacred drink of the gods, the elixir of immortality (from *a*, "not," and *mrta*, "mortal"), and metaphorically, the spirit of intoxication.

Amrta is often used interchangeably with **soma**, but the two elixirs were not originally the same. Amrta was exclusively a divine elixir whereas soma was drunk by both gods and those who served them. Whereas amrta is essentially spirit, soma is akin to the soul living in the plant from which it is liberated. In later myths the two became conflated.

Amrta's origins are not described in any myths. It was simply there at the time of creation and then as mysteriously, it was lost in the Cosmic Ocean, and then recovered as described in India's seminal myth, the **Churning of the Ocean.**

A lesser-known myth begins with amrta's existence in the body of Susna, one of the demon **Asuras.** Whenever one of the Asuras died during their ongoing wars with the **Deva** gods, Susna would breathe on him and his amrta-infused breath revived the slain demon. As a result, the Asuras could not be subdued. When **Indra,** one of the Deva gods, saw how Susna revived the dead demons, he transformed himself into a lump of honey and placed himself where Susna would notice him. When Susna saw the honey he swallowed it. Once inside the demon's body, Indra transformed himself into an eagle, snatched the amrta from the demon's mouth, and brought it to the Devas. (Dange, I: 1160–1163)

A'neglakya. In North American Zuni Indian legend, the spirit of **Datura.**

A'neglakya and his sister, A'neglakyatsi-tsa, lived deep in the earth but often came up to the surface and walked about.

During one of these sojourns, they encountered the twin sons of the Sun god, and while talking with them, A'neglakya mentioned that he and his sister could make people fall asleep and if they put a certain flower on their heads while they were sleeping, they would have visionary dreams that would enable them to find objects they had lost.

The twins decided that A'neglakya and his sister had too much magic and had to be kept from roaming the earth, so they caused them to disappear into the earth forever. From the place where the two vanished, two beautiful flowers emerged, identical to the flower A'neglakya and sister had used to give people visions. These flowers spread across the earth, enabling more people to continue to have visions. (Stevenson, 46)

Animal Tales. Stories in which animals are the main characters in a story. Many myths refer to a time when there was no difference between animals and humans and they spoke to one another in a common language. North American **tricksters** and **culture heroes** such as **Coyote** and **Raven** are often credited with creating the world and bringing culture to mankind. Animals are also the spiritual guides that lead shamans to the supernatural world; birds, for example, often represent the soul flight of a **shaman**. (Price and Kearns, 30)

Anura. In Arawak Guiana mythology, the spirit of tobacco seeds. (Levi Strauss, 426)

Apache Tobacco Origin Story *see* Coyote.

Aphrodite. In Greek mythology, the goddess of love, whose tears turned into poppies. Aphrodite loved Adonis, and when he died, she tearfully mourned for him and poppies sprouted from wherever they fell to the ground.

Aphrodite's birth place, Cyprus, was a major region for poppy cultivation. The poppy's association with Aphrodite led to its use as a love charm and an ingredient in many potions for influencing affairs of the heart. It was used by girls to induce dreams that would reveal their future husbands. (Gantz, 99–105)

Apikunni. A Blackfoot American Indian culture hero who gave his people tobacco.

Apikunni was unable to pay the bride price for the woman he loved and she was betrothed to the village chief. However, the two lovers continued to meet secretly until their trysts were eventually discovered. Humiliated, Apikunni left the village. During his wanderings, he tired one day and fell asleep near a beaver dam. While dreaming, Beaver came to him and invited him into his house where he showed Apikunni his secrets, including tobacco and how to use it, and then gave him some tobacco seeds when Apikunni left. The next day a friend found Apikunni and persuaded him to return to the village. On their way back they discovered a scout from an enemy war party secretly trying to cross a river to get closer to the Blackfoot camp. Apikunni swam under the water as Beaver had taught him, and killed the scout and then alerted the village to the imminent attack. Grateful for averting the danger, the chief welcomed Apikunni back to the tribe and made him a clan chief. Apikunni then married his former lover, called the people of the village together and taught them how to plant tobacco seeds. (Gill and Sullivan, 15)

Arawak Tobacco Myth *see* **Komatari.**

Archetype. A prototypic symbol, idea, or character, that occurs in stories from around the world. Despite cultural variations, the prototype gives the story a universality. (Powell, B., 650, 658)

Ariadne. In Greek mythology, the daughter of King Minos of Crete who became the wife of **Dionysus.**

While Theseus, the son of **Aegeus,** the king of Athens, came to Crete as part of the annual human tribute Athens sent to Minos, she fell in love with him and showed him how to escape from her father's labyrinth by unraveling a ball of string as he maneuvered through it. Theseus took Ariadne back with him to Athens but abandoned her on the island of Naxos while she was sleeping on the shore. When he came to Naxos on his way to the mainland, Dionysus saw Ariadne wakening from her sleep (a possible allegory of Dionysus retrieving the soul from death) and immediately fell in love with and married her, the only woman he ever married. Together they had six sons, one of whom was **Oenopion.** (In some variants of her story, Ariadne was killed by Artemis, the goddess of chastity, for not remaining chaste, or committed suicide in her grief at being left behind.)

Dionysus' wedding present to Ariadne was a gold crown. When Ariadne died, Dionysus turned her into the golden crowned Corona Borealis, the constellation sailors relied on for navigating the sea. (Gantz, 264–270; Price and Kearns, 51–52)

Aristaeus. In Greek mythology, the god of mead.

Aristaeus was the son of Apollo and the nymph Cyrene. Cyrene's father, Hypsaeus, was the king of the Lapiths, a community in Thessaly constantly at odds with the **Centaurs**. Apollo abducted Cyrene and carried her off to Libya where Aristaeus was born. Hermes, the messenger of the gods, then took him to some nymphs, called the Horai, who nursed and fed him **ambrosia** and nectar, which made him an immortal. On his way back to Thessaly, which became the center of his cult, he stopped in Crete where he created mead, mixing honey and water and then fermenting it (Crete was known for its honey, and the bee was important in the cult of Artemis).

Although the traditional alcoholic drink in Greece was wine (oinos), the word for drunkenness in Greek was *methuein*, which in turn was derived from Greek *methu*, an "intoxicating drink." Methu in turn was derived from the Indo-European Sanskrit *medhu*, "honey." The term may have been generic in ancient Greek and applied to any alcoholic intoxicant, such as the "mead from barley," or "wine from barley," in essence, beer. (See also **Amethyst**.)

Aristaeus challenged **Dionysus** to see whose drink was better. All the gods sampled both, but tired of Aristaeus' mead after only two cups, preferring instead Dionysus' wine. This myth reflects mainland Greece's rivalry with Mycenean Crete, and the rivalry between Apollo, the anti–Achaean god, who, along with Artemis and **Aphrodite**, fight in the Trojan war on the side of the Trojans against the Greeks, who are supported by Dionysus and the other Olympians.

Aristaeus' connection with Apollo remained a prominent feature in the latter's cult. The stone *omphalos*, at Apollo's first temple at Delphi, was in the shape of a beehive, and was where **Zagreus**, an earlier incarnation of Dionysus, was said to have been buried after being torn to bits by the Titans before he was resurrected and became a fertility god. Devotees were, likewise, buried in beehive tombs in hope of similar resurrection, and his second temple there was in the shape of a beehive. Aristaeus is also the name of the man married to Autonoe's husband. Antonoe was the sister of **Semele** and agreed to hide Dionysus while he was growing up so that his stepmother, Hera, would not be able to find and kill him. (Grimal, 60; Nonnos, 8. 270–275; Ruck et al., 2001, 71; Price and Kearns, 53; Zafiropulo, 39ff)

Arutama. In Ecuadorian Jibaro Indian mythology, the ancestral spirits ("the old ones") that animate the hallucinogenic plants ayahuasca (Banisteria caapi) and "huantuc" (Datura arborea). Arutama appears to users in drug-induced visions as anacondas, crocodiles, and other animals that speak to them in human voices that reveal the future. (Karsten, 1926, 325)

Aseni *see* **Peyote Woman.**

Asgard. In Norse mythology, the celestial home of the gods.

In Norse mythology, the world was divided into three realms, located one above the other. Asgard, at the top, was the home of the **Aesir** and **Vanir** gods and was ruled by **Odin**. **Valhalla**, the great palace where warriors who died in battle were taken, and the orchard containing the apples of eternal youth, which the gods ate to keep from growing old, were both located within Asgard, as was the well of Urd (fate) where the gods met daily in council. The level just below was Midgard, the realm of humans. Midgard was connected to Asgard by a bridge, represented as a rainbow, tree, or Milky Way, along which the gods, **shamans,** and the dead traveled from one realm to the other. Jotunheim was the realm of the giants; Nidavellir, the home of the dwarves; and Svaralfheim, the land of the black elves. The bottom, coldest level, called Niflheim, was ruled by Hel. A great ash, the World Tree, called **Yggdrasill,** passed through each level. (Fee and Leeming, 92–93, 142)

Ask. Literally the "ash tree."

In Norse mythology, Ask was the first man and was fashioned out of the ash tree which exudes a sugary sap, resembling honey, that was made into mead, implying a connection between them. His wife, Embla, was created alongside him in the same way. The world ash was called **Yggdrasil**. After Ragnarok, the end of the world, mankind would be restored from a man and woman who found shelter in Yggdrasil and were nourished by its sap. (Orchard, 38)

Asuras. In Hindu mythology, the perennial opponents of the **Devas** with whom they are always fighting. The Asuras and Devas are the Indian counterparts of the Greek Titans and Olympians, respectively.

Asura means "one without **amrta,** or **soma**" (metaphorically, "without the peace and happiness they afford"). In the myth of the **Churning of the Ocean,** the Asuras are tricked into cooperating with the Devas to obtain the amrta, which the Devas then keep for themselves, thanks to the help of Varuna. (Brown, 88)

Asvins. In Hindu mythology, twin deities who were regarded as physicians of the gods; many of the Asvins' exploits involve mead.

The Asvins were the sons of Surya, the sun god, and were depicted as horse-headed charioteers driving the sun's chariot, pulled by flying horses or birds, through the heavens. The Asvins had occult powers, and brought fortune and health to the world. They are also known as the "divine physicians," and were renowned for their knowledge of medicinal plants which gave them the power to heal, restore youth, and avoid death. When the wife of **Cyavana**, with whom they were in love, tricked them into renewing her husband's youth, they did it by bathing him in a lake from which bathers emerge with whatever age they wanted—the origins of the "Fountain of Youth." In this instance, the lake contained amrta, the drink of immortality and perpetual youth.

The Asvins were also renowned for their wisdom, including how to make mead, which they learned from a human, Dadhyanc Atharvan. When the Asvins found out that Dadhyanc had discovered the secret of making mead, they offered to become his disciples so that they could learn it. But Dadhyanc was reluctant to accept them, because Indra had threatened to cut off his head if he divulged the secret. However, the Asvins, who were expert surgeons, assured him that they had a plan: They said they would cut off his head and keep it in safekeeping, and would attach the head of a horse to his trunk temporarily. When Indra found out that Dadhyanc had divulged the secret he cut off his head as he had said he would, and took it away with him. The Asvins then attached his original head and they each went their own way. (Mahony, 25–26, Coomaraswamy, 112–113)

Atlacoaya. A female Mayan **pulque** deity. Literally "dark water" or "sad thing." (Boone, 213; Reed, 109)

Atropos. In Greek mythology, one of three **Fates**; the eponymous origins of the name of the drug, atropine. (Grimal, 294)

Aturarodo *see* **Butoriku.**

Aura. In Greek mythology, the mother of **Iacchus**, an avatar of **Dionysus**. The story describes the madness and sexual abandon associated with involvement with **Dionysus**.

Aura was a virgin hunting nymph and one of Artemis's hunting companions. Dionysus was taken with her beauty and seduced her. Artemis held Aura responsible for the seduction and made her mad. When Aura later gave birth to twins Aura tried to kill them. She tore one of the children to bits, but before she could do the same to Iacchus, the other twin, he was snatched away and brought to the **Bacchantes** at **Eleusis** who raised him. After coming to her senses, Aura drowned herself. (Nonnos, 48.243; Grimal, 71, 224)

Autonoe. The sister of **Semele**, and hence, the aunt of **Dionysus**. Because she spread the story that her sister Semele had lied by saying that Zeus was the father of her child, Dionysus, Dionysus drove her mad along with her other sisters, and they participated in the death of Agave's son, **Pentheus**. (Gantz, 472, 478)

Avagdu *see* Afagddu.

Ava'ali'i. In Samoan Polynesian mythology, the son of the island's culture hero, **Tagaloa**, from whose body his father caused the **kava** plant to grow. (Beckwith, 63–64)

Aventine Hill. One of the seven hills of Rome where many of the city's oldest temples were located, among them, those dedicated to **Bona Dea**, **Liber** and Libera, and Ceres, deities, whose worship was associated with ecstatic mystery cults. (Powell, B., 365, 617)

Awa *see* Kava.

Awa-iku. In Hawaiian mythology, helpful spirits that act as messengers that **Kane** uses to ward off evil spirits and control winds, rain and other things useful to humans. Their name indicates a connection with awa (**kava**), but there are no myths relating that association. (Beckwith, 63–64)

Awe-n-ha'i. North American Seneca Indian goddess, the Earth Mother, from whose body tobacco sprouted after her death.

In ancient times, the tobacco plant grew in the center of heaven, where the Great Chief and his people lived off its leaves and its incense. One night, the Great Chief dreamed about a girl in heaven that he had once seen, named Awe-n-ha'i. He subsequently married her but after he took her to his lodge, he discovered she was pregnant and his spirit became very troubled over her apparent promiscuity. That night the "Ancient One" appeared to him in a dream and told him that if he uprooted the celestial tobacco tree as punishment for his wife's conduct, his troubled spirit would be relieved.

When the Chief uprooted the plant, however, it led to turmoil in the heavenly world. The Chief became so angry at losing his tobacco (allegorically withdrawal), that he hurled his wife into the hole in the heavens the plant created when it was uprooted. As Awe-n-ha'i fell to earth, however, she grasped some leaves from the plant that were still growing from a root that had broken off, along with some other kinds of seeds.

A short time after she landed on earth, Awe-n-hai' gave birth to a daughter who mysteriously became successively pregnant with two boys. The older one, whom she called Good Mind, made her happy; the younger son caused her to die in childbirth. Awe-n-hai,' their grandmother, made the burial arrangements and asked Good Mind to help.

Good Mind stayed by his mother's grave and watered it until strange buds rose out of the earth. Potatoes grew from over her feet, squash from above her abdomen, corn from above her breasts, beans from over her fingers, and tobacco from over her head. When Awe-n-hai' saw the plants she taught Good Mind how to take care of them so that they would grow, and how to smoke the leaves of tobacco so that the heavenly ones, who had lost their tobacco after she had disturbed the heavenly order, would be able to enjoy its smoke once again.

In a Haudenosaunee Indian variant of this myth, a human-like family of five brothers lived in the sky which was filled with plants and animals in the time before the earth was created. The youngest of these brothers was so much in love with one of girls in the sky, that he became very weak. Although he subsequently married her, his weakness continued. In this condition, he dreamed that he could regain his health if his brothers pulled up a certain tree. His brothers did so as the young couple sat nearby, but as they ripped it up, the young girl was impregnated by the air that came out of the hole and her belly became very round. Seeing her condition, her husband threw her into the hole, but as she fell, some birds caught her and placed her onto the back of a large turtle, which supported her and the birds. After the birds rested, they flew to the bottom of the sky ocean and brought back some of its mud and created the earth on the top of the turtle's back. Soon, thereafter, the woman gave birth to a girl who grew up to become Earth Mother.

When Earth Mother was young, she wanted to play in the water, although her mother forbade her to do so. But Earth Mother disobeyed and went into the water anyway and became pregnant and subsequently gave birth to twins. One of the twins, named Tgarachiawagon, was a good spirit (Good Mind), while the other, named Tawiskaron, was evil (Evil Mind). Earth Mother died giving birth to these twins, and Good Mind buried her. Not long afterwards, tobacco and other good things like corn, squash and beans sprouted from her grave.

Good Mind then began to explore the newly created world, filling it with men and women and vegetables and other good things to eat. His twin brother Evil Mind followed him, creating monsters, diseases, snakes and other evil things in his wake. After the brothers had finished their journey far in the west, the evil twin turned into a giant, the Great World Rim Dweller, and the two began arguing about who had created the world. Finally, they decided to resolve the dispute by seeing who had the greater magic. Good Mind won and Evil Mind begged him to spare his life. Good Mind agreed if the giant promised to help the Haudenosaunee people by adopting them as his grandchildren. The giant agreed, promising that if the Haudenosaunee wore masks representing him and the other evil gods, and burned tobacco for them, he would give them the power to banish diseases, witches and high winds. (Parker, 59–73; Winter, 281–282)

Ayahuasca (also known as **Yage** or **Hoasca**). A very common **entheogen** among Amazonian Indians, especially **shamans**. Literally, it means "vine of the soul" or "vine of the dead," from "huasca," the word for "vine" and "aya," meaning "souls" or "the dead."

The hallucinogenic drink is made from the powdered bark of the *Baniseriopsis caapi* plant. Its primary mind altering components are harmine and dimethyltryptamine (DMT). Since these compounds are destroyed by enzymes in the stomach called monoamine oxidase (MAO), other plant substances that inhibit the activity of these enzymes are added.

Onset of action usually begins with nausea, sweating, dizziness and vomiting, followed by euphoria and hallucinations in which intense colors of blue, purple and gray are experienced.

Common themes in descriptions of anahuasca intoxication include sensations that the soul has separated from the body and is in flight, transformations into snakes or jaguars, and a sensation of communion with supernatural powers, visions of bright colors and complex geometric designs, fights with demons and animals, and watching one's own death. (Rudgley, 24–30; Schultes and Hofmann, 12, 19, 30, 36, 55, 59, 62–67, 124–137)

Bacchae. The Latinized form of Greek, **Bakkhai**, an alternate name for **Bacchantes** and **Maenads**. The Bacchae are women possessed by the spirit of **Dionysus**; they have the god within them (See **Entheogen**). They are followers traveling with Dionysus from Thrace to mainland Greece in his quest for recognition as a divinity. The entheogenic experience of these women is connected with his ritualistic worship and is oftentimes frenzied. (Grimal, 269–270; Price and Kearns, 80)

Bacchanalia. Cultic rites associated with worship of the Greek god of wine, **Bacchus** (or **Dionysus**), allegedly characterized by maniacal dancing to the sound of loud music and crashing cymbals, in which the revelers, called **Bacchantes**, whirled, screamed, became drunk and incited one another to greater and greater **ecstasy**. The goal was to achieve a state of **enthusiasm** in which the celebrants' souls were temporarily freed from their earthly bodies and were able to commune with Bacchus/Dionysus and gain a glimpse of and a preparation for what they would someday experience in eternity after their resurrection. The rite climaxed in a performance of frenzied feats of strength and madness, such as uprooting trees, tearing a bull (the symbol of Dionysus) apart with their bare hands, and eating its flesh raw.

This latter rite was a sacrament akin to communion in which the participants assumed the strength and character of the god by symbolically eating the raw flesh and drinking the blood of his symbolic incarnation. Because of their alleged immorality, the Roman senate banned Bacchanalias from Italy in 186 B.C. (Price and Kearns, 80)

Bacchantes. Devotees of **Bacchus** (or **Dionysus**); the Roman counterpart of the Greek **Maenads**. The Bacchantes periodically whipped themselves into a frenzied celebration of their cult called the **Bacchanalia.** (Grimal, 139, 224, 247, 264, 270)

Bacchus. The Roman name for **Dionysus**. The name came from Dionysus' Lydian name, Bakkhos, which the Romans transformed into Bacchus. The Lydian name was an epithet for Dionysus and meant "loud cries." (Grimal, 74)

Baitogogo. In Bororo South American Indian mythology, a spirit who punished those who did not share their tobacco with the gods.

One day, a fisherman discovered tobacco leaves inside a fish that he had caught, and kept his discovery to himself. During the night when everyone was asleep, he smoked the leaves in secret, but the smell woke his companions and they went looking for its source. He gave them some, but instead of exhaling the smoke, they swallowed it. Baitogogo subsequently visited them and told them they should exhale so that the spirits could share their tobacco. But the men continued to swallow the smoke. In the morning Baitogogo punished them for their gluttony by transforming them into otters and making them almost blind. (Albisetti et al., 63–66, 144–146; Levi-Strauss, 42)

Bakkhai *see* **Bacchae, Maenads.**

Balams. In Mayan mythology, gods of the winds and four directions who produced thunder and lightning by smashing large rocks together and lighted their cigars from the sparks of the colliding stones. (Winter, 47)

Balche. An intoxicating alcoholic drink, common in Lacandon Mayan culture, made from honey (or other sugar), water, and strips from the balche tree (Lonchocarpus longistylis), whose bark contains yeast. During the "balche ceremony," honey, water and balche strips are placed in a canoe especially made for the occasion. The mixture is then stirred and the boat covered. The ingredients are left to ferment for one or two days, and the mixture is stored in clay pots with the face of **Bol** molded on their sides. The clay pots are taken into a "god house," where the balche is poured into drinking gourds. Offerings are made to each of the gods by placing drops (the soul) of balche into incense pots ("god pots"). The soul of balche is transformed back into its liquid form and consumed by the gods. The initial psychoactive effect is euphoria, followed by bodily discomforts, including diarrhea and vomiting. The Lacandons are a small group (about 500 people) of Mayan descendants, living in Chiapas along the Mexican-Guatemalan border. (McGee, 8)

Baldev (or **Dauji**). In Hindu mythology, one of the manifestations of **Vishnu** who is offered bhang (cannabis) so that he will pay attention to prayers offered on his behalf. (Campbell, 1893, 251)

Ba-Maguje. In Nigerian Hausa mythology, the spirit of drunkenness. (*Probert Encyclopedia*, art. Ba-Maguje).

Bandzioku. In African Pygmy mythology, the first woman to ingest **iboga.** Bandzioku's first husband accidentally fell from a tree and died, and she married her brother-in-law, as required by her tribe's "levirate" marriage custom. Some time later, while she was fishing, she snared some human bones which, unknown to her, were her first husband's remains. She put them on shore, planning to gather them later, but an animal found them and took them away. Bandziouku followed the animal's trail until she came to a cave from which the voices of the spirits of the dead called out to her asking if she wanted to see them. When she said she did, they told her to eat the roots of an iboga plant that was growing in the corner of the entrance. After she ate it, she was able to see and talk to the spirits of dead, including the spirit of her first husband.

The next day, she returned to her village, and for several days afterwards returned to the cave with food for the spirits. Seeing her comings and goings, her second husband thought she was visiting a lover and followed her. When she came to the cave, the spirits asked her whom she had brought with her. When Bandzioku turned, her second husband asked whom she was talking to. Bandzioku pointed to the iboga plant and gave him some of its root to eat. Her husband was then also able to see and communicate with dead spirits including the spirit of his dead brother. The spirits then demanded her new husband give them an offering, but when he did, the spirits rejected it. The only other offering he could think of was his wife. The spirits accepted and he then killed his wife and sacrificed her, after which he took the iboga back to the village and built the first Witist temple. (Samorini, 5, 105–114, 119)

Bar Allei Toyon. In Yakut Siberian mythology, the god who taught humans how to make kumiss (an alcoholic drink made with milk). (Jochelson, 257–271)

Baruni *see* **Mada.**

Baugi *see* **Odin.**

Bege. In Papua, New Guinea mythology, a culture hero who discovered the **kava** plant growing out of kangaroo dung. During the night, the plant appeared in a dream and told him how to grow and use it and told him that only men were to drink it. Bege then told his people about kava and the rules for using it. See also **Culture heroes.** (Lebot et al., 124)

Beleke Belei. In Pygmy mythology, the woman responsible for the creation of palm wine.

When the world was first created, people did not drink water. Instead, when they were thirsty, they went to the marsh and squeezed juice from plants. One day, a man named Bonde Ilonga went hunting and brought the meat from an animal he had killed to his pregnant wife, Beleke Belei. But she said she didn't want that kind of meat and told him to bring her some other kind. Bonde Ilonga went out hunting again and came to a lake where his dog took a drink and suddenly fell dead. Angry over losing his dog, Bonde Ilonga filled his cup with some of the water from the lake and took it back with him. When he saw his wife, he told her that because of her demands, his dog was dead, and she should drink the water and die as well. His wife did as he told her, but the water didn't kill her. Instead, she said she liked it and wanted more.

After that, Bonde Ilonga went to the lake every day to get water for his wife. When Beleke Belei said she wanted to go with him even though she was pregnant, Bonde Ilonga refused to take her. But one day, she secretly followed him. When they came to the lake Beleke Belei jumped into it and washed herself. This made Bonde Ilonga very angry, because she was soiling the water they were drinking. But she answered that it didn't matter and told him to look at the bushes around the lake. Those bushes, she said, would grow very big and would give him a drink that was better than the water. And that is what happened. The bushes grew into large palms whose sap turned into wine. The Bangongo believed that had it not been for Beleke Beleke's bathing in the lake, the palms would still be bushes and not big trees (See also **Bunyi**). (Joseffson, 47)

Belladonna. Also known as Deadly Nightshade, Devil's Cherries, Devil's Herb, Naughty Man's Cherries. In Roman mythology, one of the ingredients in a concoction Roman priests drank in their prayers to Mars, god of war, for victory.

During the Middle Ages, it was said to belong to the Devil, who trimmed and tended it constantly and was only diverted from its care on Walpurgis, when he was preparing for the witches' sabbath, and was one of the primary ingredients of the brews and ointments said to have been used by witches to enable them to fly.

The name is derived from the use of its juice by Italian ladies to dilate the pupils of their eyes, regarded as indicating a romantic interest in a suitor (the pupils of the eyes dilate naturally when we are excited, and atropine is still used by ophthalmologists for that purpose, so that they can see into the interior of the eye more easily).

Atropa belladonna, the plant's botanical name, is a perennial that sometimes grows as high as three feet. It has green leaves, and drooping, bell-shaped purplish flowers that turn into shiny black berries. The plant grows in thickets and woods and often near old buildings.

The name of the main psychoactive substance in the plant, atropine, is derived from the Atropos, one of the Greek **Fates** who held the shears that cut the thread of human life—a reference to its deadly, poisonous nature. It also contains smaller amounts of the related substance, scopolamine. Psychoactive effects include visual hallucinations and a sense of weightlessness, the basis for its inclusion in the "witches' brew." However, the amount that causes psychoactive effects is very close to the amount that is toxic, symptoms of which include dry mouth, confusion, rapid heartbeat, cardiorespiratory failure, and coma. (Rudgley, 32–36; Schultes and Hofmann, 26, 68, 88, 107)

Berserks. In Norse mythology, fearless warriors who went into battle in a frenzy induced by a rage-inducing substance given to them by **Odin**. While the substance has sometimes been identified as fly agaric mushroom, there are no instances in which the plant or its ingredient has provoked brutal violence. More traditionally, the inciting substance has been identified as beer or mead, in keeping with alcohol's better-known potential for provoking aggressiveness. (Davidson, 71; Fee and Leeming, 20–21)

Bes. In Egyptian mythology, the misshapen god of revelry and childbirth, who was the constant companion of Hathor, goddess of drunkenness and dancing while holding bunches of grapes. (Jayne, 55; Lutz, 114)

Beyla. In Norse mythology, the goddess of ale; the wife of **Byggvir**, the god of ale. (Davidson, 108)

Bhanganath. In Sikh religion, the "lord of bhang (cannabis)." (Archer, 96)

Bhimo Raja. In middle Indian mythology, the god of **tobacco**, cannabis, and the underworld. One of the minor deities in his realm had seven sisters that no one in the underworld wanted to marry. Frustrated, the sisters journeyed to the world of humans looking for husbands. Although they fell in love with every man they saw, the men didn't feel the same about them. Despondent, they returned to the underworld. When they told their father of their rejection, he took them to Bhimo Raja and asked him what they should do to attract suitors. Bhimo Raja rubbed some dirt from his body and gave it to each sister. When they touched it they all turned to earth. Bhim Raja then struck a gong and a different plant sprang from each sister. Two of these plants were tobacco and cannabis, and the sisters now became desirable to every man. (Elwin, 1991, 328)

Bol (or **Bohr**). Lacandon Mayan god of creation and intoxication, especially from **balche**. Bol devised the ceremony for humans to become intoxicated on balche, because their gods would likewise become intoxicated, creating a mutual harmonious condition in which humans could communicate with the gods and they, in turn, would be receptive to their requests. (McGee, 148; Ratsh, 52; Thompson and Eric, 311)

Bona Dea (also known as Bona Dia or Bona Diua). A woman who was deified after being killed by her husband because she became drunk. She became a Roman fertility goddess who was primarily worshiped by enslaved women under her other name, **Fauna** (from *fatuari*, meaning "to speak for," a name related to prophecies spoken in ecstatic or intoxicated states). Bona Dea was a title, not a name. (Adkins and Adkins, 32; Grimal, 76; Hammon and Scullard, 172)

Bonde Ilonga *see* **Beleke Belei.**

Boram Burha. In middle India mythology, the god of rice beer. One day, while he was away from home and cooking rice, a root he was holding accidentally fell into his pot. After it had been in the pot for some time, Boram Burha noticed it and ate it. The root made him forget about the rice and it dried up. When he came home, after a few days, his wife was angry that he was away so long and asked where the rice pot was. Boram Burha went back to get his rice pot, and since it was dried out, he poured some water into it and heated it. Thirsty, he decided to drink it and the drink made him intoxicated and he began dancing and acting very elated. When his wife saw her husband so happy, she drank some of the potion too, and she also became intoxicated. When the people in their village asked Boram Burha what had made them so happy, he told them and after that, their people, the Bhuiyas, had rice beer. (Elwin, 1954, 208–209)

Braciaca. The Celtic god of intoxication, and personification of "bracca" malt beer; sometimes identified with the god of war in northern Spain and France. She provided alcoholic drinks to warriors before they set out to battle to excite them to greater heroics. (MacCulloch, 28; Ross, 180–181)

Bragafull *see* **Bragi.**

Bragi. In Norse mythology, the god of poetry and eloquence. Bragi was the son of Odin and became the new keeper of the mead after **Odin** stole it from **Suttung.** Bragi's wife, Idun, guarded the apples of immortality which did not cause intoxication.

As the god of mead-inspired eloquence, Bragi welcomed the **Ein-**

herjar when they came to **Valhalla.** He was so highly esteemed, that the cup of ale that a new king drank in a single draught when he toasted the gods was called the **Bragafull,** in Bragi's name. (Davidson, 164; Orchard, 20; Simek, 42)

Brahma. In Hindu mythology, one of the three main gods of the pantheon (the others are **Siva** and **Vishnu**). Brahma is the creator of the universe (he created himself) including the gods, demons, and humans and source of all knowledge. Unlike the other gods, he is not worshiped, because his work is finished. However, as in the **Churning of the Ocean,** he is sometimes consulted by the other gods for advice. The eponymous term, Brahman, means ultimate reality, the indescribable cosmic force in the world. (Mahony, 67–68, 77–78, 114–119)

Bran. In Irish legend, a **culture hero** who discovered an earthly Paradise island inhabited by women who provided him and his followers an inexhaustible supply of food and a highly intoxicating liquor. The motif of the inexhaustible food and drink and far-off Paradise were adapted into the legend of the **Holy Grail.** (Brown, 67–74)

Brew of Inspiration. In Welsh mythology, the concoction brewed by **Ceridwen,** conferring wisdom.

Buffalo Spirit *see* **Earthmaker.**

Bunyi. In African Kuba mythology, the man who discovered palm wine.

When the world and humans were first created, there was a very large lake of palm wine instead of water, close to where the Kuba lived, and they could drink as much wine as they wanted. This ended, however, when a woman, Nanchamba, polluted the lake by urinating into it. After that no one would drink from the lake anymore. The next day the lake dried up completely and a thick forest of trees appeared where it had been.

One day a pygmy called Bunyi began to wonder what had happened to the lake and concluded that it had been sucked up by the trees. He then wondered what the sap from these trees would taste like and he climbed to the top of one of them and made a hole in it, but no sap flowed and he went home. That night Bunyi had a dream in which a spirit appeared and asked him what good an idea was without perseverance and urged him to try again. When he returned to the tree the next day, he saw a thin trickle of sap flowing from the hole he had made.

Bunyi tasted the sap, found it sweet, placed a pot underneath the hole to collect it, and then returned to his village without telling anyone about his discovery. Bunyi continued collecting and drinking the sap in secret, noticing that its potency increased the longer it stayed in the pot. One day, after drinking a very large amount, he came back to his village drunk and disorderly. When the king asked him what had caused him to act that way, Bunyi told him his secret. The king then sent a servant to see if what Bunyi had said were true. When the servant returned and verified Bunyi's discovery, the king announced the great news to his people and they all went to the forest and collected seeds from the palms and planted them everywhere. After that the pygmies had palm wine and to keep them from getting drunk, the king ordered that no man was ever to drink alone; whenever he drank palm wine, he had to have a friend with him to keep him from drinking too much. See also **Beleke Belei**. (Josefsson, 46; Torday, 1919, 42; Torday, 1925, 126–127)

Butoriku. In South American Bororo Indian mythology, a snake from whose blood tobacco originated.

Butoriku often attacked the Bororo and swallowed them. One day after he killed the mother of one of the Bororo, her son avenged his mother's death by killing him. The man then cut up Butoriku's body, and gave pieces of it to all the men of the tribe, who in turn gave it to their wives to carry back. At night, the women began dancing with pieces of the snake in celebration of its death, taking care to cover themselves with leaves so that the snake's dripping blood would not have a chance to accidentally fertilize them. However, one of the women, named Aturarodo, didn't cover herself very well and she became impregnated by Butoriku's blood. Before its normal time of birth, her unborn child came out of her womb for some food and Aturarodo saw that he was a monster like his father. The unborn child returned to her womb after eating and Aturarodo returned to the village and told everyone what had happened. They told her to go back to the place where the fetus had emerged, and when the monster once again came out for food, they clubbed him to death and burned his ashes. Some time later Aturarodo went back to the grave where her son's ashes had been buried and saw that a number of plants were growing from his grave, among them tobacco.

A variation of the story says that tobacco sprouted from the ashes of a snake to which Aturarodo gave birth after she was accidentally fertilized by blood of an anaconda whose body she was bringing back to her village after it had been killed by her husband during a hunt. (Albisetti et al., 138–144; Levi Strauss, 41–42)

Byggvir. In Norse mythology, the **Vanir** god of ale; his wife, **Beyla**, was the goddess of mead. The Nordic Bryggdag, Brewer's Day (August 1), in which grains are harvested for making various Christmas ales, is named after him. As part of the ceremony, a bowl containing barley is blessed and a cup of ale is drunk in his name. (Davidson, 108)

Byrgir. In Norse mythology, a secret well located in the kingdom of **Ivaldi** containing waters that conferred wisdom and **ecstasy**. (Rydberg, 90)

Cachui *see* **Caterpillar.**

Callirrhoe. In Greek mythology, a young maiden whom Coresus, a priest of **Dionysus** in Calydonia, in western Greece, fell in love with. When Callirrhoe rejected him, Dionysus took it as a personal rejection, and drove all the Calydonian women insane. When their husbands asked his oracle what they had to do to rid them of the calamity, the oracle said the plague would continue until Coresus sacrificed Callirrhoe or someone willing to die in her stead, to Dionysus. When Coresus saw Callirrhoe being dragged to the altar, his love overcame him and he impulsively killed himself in her place, proving that his love was genuine and not simply lust. Seeing Coresus' dead body, Callirrhoe suddenly felt both love and remorse and killed herself as well, and the two were later married in the afterworld. (Pausanias, 7.21.1–5)

Cannabis. (Cannabis sativa) A tall green plant whose active psychoactive component is tetrahydrocannabinol (THC). The intoxicating preparation made from its resin-coated leaves and flowers has hundreds of names, among them marijuana, hashish, dagga, kif, bhang, ganja, charas, etc. Preparations are usually smoked, but are also eaten.

Cannabis grows throughout the world, but its THC content varies greatly depending on the geographical area where it grows. Psychoactive effects include euphoria, relaxation, disorientation, and changes in auditory, visual, and time perception. Effects are due to the resemblance of THC to anandamide, a naturally occurring **neurotransmitter** in the brain. (Rudgley, 44–57; Schultes and Hofmann, 12, 38, 72–73, 81, 92–101, 107–108, 184–185)

Cannibal Woman. In various South American Indian mythologies, a woman from whose body **tobacco** originated.

In the Toba Indian version, a man went hunting with his wife for parakeets. When he saw her eating one of the birds he became alarmed and ran off, but his wife followed and killed him. Then she cut off his head, put it in a bag, and ate the rest of his body. When she came home she put her bag down and told her children not to look in it, but when she left, her youngest child untied the bag. The sight of their father's head horrified them. Their screams brought the whole village to their house, but when they saw the decapitated head they were also horrified and ran away. When their mother returned, the village was deserted. When her children told her the people had run away because of what they had seen, she followed their tracks, killed many of them, and returned, warning her children that if they tried to run away she would catch and eat them, too.

Fearing their mother would eat them anyway, the children fashioned a trap that ensnared their mother and they ran away. But their mother escaped and pursued them. The fleeing boys eventually came to the home of Carancho, the tree spirit. When they told Carancho who they were Carancho told them that the rest of their village was hiding in hollowed out trees and let them do the same. Despite their being hidden, their mother found them and stuck her claws into the tree in which they were hiding and threatened to kill them if they didn't come out. But the next time Cannibal Woman stuck her claws into Carancho's side, Carancho held them firmly and emerging from the tree, killed her. Then her children came out of the tree and burned her body. Four days tobacco grew from those ashes.

In the Makka version, a woman becomes insane because she broke the menstrual taboo against touching food. Transformed into Cannibal woman, she kills her husband, castrates him, takes his testicles back to her village and eats them in front of the villagers. Aghast, the villagers ran away, but by then Cannibal Woman had developed wings and flew after them, killing and eating the men. Some time later, Cannibal Woman's children caught her in a trap, but when they tried to kill her she did not die. The children beat her and beat her to make her tell how to kill her, until finally, unable to stand the pain any longer, she told them. After they killed her, her sons burnt her body, except for her tail. Shortly thereafter tobacco sprouted from her ashes, and her tail, which was able to walk and talk, led them to hiding villagers and brought them back to their village. (Arenas et al., 58–70)

Cashinaua. In South American Cashinaua Indian mythology, the culture heroine who gave birth to mankind after taking **tobacco**. (Wilbert, 1987, 152)

Catamitus *see* **Ganymede.**

Caterpillar. In South American Yanomamo Indian mythology, the spirit of the **tobacco** worm who gave tobacco to a man named Kinkajou, which turned him into a **shaman**.

One day Caterpillar was walking through the forest when he encountered a man named Kinkajou sitting in a tree crying because he didn't have any tobacco. Caterpillar gave him some but it was so strong it made him vomit, but it still put him into a state of rapture, and then turned him into an animal.

In South American Ayoreo Indian mythology, Caterpillar was called **Kachui,** and was credited with planting tobacco. After he ate some of its leaves, the spirit of tobacco filled his body and he was transformed into a **shaman**. (Bormida et al., 192–193)

Cauldron. A brewing kettle that provided an endless supply of food and drink, and in some myths, intoxicating substances that conferred immortality and wisdom; by association, the symbol of fertility, wisdom and alchemy. In most myths, the cauldron's contents are inexhaustible. Cauldrons are commonplace in Indo-European mythologies. The best-known belong to Aegir in Norse mythology, and Ceridwen in Celtic mythology. The prototype is India's myth of the **Churning of the Ocean.** In transition, the miraculous cauldron became a goblet, **magic** bowl, dish, chalice or Holy Grail. In Welsh myths, the **wine** goblet also symbolized sovereignty and marriage and its theft represented the abduction of the queen and the loss of her kingdom's fertility. (Littleton, 326–333; Oosten, 72–90; Stewart, R., 119)

Cauldron of Bran. In Irish and Welsh mythology, a **cauldron** of ale belonging to the giant **Bran**. The cauldron's contents had the ability to restore health and revive the bodies of the dead that were put into it overnight. The following morning they came to life and were eager for battle; their only handicap was that they could no longer speak. The giant Bran gave the cauldron to the king as a wedding gift since he was marrying Bran's sister, Branwen. But the king mistreated her and Bran installed Gwern, his sister's son, as the new king. During the amnesty party, Gwern was murdered and fighting broke out again, with the Irish reviving their dead in the cauldron. (Jones and Jones, 256; Oosten, 73)

Cauldron of Ceridwen *see* **Ceridwen.**

Cauldron of Dagdha. In Irish mythology, a **magic** container for ale belonging to king **Dagdha** which never emptied no matter how much was drunken from it. (Oosten, 73, 84; Stewart, R., 125)

Cauldron of Rebirth *see* **Cauldron of Bran.**

Cauldron of Wisdom and Inspiration *see* **Ceridwen.**

Celestial Wine. In Chinese mythology, the wine drunk by the Eight Immortals (a group of gods with the power of life and death) that made them more intelligent and quick witted. (Ferguson, 129)

Centaurs. In Greek mythology, creatures with the lower body of a horse and the upper body of a human, who were known for their animal nature dominating their human nature, as reflected in their frequent drunkenness and violence. The centaurs are the Greek counterparts of the **Gandharas** in Indian mythology.

The centaurs were the descendants of Ixion, a minor deity whom Zeus invited to feast on **ambrosia** with the gods. However, when Ixion saw Zeus's wife, Hera, he felt lustful toward her. When Zeus learned of his passion, he created a hallucinatory cloud that looked like Hera, and Ixion mated with it. Zeus punished Ixion by tying him to a fiery wheel that whirled forever in the underworld and banished Centauros, the child of Ixion's union, with the cloud as the embodiment of a creature having neither honor among humans, nor respect for the laws of the gods. Centauros went to live with the mares that roamed around Mount Pelion in Thessaly, and had sex with many of them. It was from those unions that the centaurs were born with a human's upper body, after their father, and a horse's body and legs after their mothers. Since their grandfather had drunk ambrosia and their father was created in a hallucination, the centaurs were born with a passion for wine, its earthly counterpart, and they were known for their drunkenness.

In one of their drunken episodes, the centaurs disrupted a wedding to which they had been invited, by trying to abduct all the women, including the bride. After being defeated in the ensuing fight, they were driven from Mount Pelion.

The centaurs then went to live in Arcadia where they again got into trouble because of their passion for wine. This time the trouble started when they smelled some wine that the centaur Pholus, who was an exception to his fellow brutish kinsmen, had offered to Heracles in accord with the tradition of hospitality normally shown to strangers. Pholus had been reluctant to give Heracles any wine since it was the common property of all the centaurs. Heracles, however, insisted. When the centaurs scented the wine, they traced the scent and attacked Heracles. In the ensuring fight Heracles killed many of them and drove the rest away. (Gantz, 390–392; Kelly, 35–36; Price and Kearns, 105–106; Ruck et al., 2001, 15–21)

Centzon Totochtin. In Mayan mythology, literally, the "four hundred rabbits," the collective name for the **pulque** gods. Each god was identified with a rabbit number ranging from one to four hundred, each number embodying a different degree of drunkenness pulque can induce such as belligerence, pensiveness, sleepiness, contempt, paranoia, boisterousness, etc. The rabbit was a metaphor for drunkenness, because it was considered totally lacking in sense; 400 was the greatest stage of intoxication. The Four Hundred Rabbits was also a calendar day. Those born on that day were doomed to become drunkards. (Guerra, 248–249; H. I. Nicholson, 165,168; Mackenzie, 195–196; Spence, 1911, 104)

Ceres. The Roman goddess of fertility and agriculture; the counterpart of the Greek goddess, Demeter; like her, she was associated with opium. A statue of Ceres depicted her holding a torch and poppy pods. (Booth, 20)

Ceridwen (also known as **Cerridwen, Keridwen,** or **Kerridwen**). In Celtic/Welsh mythology, the goddesses of brewers and prophecy; a shape shifting witch whose brew of inspiration transformed an ordinary boy into a divinely inspired poet. She was symbolized as a hag, or sow, reflecting her possible earlier status as a fertility deity.

Ceridwen lived in the Underworld with her two children, a beautiful daughter, Creiwy, representing light (or good), and an ugly son **Afagddu** (also known as Morfran) representing dark (or bad). Believing her son's ugliness would prevent him from acceptance by those of noble birth, she looked for a way to offset his appearance by giving him divine knowledge and the ability to see into the future. To give him that power, she concocted a "brew of inspiration," in her **magic** cauldron, called Amen. The first three drops of the brew conferred its wisdom and prophecy on whomever they touched; the rest of the brew from the **cauldron** was lethal. To become effective, however, the brew had to be boiled day and night for a year and a day, so she put a blind man, named Morda, in charge of stirring the mixture and a young boy,

Gwion Bach, to keep the fire under the cauldron burning, while she kept it filled with water and her special herbs.

As the end of the brewing time came near, Ceridwen put her son Afaggdu by the cauldron so that she could put the first precious drops on him when the critical hour arrived, and then she sat down to rest.

When the critical moment finally came, the three magical drops bubbled out of the cauldron while Ceridwen was asleep. Either the drops accidentally spilled onto Gwion Bach's thumb, or, seeing the unprecedented opportunity, Gwion Bach shoved Afaggdu aside so they would fall on his hand, it was Gwion Bach and not Afaggdu who was instantly filled with wisdom and inspiration, including the realization that Ceridwen would kill him for his misdeed, so he ran away. When Ceridwen discovered what had happened she took off in a maddened frenzy to kill Gwion. The fleeing Gwion tried to escape by means of a series of shape-shiftings, beginning with changing himself into a rabbit so that he could run faster. But Ceridwen was also a shape-shifter, and she changed herself into a greyhound to keep up. Gwion then turned himself into a fish but Ceridwen turned herself into an otter. Next Gwion became a bird; Ceridwen became hawk. Finally, Gwion turned himself into a kernel of corn to hide among hundreds of other kernels in a farmyard, but Ceridwen turned herself into a hen and swallowed him.

The corn seed made Ceridwen pregnant. Realizing the baby inside her was Gwion Bach, she planned to kill him at birth, but when the child was born, he was so beautiful she could not do him any harm or let anyone else harm him. Instead, she wrapped him in a leather basket and put him into the river. He was later found by a fisherman named Elphin who, seeing the baby's shining brow, named him **Taliesin** (shining brow). Taliesin was able to talk when he was born and he grew up to become a great poet.

Subsequent versions of the story were set in the time of King Arthur and his Round Table. Ceridwen's ugly son was named Morfran, and when Taliesin grew up, he had a son who became Merlin the magician.

The story of Gwion Bach/Talesin is similar to the Irish story about Finn MacCool (Finn Mac Cumhail) who is given the job of cooking the Salmon of wisdom by a magician named Fintan. In that story, the salmon, a symbol of wisdom, originally swam in a well eating nuts that fell into it from some hazel trees. One day the goddess Boann, the lover of **Dagda**, tried to drink from the well but it burst and became the river Boyne, which was named after her. Many people tried to catch the salmon as it swam in the river, but only Demne was able to. Demne took the fish to his master, Fintan, who had him cook it for him. While Demne was cooking the salmon, some of the grease from the cooking pot splattered onto his thumb and he was imbued with the wisdom of the salmon and he became known as Finn MacCool. (Stewart, R., 88–90)

Chandu. In Middle India mythology, the god who created **tobacco.**

Feeling remorseful that a woman had died unmarried because of her unattractive appearance, Chandu sowed tobacco seeds at her burial site. Some time later, a goatherder noticed his animals avidly eating the tobacco leaves. Curious about what was enticing his goats, he chewed some of the leaves himself. But as soon as he tasted them, he spat them out because of their bitter taste. The goatherder forgot about the leaves, but was reminded of them when he developed a toothache he couldn't relieve with his usual remedies and decided to see if the bitter leaves might help. He chewed the leaves and instead of spitting them out as before, kept them in his mouth and soon felt his pain relieved. After that he continued chewing tobacco every day and told other men with toothaches about how it helped him. They also began chewing tobacco and like the goatherder, developed a craving for it. As a result, the girl who had previously gone unnoticed became something that all men craved (variants substitute opium for tobacco). (Bompas, 407; Elwin, 1958, 212–213; Elwin, 1991, 323–324)

Chang'o. In Chinese mythology, the moon goddess who stole the "elixir of life" from her husband and fled to the moon.

Chang'o and her husband, Yi, lived in the heavens with the other gods, but were banished to earth to live as mortals by Di Jun, the Lord of Heaven, because Yi, the master archer, had killed nine of Di Jun's sons to save the earth. All ten were suns, and when they rose together one morning their blazing heat had threatened the existence of everything on earth. In revenge, Di Jun banished Yi and his wife Chang'o from heaven to live as mortals among the humans on earth.

Chang'o let her husband know how much she resented being punished for something he had done, and she expressed her grief that they were no longer immortal and would die. Their only hope was to get some of the elixir of life from the Queen Mother of the West who lived on Mount Kunlun.

To appease his wife, Yi trekked to the Queen Mother. After hearing his story, she gave Yi enough elixir for both him and his wife to regain their immortality; but they would still have to live with humans. To become immortal and live once again in heaven, they would need twice as much, but she couldn't give them any more.

When Yi returned home he told his wife what the Queen had said, and told her that in a few days he would prepare a feast and they would take the drug. But Chang'o was not content. She wanted to be a goddess and live among the gods in Heaven again. So, while her husband was out hunting, she found the elixir and drank it all. As soon as she did, she began thinking that the other gods would resent her theft of the drug, so instead of going to live with them, she made her home on the moon.

A variation of the myth has the Queen Mother of the West giving the elixir to Yi (who is called Hou Ki) as a reward for saving the earth. A third variation makes Hou Ki a spiritual man who decides to fast for one year before drinking the elixir to demonstrate his gratitude for the opportunity to once again become immortal. One evening when Yi wasn't home, Chang'o found the magic potion and drank it all. Hou Ki returned just in time to see his wife rising into the night sky on her way to the moon. (Sanders, 32)

Charops. In Greek mythology, a Thracian who warned **Dionysus** of Lycurgus's plot against him. After defeating **Lycurgus**, Dionysus initiated Charops into his mysteries and made him king of Thrace. Charops passed his knowledge of the Dionysiac religion to his descendants, including his grandson, **Orpheus**. (Grimal, 99)

Cherri-choulang. In Micronesian (Caroline Islands) mythology, the deity who took pity on mankind for its hardships and dropped a piece of **kava** down from heaven to earth to enable humans to cope more serenely. (Christian, 190, 382)

Chi. Himalayan god of Chi, a beer made from millet. (Gorer, 96).

Chicha. A fermented Central and South American alcoholic beer made from a variety of plants, but most often from maize or manioc. During the pre–Hispanic era, it was a common everyday drink and was also used in many rituals. It was typically made by spitting into maize flour (saliva contains an enzyme, diastase, which triggers the conversion of the starches in the maize into sugar), and letting it ferment for three days. Chicha doesn't store well so it is typically drunk soon after it is made, resulting in regular period of intoxication. (Moore, 682–685).

Chimalpanecatl. A Mayan **pulque** god. (Anderson and Dibble, 2: 51; H. Nicholson, 167)

Chiu Hsien. In Chinese Taoist mythology, the spirit of wine. (Day, 163)

Chu'ang Mu. Along with her husband, Ch'ang Kung, a Chinese wine goddess, who facilitated fertility and harmony between couples. (*New Larouse Encyclopedia of Mythology*, 112)

Chuckit. Same as Tsukit, or **Hukaht.**

Churning of the Ocean. In Hindu mythology, the seminal story of the struggle between the forces of good and evil resulting in the recovery of **amrta,** the elixir of immortality, and wine.

Sometime after the creation of the universe, the amrta was somehow lost. In the ensuing time, the **Deva** demi-gods, and the **Asuras,** the demons, were constantly fighting with one another for supremacy. For a long time no side had the upper hand, but eventually the battle shifted in favor of the Asuras.

Facing annihilation, the Devas appealed to **Brahma,** the creator of the universe and source of all knowledge. Brahman was sympathetic to their plight. He, in turn, asked **Vishnu** to help them. Vishnu told the distressed Devas they had to pretend to make a truce with the Asuras and then ask them to help churn the Cosmic Ocean to recover, and ostensibly share, the amrta. Once this was done, he would get them the amrta.

After the truce was agreed to, the two sides collectively uprooted Mount Mandara, to use as a churn, and they carried it to the Cosmic Ocean where they persuaded Vasuki, the serpent king, to be the rope for them to rotate the churn; in return they promised him a share of the amrta. The Devas took one end and the Asuras another, but the mountain was too heavy and began to sink to the bottom of the ocean. To keep it from sinking any farther, Vishnu assumed the form of a Giant Turtle, and dived to the bottom of the ocean and supported the base of the mountain on his back.

The first thing to emerge from the churning was a poisonous fume that threatened to destroy everyone. Alarmed, the Devas and Asuras both appealed to **Siva** to save them. Without hesitating, Siva gulped but did not swallow the poison, which gave his throat a blue color, and earned him the epithet, blue-throated. A few drops of the poison, however, fell to the ground and were quickly swallowed by snakes, scorpions, and poisonous plants and animals.

Once the air was cleared of the poison, the Devas and Asuras resumed their churning. A series of beings then emerged from it including Sura, the goddess of all intoxicating drinks, and Dhanvantari, the physician of the gods, holding the amrta in a jar.

The Asuras immediately snatched the jar and started fighting among themselves for it until a seductive beautiful girl suddenly appeared who so enchanted them all that they stopped battling and handed the jar of amrta to her, asking her to decide who would get it. The girl, named Mohini, was actually an avatar of Vishnu. Mohini told the Devas and Asuras to form into two lines opposite one another. Holding the jar of amrta, she walked between the groups, giving each of the Devas, the demi-gods, the first sip. The Asuras assumed Mohini would give them their turn when she came to the end of the line, but instead, Mohini revealed herself as Vishnu in disguise. Just before he was about to disappear, however, he noticed that Rahu, one of the Asuras, had disguised himself to look like a Deva and had taken a place among them. As he was about to swallow his portion of the amrta, Visnu beheaded him with his discus. Although Rahu's body perished, the amrta made his head immortal and Vishnu hurled it into the moon. There, he continued to drink the amrta, but the amrta passed out of his throat.

As soon as the Asuras realized they had been tricked, they starting fighting with the Devas again. But now that the Devas had drunk the amrta, they had become immortal and easily defeated the Asuras, banishing them to the darkness of the underworld. Triumphant, the Devas retired to a beautiful palace on the top of Mt. Sumeru, the central mountain of the world where they dined on amrta forever.

In later versions, amrta was identified with **soma**. (Zimmer, 105ff)

Chyavana *see* **Cyavana**.

Cihuacoatl. The Aztec mother goddess, also known as "Snake Woman," was the most powerful of the Aztec goddesses and had an unquenchable thirst for blood. Her body was composed of tobacco and was incarnated as such on earth. She had a frightening appearance, with an exposed jawbone, and a mouth that was always gaping to eat more victims. Cihuacoatl was both a goddess of regeneration and a goddess of death. As goddess of regeneration and fertility and she was identified with other mother goddesses such as Coatlicue. As a goddess of death, she brought misery and death through warfare and human sacrifice. If she did not have human blood to drink or human hearts to eat, she would not produce tobacco. (Miller and Taube, 169; Robicsek, 17; Winter, 299, 303)

Coadidop. In South American Desana mythology, the goddess of tobacco.

At the beginning of time she lived alone with her son but they became lonesome. Wanting companions, she extracted tobacco from her body, rolled it into a cigar, and lit it. The smoke from the cigar turned into male friends for her son, and female companions for her. Then she gave tobacco to the Desana women so that they could raise plants to live on. (Leeming and Page, 34)

Coatlicue *see* **Cihuacoatl.**

Coca (*Erythroxylon coca*). A bush native to the South American Andes, from Colombia to Bolivia. The plant can grow to a height of 25 feet but is usually pruned to a height of six feet so that its leaves, which are usually harvested three to six times a year, can be more easily gathered. The leaves, which contain from 0.1 to 0.8 percent cocaine depending on where it grows, are dried and allowed to ferment slightly. The leaves are then dipped into solutions of ash or lime, which allows the plant's **alkaloid** content to be absorbed better, and it is then chewed or brewed into a tea. When chewed, saliva mixes with the powder, and the enzymes cause the cocaine in the leaves to leech out. The leaves are then spat out. Effects from chewing include mild stimulation similar to coffee, and a numb or tingling sensation in the mouth and throat. The plant was used by the Incas, and is still used by natives, to relive fatigue, pain and hunger. The far more potent cocaine hydrochloride is the white crystalline concentrate made from the leaves. (Rudgley, 58–63; Schultes and Hofmann, 12, 29, 64, 113, 117)

Coca Mama *see* **Mama Coca.**

Cohiba. In Haitian mythology, a princess who fell in love with Tabaca, a commoner from neighboring island of Cuba. However, their two tribes were enemies. When their affair was discovered, the lovers tried to flee but were captured and were put to death by fire. A new plant sprouted from their ashes that no one had ever been seen before and whose leaves gave off an irresistible odor when dried. The Haitians named the plant Cohiba after the princess and created a pipe to smoke it that they called tabaca, inhaling its smoke as a ritual recalling the burning of the two lovers by fire. (Mooney, 23)

Cohoba. A psychoactive snuff made from seeds of the yopo tree (Anadenanthera peregrine) that grows in Central and South America.

The primary psychoactive ingredient is DMT (N, N-dimethyl-tryptamine). Its main psychoactive effect is intense visual hallucinations. (Schultes and Hofmann, 26, 116)

Colhuatzincatl. A Mayan **pulque** god. (Alexander, 77; Boone, 204; H. Nicholson, 167)

Comus. The Roman god of drunkenness; he presided over banquets and festivities. (Jobes, 363)

Consciousness, Altered State *see* **Altered State of Consciousness.**

Corn Goddess. In North American Pueblo Indian mythology, the mother goddess who purified the earth using **tobacco**.

When the world was first created it was still not perfect so Corn Goddess instructed Hummingbird Man and Fly to bring some gifts to Turkey Buzzard and to ask him to purify the earth and the thunderclouds. Turkey Buzzard, however, was not satisfied with their gifts. When the messengers returned and told Corn Goddess that Turkey had not been happy with their gifts, she sent them to a hill where Tobacco Caterpillar lived for some tobacco and they brought it to Turkey Buzzard, which pleased him. After he smoked and blew the smoke to the north, south, east and west, the earth became fertile, the clouds were filled with rain, and food became plentiful.

In the Acoma variant of this myth, Corn Goddess was a recluse, because people were making fun of her. When Hummingbird Man, who loved the nectar in tobacco flowers, saw what was happening, he realized that the people were mocking Corn Goddess, because tobacco was not part of her ceremonies. When he told Corn Goddess the problem, she included the tobacco pipe in her rites, and the people no longer made fun of her. (Winter, 44)

Coyote. In various North American Indian tribal folklores, a **trickster** who gave humans **tobacco**.

In the Kawaiisu version, Coyote was in his winter house when he heard a noise like the buzzing of the bee. Curious, he went outside and noticed a black substance on the ground. He asked it who it was but the substance didn't answer. After the same buzzing occurred for several nights, Coyote demanded to know what the substance was. The substance answered that it was the juice of tobacco and had no mother or father or any other relative and hadn't come from anywhere. Since it had no family, Coyote said he would use it as a medicine so it would have many friends.

In Apache folklore, Coyote paid a visit to his cousin, Sun, but Sun wasn't home. When he saw Sun's tobacco bag hanging on the side of the house, he asked Sun's wife to give him some while he waited for Sun to return, but when she wasn't looking he stole most of it and left. When Sun returned, he noticed his tobacco bag was almost empty and asked her where it had gone. As soon as she mentioned Coyote had visited and left, he went out after him to get his tobacco back. While Coyote was escaping, however, it began to rain and the tobacco he had stolen began to grow and its leaves ripened and dried and the wind scattered its seeds. With tobacco plants growing everywhere, Sun stopped chasing Coyote and went back home.

Meanwhile, Coyote returned to the Apache camp where he was living and refused to share his tobacco. Miffed, the Apache elders held a council and devised a plan to get Coyote's tobacco. They pretended they were glad to see him back and told him they were giving him a wife, and set up a tent for him. Coyote was so appreciative, he gave them all his tobacco. But instead of a girl, they dressed a young boy as a girl and told him not to let Coyote touch him until dawn. At dawn, when the boy finally let Coyote touch him, Coyote discovered his bride was a male and became very angry at being deceived. He went to the elders and demanded his tobacco back, but they refused, and that was how the Apache first got tobacco. (Morris, 293; Zigmond, 199–200)

Cronos. In Greek mythology, the father of Zeus. Zeus plied him with mead and when he was "honey-drunk" and asleep, Zeus castrated him. (Gantz, 41–51; Porphyry, 1ff)

Culture Heroes. Benefactors associated with the origins of cultural practices such as agriculture, control of fire, tool making, or institutions, social customs and traditions such as matriarchal or patriarchal inheritance, kingship, priesthood, etc. The culture hero is often the means by which supreme beings create the world and make it habitable for mankind. Unlike supernatural beings, the culture hero is not omniscient or omnipotent and in some stories he is a buffoon or **trickster,** especially in many North American Indian stories. After accomplishing his or her task, the culture hero is often transformed into the moon or some other cosmic sign, or disappears into the earth from which a special plant later emerges.

The culture hero is often depicted in myths as twins, representing opposites such as good and bad, benefactor and buffoon. While usually human, in some myths the culture hero is an animal or insect. Culture heroes are often referred to as transformers, demiurges, and sometimes, shamans. (Price and Kearns, 137).

Cusna. In Hindu mythology, an Asura who revived other **Asuras** slain in the perpetual conflict between the Asuras and their **Deva** antagonists. (Bloomfield, 1893, 8)

Cyavana. In Indian mythology, the culture hero who bartered soma for his youth and created **Mada**, the goddess of intoxication.

Cyavana had become so aged, his body was withered and he told his sons to abandon him. They at first refused, but finally did as he asked. While he was sitting by a river, a group of boys began insulting him. Cyavana retaliated by putting a curse on them that made them sick. When their father saw what had happened to his sons he asked Cyavana to relent and tried to mollify him by offering him his daughter, Sukanya, and she became his wife.

Shortly, thereafter, the **Asvins** came by and were smitten with Sukanya's beauty. Seeing how debilitated Cyavana had become, they tried to seduce Sukanya. But Sukanya remained faithful to Cyavana. When she told Cyavana what had happened, he was pleased, and devised a plan to get the Asvins to restore his youth. The Asvins, he said, would come back the next day and would try to seduce her again. When they did, she was to tell them that they were the ones who were impaired and that her husband would tell them what their impairment was and that only her husband knew. When the Asvins came to him to ask how they were impaired, he said he would tell them if they made him young again. The Asvins agreed and threw him into the fountain of youth and when he emerged, he was young again. In return, he told them that the gods were taking **soma** and by excluding them, it indicated that the gods believed they were incompetent.

In a second variant, the Asvin twins wanted to participate in a soma party the gods were holding but Indra wouldn't let them. The Asvins appealed to Cyavana, the aged sage, for help. He advised them to make a sacrifice to the gods so they would overrule Indra. This infuriated Indra then went to kill the Asvins. The Asvins again appealed to Cyavana for help and before Indra was able to attack them, Cyavana created Mada, the goddess of intoxication, who alarmed Indra so much that he relented and let the Asvins attend the soma gathering with the other gods. (Nagar, 2:44)

Dagda (or Daghdha). The supreme god or Great Father, in Irish mythology; the counterpart of **Odin**. Also, specifically, the god of wisdom, fertility, and licentiousness, whose **cauldron** of ale never emptied. Dagda was the king of the Tuatha De Danann, the fifth wave of mythical people to invade Ireland, just before the invasion of the humans, the Gaels. Dagda and his people came from the North, the traditional origin of Underworld powers, and brought the cauldron whose ale provided perpetual nourishment and immortality. Dagda was sometimes depicted as a pot-bellied peasant whose club was so heavy it had to be carried on wheels. (Stewart, R., 125)

Dagul'ku. In North American Cherokee Indian mythology, the geese who stole the only tobacco plant.

When the world was created, people and animals lived together and shared the only tobacco plant. Then the Dagul'ku geese stole it. Without tobacco, people began to suffer. One old woman grew so thin and weak she was in danger of dying for want of tobacco. Some of the larger animals tried to get the tobacco back but they were killed by the geese before they even got near the plant. The mole tried to get to it by tunneling underground, but the geese detected his tracks and killed him when he emerged from his tunnel. Finally, **Hummingbird** offered to get it. All the other remaining creatures said he was too small, but Hummingbird said he would try anyway.

When Hummingbird finally came in sight of the tobacco plant, he saw that the geese were guarding it, but Hummingbird was so small and flew so fast that the geese couldn't see him, and he darted down onto the plant and snatched the top with the leaves and seeds and flew away before the geese noticed what had happened. Meanwhile the old woman had fainted. Everyone thought she was dead. But when Hummingbird returned, the animals blew smoke into her nose from the tobacco plant he had recovered, and she opened her eyes and came to life. (Mooney, 254–255)

Daspajka. In Middle India folklore, the culture hero who discovered palm **wine**.

One day when he was hunting, Daspajka's dog ran away and came home drunk. This happened so often, Daspajka followed the dog and saw him lapping sap that had dripped to the ground from a sago palm. Daspajka licked some of it himself and also got drunk. From then on the Kond regularly drank palm wine. (Elwin, 1954, 193)

Datura. There are three main verities, *Datura innoxia, datura metel, and datura stramonium.* Daturas grow throughout Asia, Europe and the Americas. They belong to the Solanaceae (potato family), which includes belladonna, henbane, mandrake and tobacco. These plants are found in all parts of the world in temperate and tropical climates.

The main psychoactive components in the daturas are scopolamine (hyoscine), hyoscyamine and atropine. Datura is considered to have been one of the main ingredients in the flying ointments used by witches during their "journeys to the Sabbath" where they communicated with and danced with the devil. Witches were said to rub their bodies with these ointments or salves, which allowed atropine, which can be absorbed through the skin, to enter the bloodstream.

Among native Americans, datura was used to induce a state of **ecstasy** that allowed a **shaman** to take a **magic** flight to the Upper and Under-worlds or transform into animals like the eagle or mountain lion to enable communion with dead forefathers. Among the California Chumash Indians, infusions of datura roots were given to boys and girls when they reached puberty as an initiatory rite for them to identify with an animal protector in the resulting visionary journey. The bond that forms is then appealed to whenever the individual seeks to contact the supernatural.

Datura acts in three phases. During the first phase, there is a sensation of intense thirst, blurred vision, extreme dilation of the pupils, and difficulty swallowing, symptomatic of its atropinic activity. This is followed by restlessness, disorientation, stupor, and hallucinations. Hallucinations include a sense of flying, the witches' flight and metamorphosis, the sensation of having been changed into an animal, in some instances, a wolf, a possible basis for the belief in werewolves (lycanthropy). The third stage is characterized by agitation, convulsions, and rolling eyes followed by deep sleep and coma. Too high a dose can result in death.

Datura is also known as "devil's apple," "thorn apple," "Gabriel's trumpet," and "tolache." In the United States, it became known as jimsonweed, from Jamestown, because soldiers there ground its seeds thinking it would make good flour for bread. In the Caribbean, it was called the "herbe aux sorciers" (herb of the sorcerers) and was part of the Zombie Cucumber (the other part being puffer fish poison (d-tubercucurine). In Vodu religion, the sorcerer, or Bokor, is able to communicate with Vodu, the spirit of god, and from him gains certain powers, among which is the power to overcome his enemies through use of various drugs. Sometimes, however, he abuses his power, and creates a Zombie, an "undead," a body without a spirit.

Zombification is a condition that the drug combination induces in which the physical senses are numbed and the victim develops a coma-like condition. After the Zombie is declared dead he is put into a coffin with an attached air tube and a funeral ceremony is conducted. Three days later, the coffin is retrieved. The Zombie is then given another dose of datura and initiated into the after life. He is then given regular doses of Zombie Cucumber to keep him in his hypnotic state in which his spirit remains out of his body. The Zombie is a walking corpse that eats, breathes and moves, but cannot think for himself.

(Rudgley, 76–85, 272–274; Schultes and Hofmann, 10, 26, 31, 41, 64, 68, 73, 79, 81, 93, 97, 106–111, 140–141)

Dauji *see* **Baldev.**

Deadly Nightshade *see* **Belladonna.**

Deagahgweoses. In North American Seneca mythology, the deity who created tobacco. (Gill and Sullivan, 66)

Deer Person. In Central American Huichol mythology, the avatar of Peyote who came down from the heavens to the sacred homeland, Wirikuta, bringing peyote with him on his antlers. When the Huichol hunt for peyote they attach whatever peyote buttons they find to the tines of a deer antler carried by their **shaman.** The Huichol regard peyote, deer, and corn as avatars of one another. Corn was once Deer God, and deer was once the Huichol's main food. The first time Deer God appeared on earth he left peyote in his tracks. Sometime later he became a large peyote plant.

Deer Person is also the spirit from whose semen **tobacco** originated. Before Deer became a person, he was on his way to the desert when he saw two beautiful girls at a lake and shot them both with arrows. The girls took the arrows out of their bodies and told him they would only give them back if he made love to them. Since Deer Person needed the arrows to take to **Peyote,** he agreed. While he was making love, some of his semen fell onto the ground and a tobacco plant grew from it. When Deer Person noticed the plant, he saw a small animal eating it and followed it when it left. The animal took him to a cave where Toad lived. Deer Person then hit Toad, and seeds came out of Toad's skin that grew into plants. Deer Person put some of the tobacco leaves into a gourd and cured them. When he finally came to the peyote desert, Deer Person gave the Huichol the tobacco and showed them how to use it. (Furst, 1977, 113–114; Winter, 279)

Delphi. A temple dedicated to the Greek god, Apollo, where people came to learn their future. In preparing for these prophecies, the priestess chewed laurel leaves or inhaled smoke from burning **henbane** seeds. While she was in the drug-induced ecstatic state, Apollo spoke to her and responded to the supplicant's question. (Price and Kearns, 156–159; Ratsch, 29)

Demeter. In Greek mythology, a vegetation goddess, especially of grain. Demeter was the primary deity worshiped in the **Eleusian Mysteries** where devotees celebrated her spirit by drinking barley wine, eating bread with **ergot** fungus on it, and taking **opium**. The use of opium in her rites is reflected in several statues and portraits of Demeter, portraying her with poppy flowers on her head and in her hand, and decorating her altars.

The primary myth connected with her cult involved the abduction and return of her daughter **Persephone**. After Zeus gave his brother Hades (who had replaced Hecate as the god of the Underworld) permission to take Persephone as his wife, Hades suddenly emerged from the Underworld in his chariot while she was in the fields picking flowers and abducted her and brought her back to his Underground realm.

When Persephone failed to return that day, Demeter became grief stricken and frantically went looking for her. Finally, Helios, the sun god, who had seen what had happened, told Demeter her daughter had been kidnapped by Hades, with Zeus' consent. Furious that the gods had allowed her daughter to be abducted, Demeter's grief turned to rage and she vowed to hold back fertility from the earth until Persephone was returned. Then she left Olympus, the home of the gods, and went to wander on earth disguised as an old woman. Eventually Demeter came to Eleusis, outside Athens, where she was treated kindly by a family who invited her to stay with them. The family tried to cheer her spirits, offering her barley wine. In gratitude she informed them who she was and told them to build a temple in her honor. When the temple was finished, she entered it and stayed there mourning her daughter for a year. Then she left and came to Mecone, the city of poppies. Some of the poppies were in bloom and the flowers attracted Demeter's attention. Curious, she cut open some unripe pods and tasting the sap that flowed out of them, she forgot her sorrow over losing her daughter.

By this time, the earth had become very barren. Zeus and the other gods pleaded with Demeter to restore its fertility so that humans could once again offer themselves as sacrifices, but Demeter continued to refuse unless Persephone was returned. Zeus sent the messenger god, Hermes, to Hades ordering him, in Zeus's name, to return Persephone. Hades said he would do as Zeus commanded, but before she left, he gave Persephone a pomegranate to eat. Once she tasted it, she was condemned to living in the Underworld, since once someone ate in the Underworld that person had to stay there. A compromise was finally reached such that Persephone would spend two-thirds of the time with her mother, and the other third with Hades. Demeter didn't like the arrangement, but she accepted and turned her attention once again to invigorating plant life two-thirds of the year, and leaving it barren for the other third.

Since Demeter had been treated kindly at Eleusis, she made Eleusis her central shrine and taught its devotees her Mysteries which involved a reenactment of Persephone's loss and recovery, and relied on ingestion of ergot fungus that grew on rye to intensify the ecstatic ritual. (Gantz, 63–70; Price and Kearns, 159–160; Kerenyi, 24)

Destruction of Mankind *see* **Hathor.**

Deucalion. In Greek mythology, the counterpart to **Noah**, who along with his wife survived a world flood by building an ark. After the flood, he restored the human race by casting bones (stones) of his mother (earth) behind him. His name literally means "sweet wine," and like Noah, Deucalion was the first vinter. (Gantz, 162–166; Jobes, 434; Price and Kearns, 162)

Deva. In Hindu mythology, a celestial god constantly at war with the **Asuras.** The Devas were the children of the first god-pair, Sky and Earth, who in turn were the children of **Tvastr,** a creator god. The Devas were immortal as a result of their gaining possession of **amrta** in the aftermath of the **Churning of the Ocean.** (Mahony, 18, 92, 130, 201, 239–240; Oosten, 30, 33, 53, 56, 59–60, 65)

Dionysus (or **Bacchus**). In Greek mythology, the god of beer and wine; the god of intoxication, fertility, the life force, and salvation. Dionysus is both the personification of wine and the spirit which is inherent in its effects, especially intoxication. "When we pour libations we pour the wine-god himself," says the prophet in *The Bacchae,* Euripides' play devoted to Dionysus.

Dionysus was the most complex and multifaceted deity in the Olympian pantheon, as reflected in his many epithets (see below). On the one hand, he represents the creative side of human nature, and the cultivation and processing of grapes into wine were regarded as one of the hallmarks of civilization as opposed to nomadic life. Wine, says the Bacchae prophet, is one of mankind's major blessings; the other being grain, the gift of **Demeter**. Grain is mankind's basic dry food whereas wine is mankind's basic wet food. Whereas grain nourishes the body, wine nourishes the mind. But wine's blessings are mixed; while it can cheer the heart, it can ravage the mind.

Wine's destructive side is reflected in Dionysus' dual personality. While he can be generous to those who accept him, Dionysus, the youngest of the Olympian gods and the only one to have a human parent (**Semele**), is extremely selfish, cruel and vindictive to those who refused to accept his divinity. Honored as the god who taught mankind how to transform the juice of the grape into wine, and venerated as its intoxicating principle, the dual nature of his intoxicating spirit could bring pleasure and happiness to those who imbibed that spirit in moderation, and irrationality and chaos to those who imbibed too much of it.

In keeping with his dual nature, he was sometimes depicted as an effeminate youth with flowing locks, but more often as a bull, or a fully bearded man dressed in the skins of wild animals, and an ivy wreath, one of the symbols of his fertility, on his head. He was also often depicted as surrounded by hordes of dancing women known as **Maenads,** in a drunken frenzy, by boozing satyrs, and by prostitutes carrying a giant phallus.

While best known for the effects of his intoxicating spirit, Dionysus' mass appeal derived in large part from the myths about his being reborn after his death and the promise that through participation in his **mystery religion** his devotees would, likewise, attain salvation after death. An essential aspect of all mystery cults was intoxication, combined with various repetitive activities like dancing or sounds, which freed the mind from its normal state enabling devotees to experience a sense that their spirit had been liberated from their body. In that transcendent condition, they were able to gain **enthusiasm** (from the Greek, "enthousiasmos"), a condition in which they became one with the god himself and experienced a glimmer of what they would eventually enjoy in the afterlife.

BIRTH AND EARLY YOUTH. There are two stories that describe Dionysus' earliest years. In the older of the two, Dionysus was the son of Zeus and **Persephone** and was called **Zagreus**.

Demeter, the female spirit embodying the fertility principle, was worried about her daughter, Persephone, being seduced by her philandering brother, Zeus, and hid her in a cave on the island of Crete where Persephone spent her time weaving. Despite her seclusion, Zeus discovered and came to her in the form of a snake and impregnated her. When Zeus' wife, Hera, was told about her husband's infidelity, she cajoled the Titans, who had ruled the world before being overthrown by the Olympians, to come out of the Underworld, where Zeus had banished them, to kill the young Zagreus. Dionysus tried to escape by transforming himself into different animals, but eventually they caught him in his guise as a bull, tore him apart, and ate all the pieces except for his heart which his half sister, Athena (or alternatively, his grandmother, Rhea), snatched away before the Titans noticed it and brought it to Zeus. Zeus then swallowed it, and then placed it into the body of a mortal woman, Semele, when he seduced her, and she subsequently gave birth to Zagreus/Dionysus, hence his epithet, twice born. Zeus then attacked the Titans and incinerated them with his thunderbolts in punishment for their iniquity, and from their ashes humans emerged, hence, their dual nature, one part the perishable Titanic body, the other the immortal Dionysiac soul.

Dionysus' dismemberment and return to life were symbolically reenacted as part of his mystery. Once they achieved **enthusiasm** through intoxication, his devotees, known as **Bacchantes,** reenacted his dismemberment by tearing a live animal apart with their hands and teeth, an act called *sparagmos,* following which they engaged in a form of communion by eating the animal's raw flesh and drinking its blood, an act called *omophagia.* Having symbolically eaten his body and drunk his blood, the celebrants believed they became possessed by Dionysus. The main shrines where these rites took place were at **Delphi** and **Eleusis.** The stone omphalos at Delphi was regarded as the tomb in which Zagreus was buried after being torn to pieces by the Titans, prior to his resurrection.

In the other version of Dionysus' birth, Zeus fell in love with Semele, the daughter of Cadmus, the founder of Thebes, and came to her in the form of a mortal (some versions say a snake), and told her he was a god, and seduced her.

When Hera, Zeus' wife, learned Semele was pregnant with Zeus' child, she became outraged at his betrayal of her. Unable to take out her anger on Zeus, she turned against Semele. Disguising herself as Semele's old nurse, she made her doubt that her lover was Zeus and said she should ask him to prove his divinity by showing himself in his true form, knowing that no mortal could see Zeus in his real splendor and live. The next time Zeus visited her, she asked him to grant her one wish. Zeus was so madly in love with her he agreed, swearing by the Underworld river Styx, an oath that couldn't be broken, that he would grant her whatever she wanted. When Semele asked him to appear to her as he did to Hera, Zeus immediately regretted his promise. Although he tried to dissuade her, Semele insisted. The heat from his thunder and lighting was so overwhelming, Semele was burned to ashes, but before she perished completely, Zeus plucked the unborn Dionysus from her womb and implanted it in his thigh. A short time later, Dionysus was born from his father's thigh, hence, one of his epithets, Dithyrambus, meaning twice born.

To protect Dionysus from his wife's jealousy, Zeus gave Dionysus to Hermes to hide. Hermes took Dionysus to his aunt, Semele's sister, Ino, who was nursing her own son at the time, and told her to keep him in a dark room and dress and raise him as a girl so as not to attract Hera's attention. But the ruse didn't work and Hera drove Ino and Athamas her husband mad, causing them to murder their own children. Before Ino could harm Dionysus, however, Hermes snatched him away and disguised him as a goat which he gave to the care of nurses called Nymphs who raised him in a cave on a mountain called Nysa. In reward for their attention to Dionysus, Zeus later placed their images among the stars, naming them the Hyades. During this time on Mt. Nysa, Dionysus discovered how to make wine from the fruit of the vine. Since Nymph was another term for "water spring," putting him in the care of Nymphs may been an allusion to the mixing of water with wine. After king **Amphictyon** was taught the practice of mixing water with wine, he set up an altar in honor of the Nymphs along with an altar to Dionysus Orthos.

YOUTH. When Dionysus was old enough to leave his cave home, he became friends with another youth named **Ampelos**. Still vengeful, Hera engineered Ampelos' death and drove Dionysus insane, a foreshadowing of the insanity he himself would later visit on his enemies. In his demented condition, Dionysus wandered into Egypt, Syria, and finally Phrygia, in central Asia Minor, where his grandmother Rhea (whom the Phrygians called Cybele, the Great Mother) cured him of his madness.

After he regained his sanity, Cybele's female followers, who played the flute and regularly danced themselves into a frenzy that included

sexual orgies, joined Dionysus and accompanied him on his journey farther east. The female members of his entourage were called Maenads
(from the Greek, "raging women") or **Bacchae** (women possessed by
Bacchus). The male followers were satyrs, half men with the ears and
tails of horses, and large erect phalli. The oldest of these satyrs, **Silenus**,
was a very fat and ugly, rode a donkey and was always drunk.

Dionysus, now traveling in a chariot pulled by tigers, made his way
along with his followers across the Euphrates river over a bridge they
made of grapevines, and crossed into India, where they defeated all
those who tried to stand in their way. Then they returned to Phrygia
where Silenus wandered off and was found by King Midas, the son of
Cybele. Midas treated Silenus well and returned him to Dionysus, who
rewarded him by granting him a single wish. Without thinking Midas
said that he wished that everything he touched would turn to gold.
When he turned his food and drink and even his own daughter into
gold, Midas realized his mistake and begged Dionysus to undo the
wish. Dionysus agreed and told Midas to bathe in a nearby river that
flowed by the city of Lydia. The river carried the golden touch to Lydia
where it embedded in its sands and made it a wealthy kingdom.

RESISTANCE. Dionysus then began his journey to mainland Greece
to establish his cult there, but on the way he encountered considerable
resistance on the part of many kings and other prominent people. The
first of these encounters occurred in Thrace, where King **Lycurgus**
refused to recognize his divinity. Dionysus retaliated by driving Lycurgus insane. In his demented state, Lycurgus killed his own son with an
axe, imagining he was lopping off pieces of a vine. By the time he came
to his senses he had begun to prune the nose, ears, fingers and toes of
his son's corpse. The entire land of Thrace then became barren and
remained that way until an oracle told them that the plague would only
be lifted when Lycurgus was punished for his crime. When they heard
this judgment, the Thracians tied Lycurgus to wild horses and whipped
them until they tore his body apart.

In a variant of the Lycurgus story, one of Dionysus' followers, a
nymph named Ambrosia, turned her lower torso into a vine, wrapped
it around Lycurgus and suffocated him. Lycurgus's half-brother, Butes,
was also punished for resisting. A thief and pirate, Butes attacked
Dionysus' female worshippers on the island of Naxos. Most of them
escaped except for Coronis, Dionysus' nurse who prayed to Dionysus
for help. Dionysus answered her prayer and made Butes insane. Brutes
then killed himself by throwing himself down a well.

Next Dionysus came to his birthplace, Thebes, where neither **Pentheus,** his cousin, who was now king, nor Pentheus' mother Agave, Dionysus' aunt (Semele's sister) acknowledged his divinity. Dionysus punished Agave by driving her insane, and in that condition, she, like Lycurgus, killed her son and tore him to pieces.

From Thebes, Dionysus went to Argos where all the women except the daughters of King Proetus joined in his worship. Dionysus punished them by driving them mad, and they killed the infants who were nursing at their breasts.

Dionysus then headed for mainland Greece. He hired a ship at Icaria which he didn't know was manned by pirates. Seeing the beauty of their passenger and his rich clothes, the pirates decided to kidnap him and sell him for ransom. Acetes, the ship's pilot, immediately realized their passenger's divinity but the others refused to believe him and tried to tie him so that he would not be able to escape. Amused at their feeble efforts, Dionysus caused vines to grow out of the sea which entangled the ship's mast and sails. Then he turned himself into a lion and ate one of the sailors. Panic stricken, the other pirates jumped into the sea and were turned into dolphins. The only one to escape was Acetes, whom Dionysus spared because he had been respectful to him. Acetes then piloted the ship and docked first at the island of Naxos where Dionysus encountered **Ariadne,** who had been deserted by Theseus. Dionysus fell in love with and married her in a big wedding to which he invited all the gods. After that, Dionysus continued on to mainland Greece.

At Argos, the daughters of King Proteus refused to recognize his divinity. Dionysus punished them by driving them mad and did the same to the daughters of Minyas, King of Orchomenos in Boetia, and then turned them into bats.

RECOGNITION. When he at last came to Athens Dionysus was welcomed by a farmer, **Icarius.** In return for his hospitality and courtesy, Dionysus showed him how to cultivate vines to make wine (for a different version see **Orestheus**). Later, when one of his male goats began gnawing at the first vines, he sacrificed him to Dionysus, and a sacrifice of a goat became part of the ritual celebrations for Dionysus. After Dionysus left, Icarius shared some of the unmixed wine with his neighbors. Not used to its effects, they believed Icarius had poisoned them and they killed him. When Icarius' daughter **Erigone** found his body, she hanged herself in grief. Dionysus subsequently taught the Athenian king, **Amphictyon,** to mix wine with water to avoid its undiluted power.

DESCENT TO THE UNDERWORLD. Once Dionysus' divinity was acknowledged and his worship firmly established throughout the world, Dionysus was allowed to ascend to Mt. Olympus and take his place among the other Olympians. Even Hera, his longtime enemy, finally accepted him.

Now entrenched among the other gods on Olympus, he descended to the Underworld to try to bring his mother, Semele, to Olympus. On his way to find Hades, Dionysus became lost until he met a shepherd named Prosymnus, who gave him directions. After he found Hades, Dionysus was able to persuade him to allow Semele to leave, but only on condition that Dionysus give him something he highly valued in return, and Dionysus gave Hades his myrtle plant. When he emerged from the Underworld with his mother, Prosymnus himself had died and Dionysus erected a phallus-shaped object on his tomb as his symbolic gift to him. To keep the spirits left behind from knowing about his mother's resurrection, Dionysus changed Semele's name to Thyuone and Zeus made her immortal. Hera wasn't pleased with Semele's reappearance, but she resigned herself to accept it.

FESTIVALS. A number of festivals honoring Dionysus were held throughout Greece and Asia in which various episodes from his myths were reenacted. The Lenaia was held in January to arouse him from his wintry slumber. It was celebrated at the Lenaeon, the oldest of Dionysus' temples, and featured a great feast along with a nocturnal procession of women, clowning, and bawdy comedies.

The Anthesteria was a three-day festival held in Attica during the middle of the month of Anthesterion (mid–February) commemorating various episodes in the life of Dionysus and those associated with him, and representing Dionysus' dual aspect as the god who brought new life and **ecstasy**, and the god who influenced the fate of the soul. The light-hearted side of the Anthesteria celebrated the renewed promise of fertility in the spring, whereas the somber aspect acknowledged the end of the growing season (i.e. death) in the winter.

The first day, called "cask-opening day" (Pithoegia) was when new wine casks were opened for the first time and the wine was tasted. People put pitch on their doors to ward off the spirits of the dead that were said to rise on that day, and everyone over the age of three came to a sanctuary dedicated to Dionysus and sat at a table and at the sound of trumpets, in complete reversal of the animated conversation and friendliness that characterized drinking, they drank without talking to one another. After the silent drinking was over, a contest was held to see who could empty a two liter container of wine the fastest.

The second and third days were more festive. On the second day, called "cups" (Choes), young children who reached the requisite age were given their first taste of wine. This commemorated Dionysus' marriage to Ariadne. At the Lenaeon, the oldest of Dionysus' temples, celebrants brought their drinking cups back to the sanctuary and handed them to a group of women and their "queen." That night, the queen, in the role of Ariadne, engaged in the central rite of the festival, the "sacred marriage," with the king taking the role of Dionysus.

The third day called "pots" (Chytroi) was an homage to the spirits of the dead. During the festival, a contest was held in which virginal girls sat on swings hanging from trees to commemorate **Erigone's** suicide by hanging when she found the body of her dead father, Icarius (an avatar of Dionysus), after he had been killed by drunken herders.

The Greater or City Dionysia, the most elaborate of the major Athenian festivals, was held in March when Dionysus supposedly awoke after his long sleep and liberated the land from the barrenness of winter. The festival lasted for five days and attracted people from all over Greece. During the festival, ordinary business was stopped and prisoners were released to take part. The most memorable part of the celebration was the Thymele contest, named after an altar to Dionysus that stood in the center of the orchestra in Greek theaters, during which new tragedies and comedies were performed in open air theater and competed for the honor of best play.

Dionysus' position as patron god of the theatre originated from songs praising Dionysus called *tradoidia*, literally "goat songs," that commemorated Hera's persecution of Dionysus, and his disguise as a goat on the Island of Nysa. These *tradoidia* were transformed into plays honoring Dionysus that came to be known as tragedy. The essential characteristic of these plays was a hero's tragic flaw, a defect in character or inability to understand his or her situation that made the character's destruction inevitable. Eventually he would realize truth of his situation and would accept his fate. The audience identified with the hero and felt pity or fear; catharsis of these feelings left the audience exalted or in tears.

The Eleutherai was a fall celebration held at Eleutherai, a small community near Athens. Phallic images were a prominent feature of the celebration, since wine was credited with promoting sexual intercourse and therefore human generation. The Lesser Dionysia was held in December when Dionysus was supposedly languishing in slumber. Devotees believed Dionysus rose from the dead each year at Delphi and "reigned" there during the three winter months when Apollo was away.

EPITHETS. Dionysus had many epithets that referred to various aspects of his character, among them: Agrios ("wild one," reflecting the lack of restraint his intoxication could produce); Aigobolos ("Goat slayer," which referred to a cultic celebration in Boetia, at which the worshippers became so violently drunk, they killed Dionysus' priest who was conducting the services. Immediately after the murder, Dionysus sent a pestilence on the city as punishment. When the inhabitants consulted the Delphic oracle as to what they had to do to appease him, they were told they had to sacrifice a healthy young boy. Sometime later, Dionysus regretted his decision and allowed them to substitute a goat as a victim in place of a boy); Antheus ("Flowering One"); Areion ("Warrior"); Arretos ("Ineffable"); Bromius, "Thunder," from the thunderous noise which accompanied his birth; Bassareus ("Fox"); Botriephoros ("Carrier of Grape Clusters"); Bougenes ("Oxborn"); Boukeros ("Ox-Horned"); Brisaeus, from Brisa, the name of one of the nymphs who raised him; Charidotes ("Giver of Grace"); Choreutes ("Dancer"); Chthonios ("Underworld"); Dendrites ("Tree God"); Dikerotes ("Two Horned God," from his representation as a bull); Dimorphos ("Two-faced God") a reference to alcohol's dual nature; Dithrambos ("He of the Double Door") referring to his death and second birth or resurrection from his father Zeus' thigh after being snatched from his dying mother's womb. The term dithyramb came to be used in a spontaneous choral song to Dionysus, sung under the influence of wine. During the Great Dionysia, it was sung by a large chorus, dressed as satyrs with especially large penises. Around the beginning of 5th century B.C.E., three playwrights, called "poets," competed for best play, during the festival.

Other epithets for Dionysus included Eiraphoiotes ("In-sewn One"); Ekstatikos ("Ecstatic One"); Eleuthereus or Eleutherios ("Emanipator"), referring to his power to liberate the mind of its worries and the soul from its earthly body; Eschatos ("Farthest, the End"); Euanthes ("Fair Blossoming One"); Euaster ("Reveler"); Eurbouleus ("Good Counselor"); Euergetes ("Benefactor"); Euios, Euhoe, Euae ("Reveler"), a wild cry uttered by his followers during his celebration; Gynaimanes ("He Who Makes Women Mad"), referring to his female devotees who became frenzied; Hagnos ("Holy One"); Kallikarpos ("Lovely Fruit"); Kissobryos ("Ivy Wrapped"); Kissokomes ("Ivy Crowned"); Kryphios ("Secret One"); Lenaeus ("Winepress"), honoring him as the god who taught mankind how to crush grapes in vats); Lampter ("Bringer of Light"); Liknites ("Cradle"); Limnagenes and Limnaios ("Marsh Born"); Lyaeus ("Loosener"), because of the relaxing effect of wine; Lysos ("Redeemer"), the god who released people from their mundane lives through the ecstasy of rebirth and resurrection, the vine being a metaphor for new life arising from death. In the Phaedrus, Socrates says that mankind's "greatest blessings came from madness, his term for divine inspiration, not mental illness; Socrates called such inspiration mental liberation); Pyrigenes, from his birth in fire; Tauokeros ("Bull Horned") and Tauroprosopos ("Bull Faced"), referring to his virility. (Dalby, 1ff; Gantz, 112–119, 264–269; 736–737; 742–743; Guthrie, 148ff; Oosten, 91–99, 108–109; Parry, 150–151; Price and Kearns, 169–174)

Divine Banquet. A common motif in many myths during which the gods of a pantheon dine together and consume intoxicating drinks. In virtually every instance in which banquets are mentioned in ancient Near Eastern mythology, the gods and goddesses sit down to a communal meal during which there is considerable drinking. In Mesopotamia, two synonyms for "banquet" were "the place of beer and bread," and "the pouring of beer." When wine became generally available, it replaced beer. In Greece, the divine banquet took place on Mt. Olympus; in Persia, on Mt. Hara, in Scandinavia, in Asgard. (Campbell, 1968, 176–177; Price and Kearns, 338)

Divine Smiths. The gods who made the cups out of which the other gods drank their intoxicating drinks. The best known of the divine smiths are Tavastr (India), Hephaistos/Vulcan (Greece/Rome), and Gobineau (Wales). In Wales, the smith was accorded the privilege of drinking the first drink in the divine banquet. (Stewart, R., 118–119)

Doini-Botte. In northeast India folklore, a culture hero who along with his wife cleared a forest on side of hill where they lived but didn't sow any seeds because everything grew of its own accord. Just before their crop was ready to be harvested, wild animals ate all the plants except for **tobacco.** Doini Botte and wife wondered why they had left them and picked some tobacco leaves and took them home. A few days later one of their children died. They were very sad and had no interest in anything and stayed crying in their house. With nothing to eat the couple became very hungry and thought they might as well eat the tobacco leaves. The leaves took away their hunger and they began to cultivate the tobacco plant. (Elwin, 1958, 221)

Donar *see* **Thor.**

Drunkard Boy. In Japanese folklore, a cannibalistic giant ogre with the face of a boy, who was overcome by intoxication. When Drunkard Boy's followers began feasting on noble ladies, the governor ordered his general to kill him. The general and his men disguised themselves as wandering priests and set out on their mission. On the way they met a mysterious man who gave them a magic drink to intoxicate Drunkard Boy. When the disguised priests came to Drunkard Boy's home where he was living with a number of ogres, they were welcomed and when evening came, the priests offered their hosts some of the magic drink. When Drunkard Boy and the ogres became drunk, the warriors threw off their priestly robes and after a hard fight, they killed the ogres and cut off Drunkard Boy's head and returned to the governor in triumph bearing the severed head. (Anesaki, 306–307)

Du Kang. In Chinese legend, the culture hero who created **wine**. When he tasted it he found it so energizing he gave some to the emperor. The wine not only energized him as well, but also restored his appetite. As a reward, the emperor named Du Kang an "immortal of wine."
A different story involving Du Kang begins with a man who had developed a liking for wine and came to visit Du Kang's wine cellar. After tasting his wine and lavishly praising his host, he offered to pay, but Du Kang said that instead of paying him then, he should pay him in three years. After the man returned home still under the influence of Du Kang's wine, he fell into a deep sleep. When he failed to awake after three days, his family thought he was dead and buried him. Three years later, when Du Kang came to the man's house asking for payment, the family accused him of murder and was about to kill him in retribution. But Du Kang only smiled and told them to dig up the grave and open the coffin. When they did, the man immediately sat up and told his family how wonderful Du Kang's wine had been. (Yu, 1ff)

Dumuzi. In Sumerian mythology, the archetypal fertility god who annually dies and is resurrected; the shepherd, who was originally a nomad and gave up that life to become a farmer. The inventor of beer, and god of its related effects on creativity and inspiration.
Dumuzi was the divine bridegroom of **Inanna** the fertility goddess. Inanna journeyed to the Underworld but was not allowed to return unless she sent a substitute in her stead. When she returned to earth,

she was enraged that her husband Dumuzi, the god of beer, had not mourned for her and instead, had been dallying with **Geshtianna**, the goddess of the vine, and named him as her substitute. Dumuzi then died and was then banished to the underworld but was allowed to return to earth for six months to soothe his lamenting worshippers. As part of the rituals held in his honor, his devotees annually journeyed from the mountains to the temple of Geshtianna. (Jacobsen, 1ff)

Duraosha *see* **Frashmi.**

Dusares (or **Dushaa**). In Nabataean (South Arabian) mythology, the god of wine and fertility. (Langdon, 17; Lutz, 152)

Dushaa *see* **Dusares.**

Eagle. A prominent animal in myths representing either the spirit of the **shaman** during his trance-induced journey to the gods, or a bird that descends from its perch on the cosmic tree and brings, sometimes by theft, entheogenic drinks to the gods or humans. **Indra, Zeus, Odin,** and other gods who have characteristics of the **shaman**, e.g., shapeshifting, all assume the guise of, or ride on eagles. In India, **Garuda** steals Indra's **soma**. In Scandinavia, Odin takes the form of an eagle when he steals the giant Suttung's **mead** from his mountain stronghold, and is pursued by Suttung, who also changes into an eagle. In Greece, Zeus rides an eagle when he abducts **Ganymede**, whom he makes cupbearer to the gods. (Price and Kearns, 84–85)

Earthmaker. In North American Winnebago mythology, the god who gave humans tobacco to compensate for their powerlessness.

When Earthmaker created the world he gave each of his creations a special power. When he finally fashioned mankind, the last of his creations, he was out of powers. Feeling remorse, he created a weed whose leaves he mashed and lighted. When he and the spirits inhaled it they all liked it. The spirits thought Earthmaker would give the plant to them, but he told them he was giving it to the humans, because they were the only one of his creations that had not been given a special power. Earthmaker told humans to call the plant tobacco and said that his desire and the desire of the spirits for it was so strong that whenever they offered it to them, they would not be able to refuse any request made of them. In that way, even though humans had no special powers of their own they would be able to influence the powers the Earthmaker had conferred on the spirits.

In a related Winnebago myth, the Winnebagos sacrificed tobacco to the Buffalo Spirits. The chief of the Buffalo Spirits warned the younger Spirits not to get too close to the fumes, because the odor was so powerful that if they inhaled it they wouldn't be able to control their desire for it. Once they inhaled the smoke, he said, there would be no power that could save them and they would have to go down to the earth where they would be killed. (Radin, 1990, 18, 389)

Earth Mother. In North American Haudenosaunee Indian mythology, a goddess from whose brain tobacco grew (Winter, 309)

Eboka *see* **Iboga.**

Ecstasy. A mystical condition, or rapture; a visionary condition induced by various techniques such as fasting, dancing, drumming, or **entheogen** consumption that results in a sense of being possessed by or united with God. From the Greek, *ekstasis*, literally, the flight of the soul from the body; figuratively, an abnormal mental condition such as madness. More specifically, it also came to mean a divinely inspired mental state providing insights into reality. Ecstasy carries with it the idea of a trance state in which the soul leaves the body and sees visions; it is the primary condition required for the soul's escape from the body or from rationality so that it can achieve union with a god. (Fuller, 1–7; Powell, Barry P., 275–276; Price and Kearns, 183)

Einherjar. In Norse mythology, brave warriors slain in battle, who were brought to **Valhalla.** The Einherjar spent the rest of eternity fighting every day, but at night they returned to Valhalla where the Valkyries served them endless amounts of meat and **mead.** The Einherjar remained at Valhalla until Ragnarok, the end of the world, when they were called upon to fight with Odin. (Lindow, 102–3)

Elder Brother. In North American Papago Indian mythology, the god of fermentation who showed the Papago how to make wine from the sahuaro cactus.

When there was drought in the land, Elder Brother created the sahuaro cactus from beads of his sweat. After the plant bore fruit, Elder Brother put the juice of its fruit into a jar, mixed it with water, fermented it into wine, and drank so much of it he became drunk. While still intoxicated, Elder Brother poured the wine over the thirsty soil and it immediately began to rain. After that, whenever there was a drought, the Papago made sahuaro wine and held a great drunken feast so that the rain would come just as it had when Elder Brother became drunk.

In a related myth, an infant disappeared after sinking into the earth and the animals went searching for it. Finally Crow found it at the top of a mountain where it had reemerged as a sahuaro cactus. Crow nibbled its fruit and then spat the red pulp into a basket where it began to ferment. When the animals drank some of the ferment, they became so quarrelsome that Elder Brother decided to get rid of the cactus. Elder Brother sent Badger to throw its seeds into the waters, but when Badger met Coyote, Coyote asked him to show him the seeds. When he did, Coyote struck his hand, scattering the seeds to the wind. Since the seeds were scattered everywhere, Elder Brother relented and showed women how to gather its fruit to make wine, and told them to make themselves drunk on it yearly, to bring rain.

In North American Pima Indian mythology, Elder Brother was the spirit who showed the Pima how to use tobacco. Earth Brother was born when the male sky and female earth united. Sometime later he killed an evil monster. When an old woman drank some of the monster's blood, she died and shortly thereafter the first tobacco plant grew from her grave. (Lumholtz, 48; Underhill, 42–43, 84; Winter, 44)

Elder Sister. Goddess of peyote in Huichol mythology. Also known as Mother Peyote. (Schaeffer and Furst, 17)

Eleusian Mysteries. Secret initiation ceremonies into the cults of **Demeter** and her daughter, **Persephone**, which were held at **Eleusis** beginning around 1,500 BCE, and annually, thereafter, for the next two thousand years. The cult became a recognized state religion around 300 BCE and was opened to anyone, male and female, including slaves. The only requirements were being able to speak Greek, and the absence of "blood guilt," i.e., not having murdered someone. Participation continued until banned in 392 CE by the Roman emperor Theodosius I who closed down the cult's sanctuaries to eliminate resistance to Christianity as the state religion.

The cult's mythical basis derived from the story of Persephone's resurrection from the Underworld and her reunion with her mother, Demeter. Initiates were promised special rewards in the afterlife, and once initiated, were not allowed to say what was seen or done during the rites. The punishment for violating the injunction was death. As part of those rites, devotees ate cakes containing opium, and drank a concoction called "kykeon," made from barley, water, and mint. The barley is believed to have contained **ergot,** a fungus that affects rye and barley (the latter was closely associated with Demeter) and induces hallucinations. These hallucinations were regarded as mystical communions with Persephone and Demeter. (Wasson et al., 1ff)

Eleusis. Located about 12 miles from Athens, the site of the secret **Eleusian Mysteries** devoted to **Demeter** and **Dionysus.** Revered as the place where **Persephone** was first reunited with her mother Demeter, after Zeus persuaded Hades to let her return to earth for part of the year. (Price and Kearns, 186)

Eleutherai. A small community near Athens where a Fall celebration originated in honor of **Dionysus.** Phallic images were a prominent feature of the celebration since wine was credited with promoting sexual intercourse and therefore human generation. (Wasson et al., 1ff)

Elixir. An intoxicating drink or **magic** concoction, typically brewed in a **cauldron,** that rejuvenates youth, cures sickness, brings wealth, confers eternal life, or endows wisdom and knowledge. From the Arabic *al-iksir,* meaning a dry powder. Divine elixirs are sacred beverages such as **ambrosia.** An earthly elixir that brings users into communion with the gods is called an **entheogen.**

The oldest elixir quest comes from Mesopotamia, where **Gilgamesh,** the legendary king of the Sumerian city of Erech, goes out in search of the plant of immortality. After maneuvering by lions that guard its foothills and scorpion men who watch the heavens, Gilgamesh arrives at a mountain paradise watched over by Siduri-Sabitu, an avatar of Inanna. Siduri admits him and after he tells the purpose of his quest, she advises him to go back to his home and be content with the mortal joys of life. But Gilgamesh persists, and Siduri lets him pass.

Norse mythology has several quests involving intoxicants. The best known is **Odin's** quest of the **Mead of Inspiration and Poetry;** another is Thor's quest for a cauldron large enough to brew beer for all the gods. Indian mythology has a **soma** quest. The Cherokee Indians have a version of this quest, in which tobacco is guarded by geese and sought after by a **shaman.** (Worthen, 39–69)

Embla *see* Ask.

Enki. In Sumerian (Mesopotamian) mythology, a creator god whose lechery and weakness for alcohol resulted in the creation of humans with deformities.

Before the creation of earth, when Enki lived in his shrine on the shores of the primordial sea, Ninhursag, the mother goddess, asked him to help her make the earth productive. Enki agreed and created rivers and canals and filled them with fresh water from the north, so that the earth became fertile and ready to produce grain. In return for his benevolence, Ninhursag copulated with Enki, and she gave birth to a daughter whom Enki subsequently seduced. Sometime after his daughter herself gave birth to a daughter, Enki also seduced her and she too became pregnant. Enki was about to do the same to his great-granddaughter, Uttu (a word meaning "vegetation"), but his plans were thwarted by Ninhursag, who told Uttu not to have anything to do with Enki until he brought her fruits and vegetables as marriage gifts. Enki then caused fruits and vegetables to grow, and brought them to Uttu which pleased her, and she let him into her house. Enki then got Uttu drunk, raped her and left her in pain with the fetuses she had conceived. Ninhursag heard her cries and removed the fetuses, planting them in the earth.

When Enki learned where his children were growing as plants in the earth, he ate them. This was the last straw for Ninhursag and she cast an evil spell on Enki that made him ill.

Enki pined away until Ninhursag relented and she agreed to restore Enki's health. Sitting next to him, she asked where he felt pain. Each time Enki pointed to one of his bodily organs, Ninhursag created a new deity from that organ and some of the pain dissipated. Eventually, eight new deities came into existence, among them Ninkasi, the "goddess of beer" whom Ninhursag created when Enki said he felt pain in his mouth.

Some time later the gods complained that they had to work too hard digging canals and hauling away the earth so they could sow and raise crops to feed themselves. The gods appealed to Enki who told the mother goddess, Ninmah, how to make humans out of clay. Afterwards, the gods held a party celebrating the creation of humans, because they would now be doing all the work they had formerly had had to do and the humans would now provide them with food and drink through their sacrifices. During the festivities, Ninmah became drunk and challenged Enki's creative powers, claiming that she could make humans with misshapen bodies as well as those good in form. Enki, who was also intoxicated, took up the challenge and boasted he could mitigate any shortcomings she created. Ninmah created six adult men and women out of clay, each with a different congenital physical handicap. Some were crippled, one was blind, another was sterile, and one lacked genitals. Enki then showed his superior power by finding a useful work for each so that they could earn a living, despite their handicaps; for example, he found a job for the blind man as a singer; the barren woman was given a place in a harem; and the eunuch was put to work in the service of the king. (Abel, 1997, 3–7)

Entheogen. A psychoactive substance that produces a sense of dissociation between the mind and body (called "**ecstasy**"—no relation to the drug of that name), inspiring a mystical feeling of ecstatic possession, or direct communication with God. From the Greek, *entheos*, meaning the "god [*theos*] coming [*-gen*] within." The term was coined in 1979 to replace "hallucinogen," which had come to suggest mental aberration, to refer instead not only to mystical states, but also prophetic seizures, erotic passion, and artistic inspiration. In some cultures, entheogenic plants or the derivatives made from them, such as soma and peyote, were regarded as containing the spirit of a god and the source of his divine power, and as such were deified and worshiped in their own right. (Fuller, 2; Ruck et al, 1979, 144–146; Rudgley, 93–94; Schultes and Hofmann, 12)

Enthusiasm. Literally, "inspired" or "being filled with god." From the Greek, *enthusiasmos*, meaning possessed by or communion with God. The intense emotional feeling that god has entered one's body. In many religions, devotees attempted to attain ecstatic communion with the life and power of the world, so as to achieve the enthusiasm that made them one with a god. Enthusiasm was the special goal of Dionysus' followers, who sought to lose themselves in his sudden overpowering spirit. Once their personal identity was lost, those so possessed expressed their enthusiasm in irrational behavior. Various ways were used to achieve this enthusiasm such as dancing, chanting, self-mutilation, and **entheogen** use. Religions emphasizing such communion offered the promise of immortality and release from earthly bondage. (Powell, B., 275–276)

Epena. The sacred snuff from the virola plant (*Virola theidora, Virola callophylla, virola callophylloidea, virola elongata*) containing the spirit of **Viho-mahse**, the snuff person. Virola is a type of vine that grows in the Amazon area of South America. Its bark, which contains hallucinogenic tryptamine **alkaloids**, such as DMT (Dimethyl-tryptamine), is eaten or powdered into a snuff called Nyakwana and Waika. The snuff is made by scraping the soft inner layer of the bark and slowly roasting the scrapings. The scrapings are then pulverized and sifted and stored in containers decorated by a bird (usually an eagle) or mammal (usually a jaguar). The animals are representative of the **shaman**'s alter ego. When wanted, the dried material is then taken into the nose through bird- or mammal-shaped nose pipes or tubes. In some cultures, the snuff is blown through the tube by one individual into another's nose.

The immediate response is a runny nose and salivation. Onset of intoxication is very rapid, beginning with a tingling or itching sensation at the top of the head, then numbness, loss of motor control, and nausea, followed by brief ecstatic visual and auditory sensations often interpreted as communion with the spirit world. (Goodman, 97–100; Schultes and Hofmann, 29, 60, 73, 81, 138, 176–181)

Epiphany. An experience in which a god reveals himself or herself in human form or in the guise of an animal or as a disembodied voice, or manifests his or her power; a revelation of divine presence or power. (Price and Kearns, 194)

Ergot. A fungus (*Claviceps purpurea*) that grows on cereal grains, especially rye and barley, and produces a telltale purple spike. The fungus, which contains various **alkaloids**, was scraped away and mixed with water and mint and drunk. Because of its association with barley, which was one of **Demeter**'s symbols, ergot is believed to be the main **entheogen** used in the **Eleusian mysteries**. Many people experience a sensation of being on fire after eating ergot. Ergotism, the disorder it causes, was called St. Anthony's Fire in the Middle Ages; symptoms included high temperature, tremors, vomiting, and convulsions. Ergot's alkaloid chemical structure is similar to LSD, and its hallucinatory effects are believed to result from changes in the **neurotransmitter** serotonin. (Rudgley, 95–98; Schultes and Hofmann, 26, 39, 68–69, 102–105)

Erigone. In Greek mythology, the Athenian daughter of **Icarius**, the farmer whom **Dionysus** had shown how to make **wine** out of grapes. After his friends became drunk from the wine Icarius gave them, his neighbors, believing he had poisoned them, killed Icarius. When Erigone noticed her father was missing she went looking for him and found his dog who led her to his body. Finding him dead, she was so grief stricken, she prayed to **Dionysus** that all Athenian daughters would suffer a death like hers until her father was avenged, and then hanged herself.

When Athenian girls began to be found swinging from trees, the Athenians consulted an oracle which told them that Dionysus had caused the suicides in response to Erigone's prayer. The Athenians then sought out the peasants who had murdered Icarius and killed them, and the curse was lifted.

This myth was annually reenacted during the Athenian Anthesteria festival in honor of Dionysus. (Graves, 1992, 262–263)

Eurypylos. In Greek mythology, a Greek king who brought the **Dionysus** cult to the Island of Patras.

Eurypylos was one of the Greek kings who conquered Troy. During the looting of the fallen city, Eurypylos found a chest containing a statue of Dionysus which caused the first person to look at it to become insane. Eurypylos was immediately affected and continued to be insane except for occasional lucid periods. During one of those periods he consulted the oracle at **Delphi** to ask how he could cure himself. The oracle told him he should carry the chest with its statue with him and when he encountered a people offering a strange sacrifice, he should show them the statue. In the course of his wanderings, Eurypylos eventually came to the Island of Patras, where a beautiful girl and handsome boy were about to be sacrificed at the altar of the goddess Artemis as the annual expiation for a sacrilege that had once been committed at her temple. Realizing this was the sacrifice foretold by the oracle, Eurypylos brought out the statue of Dionysus. For their part, the people of Patras had also been told by the Delphi oracle that they would no longer have to make the annual sacrifice once it was witnessed by a foreign god. Eurypylos then settled in Patras and the inhabitants became worshippers of Dionysus. (Pausanias, 7.19.6–7.20.1; Graves, 1992, 237; Grimal, 158–159)

Ewa. In Hawaiian legend, the female culture heroine who was the first to discover and try awa (kava) and become intoxicated from it. She told those with her that if she died, they should not bury her. When she recovered from her intoxication, she called the plant "awa." (Titcomb, 108)

Faflon *see* **Fulfluns.**

False Faces. In North American Iroquois Indian mythology, evil spirits who are addicted to **tobacco.** Although defeated in their attempt to rule the world, they still wield great power. They can be made allies if their addiction is appeased or enemies if those with tobacco do not offer it to them. (Winter, 283)

Fates. In Greek mythology, three daughters of the goddess, Necessity, and Zeus, whose decisions cannot be undone. Named Clotho ("Spinner"), Lachesis ("Apportioner"), and Atropos ("Inflexible"), the Fates used a thread to determine human longevity and life. Clotho spun the thread; Lachesis apportioned its length; and Atropos cut it. Despite their implacability, they were not immune to the power of intoxication. When **Admetus** was scheduled to die, Apollo got Atropos drunk and was thereby able to postpone his death until a substitute could be found.

While there is no mythological link with the plant **belladonna**, Atropos became the eponym for atropine, the main compound in belladonna. Atropos' mythological link comes from its potential lethality if ingested. (Gantz, 195, 396–397; Price and Kearns, 212–214)

Fauna. In Roman mythology, a goddess of fertility and virginity, venerated by married women who worshiped her under the title Bona Dea ("Good Goddess").

In Rome, secret rites in her honor were held on December 3rd, at a prominent magistrate's house. No men were allowed to participate, and during the celebration, no one was allowed to say the word "**wine**," and although the participants drank from a vessel covered with a cloth that contained wine, it was called milk. Her public celebration was held in May at her temple on the **Aventine Hill**, but again only women were allowed to participate. (Grimal, 76)

First Wine Drinkers *see* **Icarius.**

Fjalar. In Norse mythology, one of the dwarfs who created the **entheogenic mead** of inspiration from **Kvasir's** blood. In another story, Fjalar is a giant who is given the mead by **Ivaldi** in return for marrying Fjalar's daughter. When **Odin** found out about the wedding, he disguised himself as Ivaldi, and when no one was watching, stole the mead. (Rydberg, No. 123)

Fly Agaric *see* **Amanita Muscaria.**

Forbidden Fruit. In early Israelite mythology, fruit from a tree growing in a Paradise that no one was allowed to eat. In later Christian and Jewish tradition, the grapevine was identified as the Tree of Knowledge and grapes an **entheogenic** fruit, that made Adam think he was himself godlike, thereby causing his fall from God's grace. Adam secretly cut a piece of the vine from the Tree of Knowledge, and illicitly brought it out of the Garden of Eden. When **Noah** discovered it, he planted it and watered its roots with the blood of four animals, a lamb, lion, pig and ape. In a variant of the story, it is the Devil who waters the roots with the blood from these four different animals, thereby imbuing the juice of grape with four stages of drunkenness: the innocence of the lamb associated with drinking lightly; the courage of the lion that comes with moderate drinking; the brutishness of the pig that comes with more drinking; and finally, the foolishness of the ape that comes with complete drunkenness. During the 15th and 16th centuries, these four animals became metaphors for the different types of drunkards, rather than the progressive stages of drunkenness, and the lamb was replaced by the lecherous goat or stag, symbolizing the cuckold. (Ginsburg I, 168; Janson, 241)

Four Hundred Rabbits *see* **Centzon Toltochtin.**

Four Manido. The North American Chippewa Indian god who gave the gift of **tobacco** to his son, Nanbush, after an epic battle. Nanbush in return he passed it on to the Chippewa, who used it to compose their minds and spirits. (Johnston, 21–31)

Frashmi (or **Duraosha**). In Persian mythology, a prophet who discovered the **haoma** plant in the mountains. After eating some of its leaves, he felt invigorated and brought it down for the rest of the world, and instituted a special ritual for its usage that would give users divine wisdom. He subsequently died from immolating himself, and divine wisdom, courage, and exhilaration streamed from his body. (Modi, 506–507)

Fulfluns (also known as **Faflon** or **Fuflunu**). The Etruscan god of **wine**. Fulfuns was also a prankster who scattered the harvested grapes and ruined them if his pranks were not taken with good humor; if they were, he would return the grapes to their baskets. (Fox, 318; Hamblin, 92)

Fulflunu *see* **Fulfluns.**

Fum Mbombo. In Luba (African) mythology, a monkey who initiated the separation between humans and animals by stealing **wine** calabashes from humans.

　　When they were first created, animals and men got along well, but war between them erupted when the monkey Fum Mbombo stole some wine-filled calabashes from a palm wine tapper. The man killed Fum Mbombo and was in turn killed by a leopard to avenge Fum Mbombo's death. After that animals and humans became enemies and the animals left the village and went to live in the forest. (De Heusch, 104–105; Josephsson, 45)

Gadaba Brothers. In Middle India mythology, 12 brothers who discovered **tobacco**.

By chance a cuckoo carrying a tobacco seed in its beak happened to perch in a tree near where the Gadaba brothers lived and accidentally dropped it. The seed sprouted and grew into a tobacco plant whose leaves their goat ate. The intoxicating juice passed through its body and into its milk and in the evening when the brothers drank some of the milk, they experienced a pleasurable sensation. After that they brought the goat to the plant every day so that it could feed on its leaves. One day, however, they decided to dry and burn the leaves. When they inhaled the smoke they enjoyed the sensation so much they kept the plant to themselves and wouldn't let the goat get near it. (Elwin, 1954, 177)

Gahpi Mahso. In Colombian Desana mythology, the mother of the **yage** vine (Banisteriopsis capi). (Reichel-Dolmatoff, 1975, 134, 146)

Galar *see* **Fjalar.**

Gama Sennin. A legendary Japanese **shaman** who lived in the mountains with a giant toad ("gama") which taught him how to make drugs that could transform humans into toads and induce visions of celestial paradise. (Furst, 1976, 162)

Gandharas. In Hindu mythology, male spirits part human and part horse, living in the forests, mountains or air. Known for their musical abilities and power to cast illusions, they are variously described as either protectors or abductors of **Soma.** As abductors, the half-man, half-horse Gandharas are the counterparts of the Greek **Centaurs.** Like them, they do not like to share their divine drink. (Kelly, 35)

Ganymede. In Greek mythology, the cupbearer to the Olympian gods.

Ganymede was the son of Tros, the founder of Troy. One day Zeus saw him playing and was so struck with his beauty he transformed himself into an eagle (some versions say he sent an eagle), and carried Ganymede off to Olympus. There he made Gandymede an immortal and installed him as cup bearer of the gods, replacing Hebe, his own daughter. Zeus later transformed Gandymede into the constellation of Aquarius, the water carrier, and placed the eagle that had kidnapped him alongside him as the constellation Aquilla. In Roman mythology Ganymede was called Catamitus. (Gantz, 557–560; Price and Kearns, 226)

Garuda. In Indian mythology, a creature with the beak, talons and wings of an eagle and the body and limbs of a man. Garuda is best known for stealing the **amrta**, the **elixir** of immortality, from the gods.

Garuda's mother, Vinata, and her sister, Kadru, were rivals. Kadru's children, the Nagas, abducted Vinata and said they would only release her if Garuda stole Indra's amrta and gave it to them. It was a seemingly impossible challenge because the amrta was protected by guards. Even if they were overcome, access to it could only be accomplished by first passing through a revolving wheel that had razor-like spokes. Then whoever managed that had to avoid the glare of two great serpents which turned whatever they looked at to ashes. Garuda managed to defeat the guardians and pass through the wheel. Then without hesitating for a moment, he threw ashes into the eyes of the serpents so they would not be able to look at him, snatched up the amrta, and brought it to the Nagas who then released his mother.

While Garuda was stealing the amrta, **Vishnu** saw what he was doing and was so impressed with his resourcefulness and courage, he told him he could have any favor he requested. Garuda asked that he be given immortality without tasting the amrta, and Vishnu granted him his request. In the meantime, **Indra** had found out about the theft of the amrta and went after Garuda to get it back. Since Garuda was now immortal, Indra couldn't kill him. Instead, he promised to help him kill the Nagas in return for the amrta, which Garuda now stole back from the Nagas. (Knipe, 328–360; Walker, B., 1: 381–382)

Geeheesop *see* **Siuuhu.**

Geirhild. Norse goddess of brewing.

A pregnant Geirhild competed with Signy to see who could make the best ale for King Alrek. The winner would become Alrek's queen. Geirhild asked **Odin** for help. Odin said his price for helping her was what was between her and her mash tub. Geirhild understood but nevertheless agreed. Then Odin spit on her mash, and her ale won the contest. Odin then demanded her unborn child, who was sacrificed to him when he became a man. (Bachman and Erlingsson, 3–4; Davidson, 141)

Geshtinanna (or **Gestin-anna**). In Sumerian mythology, the "Lady of the grape"; the goddess who incarnated the vine. When **Inanna** returned from the Underworld after her unsuccessful attempt to dethrone her sister, she found her husband, **Dumuzi**, who had invented beer, drinking **wine** with Geshtinanna. In anger at what she interpreted as a carnal relationship between them, she banished Geshtinanna to the Underworld for the six winter months and Dumuzi for the six summer months. The myth was meant to explain why beer and wine were not produced at the same time of year. (Lutz, 130–131; Mclish, 287)

Gilgamesh. The Mesopotamian culture hero of the world's oldest **elixir** story. Gilgamesh found the herb of immortality but had it stolen from him by a snake, During his wanderings he encountered **Siduri**, who tended the vineyard of the gods and although she tried to discourage him in his quest, Gilgamesh would not be dissuaded. (Lutz, 130–131)

Girl that Nobody Loved. A common folklore theme, wherein a homely girl is rejected by all men until she is turned into an **entheogenic** plant that all men cherish (See **Chandu**).

In one variant of this story from India, the main character is an angry wife from whose body **poppies** grow after she commits suicide to revenge herself on her husband for ignoring her. Implicit in the story is that she was finally able to gain her husband's attention through the poppies that sprang from her body after her death.

In another Indian variant, eight princes continually quarreled with one another over the right to marry a beautiful princess. Their constant pleadings over who was the most worthy made her so unhappy, the princess told them she had become so weary of their bickering that she was dying. However, she told them they could still enjoy her if they burned her body five days after her death. On the fifth day when they came to her grave, they found two plants growing from it, one **opium**, the other **tobacco**, so that even though they had not been able to marry the princess she was still able to please them. (Elwin, 1954, 213, 220)

Gitche Manitou. Among Ojibway and other woodland native American tribes, the great spirit who lives in the heavens. Gitche Manitou created and gave **tobacco** to humans to assuage their anxieties about the shortness and infirmities of life and to enable them to ask favors of all the Manitous, the spirits who animated the world and to whom tobacco originally belonged.

After creating humans, Gitche Manitou asked the Manitous to give them tobacco, but they were reluctant to do so because they would then be at the mercy of humans for their tobacco. They finally agreed, provided people made them regular tobacco offerings in the form of smoke whenever the ceremonial pipe was lit. (Underhill, 185; Wilbert, 1987, 182)

Gobind Singh. In Sikh mythology, a culture hero who introduced bhang (a form of **cannabis**) to the Sikhs. When the Sikhs were at war with India, the Indian Rajas sent an elephant that had been specially trained to break down gates of fortifications and attack with a sword in his trunk, against the Sikhs. In a variation of the David and Goliath confrontation, Gobind Singh gave one of his followers some bhang and a little **opium**, and told him to face the elephant. The man stood his ground when the elephant attacked and killed him. The event was subsequently celebrated in a festival called Dasehra, in which bhang is ritually taken to commemorate the event. (Campbell, 1893, 162)

Goibniu (also known as **Goibhniu** or **Goibnll**). In Celtic mythology, the god of metalsmiths and cupbearers. Goibniu was also a master brewer, whose ale was served at a **divine banquet** called the "Feast of Goibniu" or "Feast of Age." Those who drank it acquired divine wisdom and immortality and no longer decayed or became older. (MacCulloch, 31; Mackillop, 28)

Grail *see* **Holy Grail.**

Grandfather Tobacco. In North American Delaware Indian mythology, the Creator who gave the Delaware **tobacco**. (Winter, 18)

Great Raven. In Siberian mythology, the culture hero and ancestor of mankind who gave it **fly agaric.**
  One day Great Raven found a great whale and tried to haul it back to his home in the sea but it was too heavy. Frustrated, Great Raven asked Vahiyinin, the god of Existence, for help. Vahiyinin agreed and spat on earth and from his spittle, spirit beings called wapaq appeared in the form of fly agaric, beautiful plants with white stalks and spotted red hats. Vahiyinin told Great Raven to eat some of the plants, and when he did, he felt much stronger and was able to carry the whale. The wapaq spirits showed Great Raven the way back to the sea and after he got the whale home, Great Raven thanked the wapaq and told his people about their powers. (Furst, 1976, 94)

Great Spirit *see* **Gitche Manitou.**

Gwion Bach. In Celtic mythology, the shape-shifter who stole the power of wisdom and prophecy from the witch **Ceridwen**'s son and was subsequently reborn as **Taliesin.** (Stewart, R., 88–90)

Gymir *see* **Aegir.**

Hallucinogen. From the Latin, *alucinare*, "to wander in the mind." A chemical substance that alters auditory, visual and other sensory perceptions, including the sense of time and space. Hallucinogens do not cause hallucinations, which are perceptions in the absence of sensory stimulation such as those associated with schizophrenia. The term, when used in the context of myth and religion, has begun to be replaced by **entheogen.** (Goodman, 41–42; Rudgley, 126–127; Schultes and Hofmann, 10–14, 73–79).

Haoma. In Iranian mythology, the counterpart to the **elixirs, ambrosia** and **soma** of Greek and Indian mythology, respectively; also a god, the counterpart to soma in Indian mythology, and a prophet. Haoma gave the gods immortality. In mortals it induced the illusion of immortality.

The first four men who pressed haoma were rewarded by the gods with fathering great sons, one of whom was the prophet, Zoroaster.

Like soma, haoma was stolen from the gods by an eagle (cf. **Garuda**), but in this case, all of it fell to earth. From then on, the gods were dependent on humans; if humans lost their faith they would no longer press out the haoma for the gods, and like humans, the gods would know death and disappear.

A variant of the world tree motif has haoma growing in heaven near another tree called "inviolable" or eagle's tree, because an eagle sat in its top. The eagle tree contained seeds from every kind of plant. Whenever the eagle rose from his perch, a thousand branches sprouted from each tree; when he returned, the thousand branches from each tree broke and their seeds fell to earth.

As a God, Haoma was created from the haoma plant by the supreme god, Ahura Mazda, to be his son, and was empowered by him to be the adversary of death. After Zoroaster eliminated polytheism, it was no longer possible to recognize a god in the plant, but people continued to see it as manifestation of his divine power and continued to use it as part of the Zorastrian religion.

As prophet, Haoma spent much of his time meditating on the peak of mountains before the time of Zoroaster. He discovered the haoma plant growing in the mountains and ate it. The plant invigorated him and he subsequently taught its use to humans.

Traditions involving Haoma were later incorporated into Zoroastrianism, among them a temple ritual for preparing haoma called the yasna. As part of the ritualistic observance, haoma was presented to Zoroaster as an offering so that he would make all humans immortal when world history finally ended. (Boyce, 62–80; Hinnels, 33; Kelly, 138; McLeish, 239; Modi, 507)

Hashish. A potent combination of the leaves and resin of **cannabis sativa.** (Rudgley, 44–57; Schultes and Hofmann, 72, 74, 92–101)

Hashoriwe. In South American Yanomamo Indian mythology, the ancestor from whose spittle **tobacco** originated. (Albert et al., 164)

Hathor. In Egyptian mythology, the goddess of sex, fertility, motherhood, and drunkenness; had she not gotten drunk, Hathor would have destroyed the world.

One day, the aged sun-god Re became angry because he felt the Egyptians were no longer showing him the respect owed him, and he summoned several of the gods still loyal to him and asked them what he should do about the insolent Egyptians. They advised destroying the ingrates. Re agreed and sent Hathor, in the avatar of Sekhmet, the raging lioness, to do the job. Obediently, Hathor started in the desert region and slaughtered everyone in sight. Seeing the carnage, Re had a change of heart and decided to save those still living. But Hathor was now frenzied and couldn't be controlled. The bloodshed continued until she tired and went to sleep, intending to finish off those who had temporarily escaped her deadly mission, when she awoke.

While she was sleeping, Re attempted a ruse. He ordered the high priest of his still dutiful temple at Heliopolis to send him 7,000 jars of barley beer mixed with red ochre, and he poured it over the desert so that it looked like a sea of blood. When Hathor woke up, she saw her reflection in the reddened beer and began to lap it up, drinking so much beer she got drunk and forgot about her murderous mission. She was then transformed back into the beautiful Hathor and mankind was saved for the time being. However, death and destruction had now been unleashed, and to prevent a recurrence of the holocaust, Hathor's devotees attempted to appease her rage by celebrating their mythical deliverance every month at her temple, the "house of drunkenness," in a rite called the Bubastis festival or "the Feast of Drunkenness."

The annual festival was one of the country's most drunken public holidays. Men and women traveled by boat to Hathor's temple at Bubastis, singing, clapping their hands, playing pipes and drinking large quantities of beer or wine. Once they arrived at their destination, the celebrants drank more wine than during the whole year. (Lesko, 110–111; Piankoff, 29)

Haydar. Persian founder of Sufis, who discovered **hashish**, sometimes called the "**wine** of Haydar." After falling into a state of depression, Haydar wandered out of his monastery into the surrounding fields to be alone. When he returned he appeared unusually happy and whimsical in contrast to his previous reclusive nature, and he allowed his disciples to enter his room. Surprised at their teacher's dramatic mood change they asked what had happened. Haydar told them while he was in the field he noticed an unusual plant which unlike all the other plants standing motionless in the heat, seemed to be dancing in the sun's rays. Curious, he ate some of its leaves and they put him into this new euphoric state. When his disciples asked if he would let them share in his pleasure, Haydar agreed but not before they promised not to reveal its secret to anyone but the Sufis. (Rosenthal, 49–50)

Hebe. In Greek mythology, the goddess of youth and first cupbearer to the gods. Her Roman counterpart was Juventas.

According to one story, she resigned as cupbearer to the gods after marrying Heracles, who had just been deified. In another, she was dismissed from her position after presumably becoming drunk and falling down and exposing herself while serving the gods. Hebe's position as cupbearer was taken over by **Ganymede**. (Gantz, 81–82, 460–463; Price and Kearns, 241)

Heidrun. In Norse mythology, a she-goat who grazed at **Valhalla** on leaves from the world ash tree, **Yggdrasil**. In the process of being digested, the leaves fermented inside her body so that instead of milk, endless amounts of heavenly **mead** came out of Heidrun's udders. The mead was collected into large jars that were taken by the Valkyries into Valhalla for warriors to drink. (Gayley, 376; Turville-Petre, 54; Simek, 135)

Henbane. Henbane (Hyoscyamous niger) is also known as "Devil's herb, "murderer's berry," "sorcerer's cherry," and "witch's berry." It belongs to the same family of plants (Solanacea) as **tobacco, belladonna, datura,** mandrake, and the tomato and potato. Henbane's primary psychoactive ingredients are scopolamine, atropine and hyoscyamine. It is eaten or smoked. Psychoactive effects including visual hallucinations and intoxication, but it also produces dizziness, confusion, headache, and amnesia. In Greek mythology, it was the plant worn on the head by the dead in Hades as they wandered hopelessly beside the Styx. The Greeks also believed that henbane imparted the gift of prophecy. As such, henbane was an active component in the incense used by Pythia, Apollo's priestess at Delphi, to induce the clairvoyant **ecstasies** that enabled her to contact Apollo for the answers to the questions posed to the god by supplicants. In Norse mythology, it is associated with Donar (Thor), the god of weather and storms; in Roman mythology, with Jupiter. During the Middle Ages, it was believed to be one of the main inebriating substances used by witches in their "flying ointments." (Rudgley, 127–132; Schultes and Hofmann, 13, 26, 70, 81, 86–91)

Hera. In Greek mythology, the wife of Zeus and goddess of families and childbirth. Hera persecuted **Dionysus** because as the son of Zeus, he embodied the betrayal of marriage that often came with drunkenness. Once he was accepted into the Olympic pantheon, Hera was reconciled to him. (Gantz, 474–476)

Hero Twins. In Central American Maya Indian mythology, rulers of the Upperworld who used **tobacco** to protect themselves from the evil rulers of the Underworld.

The Underworld rulers challenged the Hero twins to keep two cigars lit throughout the night. The Hero twins lit the cigars but when the Underground rulers weren't looking, put them out and placed fireflies on the tips of their unlit cigars and pretended to smoke without stopping. In the morning the twins lit them once again, proving their superiority. (Furst, 1976, 26–27)

Hierophant. A priest of a mystery religion who explains its rituals and mysteries to newcomers. Hierophantes was the chief priest of the **Eleusian mysteries.** (Powell, B., 244–246)

Hikori. Among the Huichol and Tarahumara Indians of Central America, the spirit of **peyote.** In Tarahuma mythology, Hikori is called "uncle," because he sang in the fields when it was growing to make it easier to find. After being harvested, peyote was kept in a special warehouse instead of private homes, because Hikori might be offended by what happened in the latter, especially activities of a sexual nature. (Bonnefoy, 1186; Petrullo, 3, 17)

Hinon. A North American Seneca Indian deity, "the Thunderer," who lived in a cave beneath Niagara Falls; he protected people from evil and taught humans how to make **tobacco** offerings so that they could thank him. (Gill and Sullivan, 122)

Hiro. Tahitian god of **kava** plant. (Beckwith, 251)

Hitchiti. North American Indian **tobacco** origin story.

By chance, a man and a woman who had both lost their horses at the same time and were both looking for them, happened to meet. They started talking to one another, became friendly, had sex and then departed.

The next summer the man happened to lose his horse again and in searching for it came by the place where he and the woman had had sex and noticed a weed that he had never seen before growing from where they had lain. When he told the old men in his tribe about it they advised him to go back to the place periodically and watch it grow. Each time the man returned to the place, the plant was bigger. It finally blossomed with pretty flowers and when they eventually ripened, he took the seeds and leaves to the old men. The men didn't know what the plant was useful for, but one of them pulverized the leaves and put them in a pipe and smoked them and found its effects pleasing and from then on the Hitchiti smoked tobacco. (Grantham, 239; Swanton, 87)

Hler *see* **Aegir.**

Ho. Among the North American Apache Indians, the spirit of **peyote.** (Bonnefoy, 1186; Petrullo, 3)

Hoasca *see* **Ayahuasca.**

Ho Hsien Ku. In Chinese mythology, a **wine** goddess, the only female among the Chinese immortals. (Werner, 296)

Holy Grail. In Christian mythology, the counterpart of the magic **cauldron** mentioned in various ancient myths, believed capable of providing inexhaustible amounts of food and **wine**. The search for its retrieval became the spiritual quest for everlasting life and happiness and the basis for most of the adventures of the legendary Arthurian Knights of the Round Table. In the Arthur legend, the cup appears unexpectedly at feasts and confers supernatural benefits on those able to possess it, but only the purest heroes can do so. Lancelot, the most courageous and ablest of the knights, is prohibited from possessing it because of his adulterous romance with Arthur's wife, Guinevere.

The Grail myth in England Christianized much of the earlier Celtic myths featuring cauldrons, e.g., Cauldron of **Dagda**, and also borrowed from Irish quest myths such as the Voyage of **Bran** where the quest takes the voyagers to an island with intoxicating fruit and endless alcoholic drink.

Some modern scholars contend that the grail, like all magic cauldrons, is a metaphor for the mushroom, **amanita muscaria**, the shape of the cup or cauldron, representing the mushroom, and the blood representing the **elixir** of immortality. (Brown, 385–404; Littleton, 326–333; Oosten, 85–86)

Hou Ki *see* **Chang'o.**

Hrungnir. In Norse mythology, a giant or demon whom the **Aesir** invited to visit **Asgard** while **Thor** was away. Hrungnir drank so much ale he became very drunk and began boasting that he was going to drink all their ale and then kill them. Realizing the imminent danger, the gods immediately summoned Thor, who came at once. In the ensuing duel, Thor defeated Hrungnir and restored order. (Haustlong, 14–18; Fee and Leeming, 37–39)

Hsi Wang Mu *see* **Queen Mother of the West.**

Huitaca. In South American Chibcha Indian mythology, an evil goddess of drunkenness and licentiousness who came to earth to destroy good and teach men evil. Huitaca was constantly arguing with her husband, the supreme god Bochica, who represented hard work and self control. Eventually, her malevolence became so unbearable he transformed her into an owl. (Mercatante, 329)

Hukaht (Kitanemuk, Pamashiut, Pichurey, Tsukit Ukut). In North American Chumash Indian mythology, the god of **datura.** (Hudson and Underhay, 57)

Hummingbird. In many origin of **tobacco** mythologies, the bird that retrieved tobacco after it was stolen.

In a variant of the **Dagul'ku** myth in which geese stole their tobacco, the Cherokees had used up all their tobacco and were suffering from its absence. One old man had only been kept alive by smoking it. To keep him from dying, his son, a **shaman,** went on a quest to find some. The area where it grew, however, was far to the south and had high mountains all around and the tobacco field itself was constantly guarded. When he came to the mountains, he opened his medicine bag and took out a hummingbird skin and draped it over himself. Transformed into a hummingbird, he flew over the mountains and came to the tobacco field. In the guise of a hummingbird, he was so small and quick that the guards didn't see him, and he was able to pull some of the leaves and seeds and put them in his bag without being detected. When he returned, his father was still alive and he gave him some of the tobacco leaves and revived him. The Cherokees planted the seeds and after that they always had tobacco. (Mooney, 255)

Hyas. In Phrygian mythology, the god of **wine** and vegetation. (Jobes, 810)

Hymir. In Norse mythology, the giant who possessed the largest **cauldron** in the world, the only one big enough to brew enough beer for the **Aesir's** yearly **divine banquet.**

   The Aesir wanted to have a huge annual banquet and asked the giant, **Aegir,** known for his brewing skill, to make the beer for them. Aegir didn't want to, but since he couldn't refuse outright, he thought he could evade his obligation by telling the Aesir he didn't have a cauldron that was big enough for such a banquet. When Tyr, one of the Aesir gods, said that his father Hymir had a cauldron that was big enough, he and **Thor** journeyed to Hymir's home to get it from him. Hymir fed Thor and Tyr when they arrived and after being told what they wanted, promised he would give it to Thor if he could break a mug he gave him into bits. Thor threw the mug against a stone pillar with all his strength, but the pillar broke instead of the mug. When she saw what was happening, Tyr's mother secretly told him to tell Thor to throw it against Hymir's head; this time the mug broke. Disgruntled, Hymir tried one more ploy to keep the cauldron by making its removal contingent on only one of them being able to carry it out of his house. First Tyr tried to lift it, but couldn't budge it. Thor then tried. When he lifted it, his feet broke through the floor but he nevertheless managed to sling the cauldron over his shoulders. Although it was so large that its handles clattered to the floor, Thor nevertheless made off with it. When he finally returned to Aegir's palace, Aegir was finally compelled to brew the beer for the yearly banquet. (Lindow, 189–190)

Iacchus. In Greek mythology, an avatar of **Dionysus,** usually depicted as a child holding a torch and leading the procession for initiates at the **Eleusian Mysteries.** (Grimal, 225; Nonnos, 48.848; Price and Kearns, 277)

Iboga (or Eboka) (*Tabernanthe iboga*). A bush-like plant with several varieties common to Equatorial Africa. It produces yellow and pinkish white flowers, and small orange fruit. The primary psychoactive component, ibogaine, is produced primarily in its roots, which are ground into a powder and eaten, or are soaked in water and drunk as a tea. Psychoactive effects include visual hallucinations, a sensation of floating, and alterations in time perception that can last for more than a day because ibogaine is metabolized very slowly by the body. (Rudgley, 87–88; Schultes and Hofmann, 64, 70–71, 112–115)

Icarius. In Greek mythology, an Athenian farmer whom **Dionysus** rewarded for his hospitality by giving him grape vines and teaching him how to turn their fruit into **wine**. Wanting to share his gift with his neighbors, Icarius offered some of the new drink to them. Unaccustomed to its effects, and drinking it without water, they became drunk. In one variant, their drunkenness caused them to imagine Icarius had poisoned them and they murdered him. In another variant, they fell into a deep drunken sleep, and when they didn't come home that night, their families went out looking for them. Finding them drunk and believing Icarius had poisoned them, they murdered him. In both versions the murderers buried his body under a tree.

The next day Icarius' daughter **Erigone** went to look for him and while searching, was led to his corpse by the family dog. When she discovered the body, she became grief-stricken and hanged herself from the tree over her father's grave. Angered at the murder-suicide, Dionysus carried the father, daughter and the dog to the heavens, transforming Icarius into Bootes, the "grape harvester," the constellation that rises in autumn at the time of the grape harvest, Erigone into the constellation Virgo, and her dog into the dog star, the constellation called Canis. Then he caused girls in Athens to hang themselves as punishment for Icarius' death and Erigone's suicide. Unable to understand why they had been so afflicted, the Greeks consulted the oracle at **Delphi** and learned of Dionysus' anger. To appease him, they began worshiping him and instituted a festival called Aiora, the day of wine mixing, on the second day of the Anthesteria (see Dionysus) in honor of Erigone, in which little girls swung from ropes.

Dionysus' gift of grapes to Icarius and his teaching him how to turn them into wine were regarded as the beginnings of civilization by many Greek and Hellenistic writers because viticulture was considered a watershed in cultural evolution, since it meant settling in one place as opposed to the wandering associated with hunter cultures. (Grimal, 226; Nonnos, 47.34–55; Price and Kearns, 278)

Ilako. In Polynesian mythology, a god of **kava**. (Christian, 384)

Im-dugud. In Sumerian mythology, a gigantic bird, similar to **Garuda**, who carried off the tablets of destinies, by which the gods maintained their positions as masters of the universe. Lugalbanda, the sun god, who was delegated to recover them, found the bird nesting and with the help of **Ninkasi**, the goddess of fermentation, succeeded in intoxicating the bird and regaining the tablets. (Albright, 268)

Inanna. In Sumerian (Mesopotamian) mythology, a dual natured androgynous goddess associated with the planet Venus. Inanna, whose name means "Lady of Heaven," was the most important female deity in the ancient Near East. Her counterparts in other mythologies were Anat (Canaan), Ashoreth (Israel), Astarte (Phoenicia), Athena (Greece), **Hathor** (Egypt), and Kali (India).

Inanna was at the same time mankind's benefactor, the counterpart of Prometheus and the goddess of sexual love.

In her role as the Mesopotamian Prometheus, she stole the "me" from **Enki**, the god of wisdom, after getting him drunk, and gave them to humans. The "me" were the norms of civilization, i.e., the rules, customs and mores that distinguished culture from nature, e.g., family, crafts, writing, and rules of conduct.

The theft occurred after Inanna was invited by the lecherous Enki to dine at his heavenly table. The two deities drank one beer after another, but Enki was the only one to become totally drunk. Inebriated, he offered Inanna one set of "me" after another. After he sobered up, Enki asked his servant where all his "mes" had gone. The servant told him he had given them all to Inanna. Enraged, Enki realized he had given away all of the prerogatives of civilization by which he controlled mankind. Desperate to regain his "mes," and thereby keep mankind subservient to him, Enki sent several demons after Inanna to bring her back before she reached her throne city, Uruk. But Inanna had her own demon, and he overpowered Enki's. After she arrived in Uruk, she turned all the "me" over to the people of Uruk.

Inanna was also responsible for the cycle of **beer** and **wine** making after returning, like **Persephone**, from the land of the dead. Inanna had gone to the Underworld to usurp the place of her sister, Ereshkigal, "the queen of death," but was unable to win over the "seven judges of the dead," and was taken prisoner and hanged from a hook, where her body began to rot. When she didn't return after three days, the gods sent an emissary who persuaded them to let Inanna go. They agreed on the condition that she found a substitute. When she returned to Uruk, she was outraged that her husband **Dumuzi** had not been grieving for her, and was instead drinking wine with her sister. Angered at their apparent carnal relationship, she chose Dumuzi and **Geshtinana** as her substitutes, each of them having to spend six different months in the Underworld (reflecting the annual beer and wine making cycles). (Jacobsen, 55ff; Wolkstein, 34ff)

Indra. The most celebrated of India's Hindu gods; venerated as the god of atmosphere, storms, rain and battle. Before each battle, he drank vast amounts of **soma** which empowered him to accomplish his heroic deeds.

Indra was the son of Earth and Sky and the grandson of **Tvastr**, the god who created the world, and gave Indra his most powerful weapon, the thunderbolt. When Indra was first created he was weak, but after he either stole or found soma in his father's house (i.e. the earth) or his mother's breast's (i.e. the mountains), and drank it, he became very powerful and the champion of the gods in their ongoing battles with the demon **Asuras**.

One of his best-known deeds was his conquest of the serpent demon Vrtra, who had swallowed the Cosmic Waters, and the sun, the source of those waters, so that there was no rain and dew to nourish the earth. To prepare for battle Indra drank soma for three days. As the conflict raged the heavens and the earth trembled reflected in recurring thunderstorms. When Indra finally defeated Vrtra, a victory that earned him his best-known title, Vrtrahan, "slayer of Vrtra," the Cosmic Waters and the sun were freed and life was regenerated on earth. The fight between Indra and Vrtra symbolized the conflict between the destructive forces of darkness (night, winter) and regenerative forces of light (day, summer). For Indra's other exploits, see **Asvins**, **Garuda**, and **Namuci**. (MacDonell, 66–69; Brown, 88–96; Mahony, 127–128)

Ino. In Greek mythology, the sister of **Semele**, and wife of Athamas, king of Orchomenus. She took care of **Dionysus** while he was a child. **Hera** hated her and her husband for helping Dionysus and made them both mad. In her demented state, Ino drowned herself along with her son. (Dalby, 36–42)

Inti. In Inca mythology, the sun god and creator of coca. He instructed the moon goddess to plant coca in humid valleys and ordered that only his descendants be allowed to chew it. (Gagliano, 15)

Intshanga *see* **Fum Mbombo.**

I-ti. The Chinese god who invented wine; also the god of **wine** making. (Werner, 204)

Ivaldi. In Norse mythology, a dwarf king who lived in Jotunheims, the land of the giants, and discovered a well, called **Byrgir,** whose water contained a **magic** mead that conferred wisdom and **ecstasy.** To keep the **mead** secret, Ivaldi sent his son Hjuki and daughter Bil with a pail to empty the well out at night and bring the mead back to him. One night, however, Nepur, the Moon God, whose children Ivaldi had earlier abducted, and who was waiting for an opportunity to retaliate, noticed Ivaldi's children and kidnapped them in return. When he brought them and their pail back to his home in the moon he discovered the mead's magical effects and gave some of it to the **Aesir** gods. When Ivaldi learned what had happened, he became infuriated, and waited for Nepur to pass through the Underworld on his nightly journey, captured him, rescued his children and got his mead back. Ivaldi knew that the Aesir would try to get the mead, so he formed an alliance with their enemies, the frost giants, and entrusted his mead to the giant, **Fjalarr,** for safekeeping. In return, Fjalarr gave him permission to marry his daughter, Gunnloo. On the day before the wedding, **Odin** arranged to have Ivaldi ambushed and killed. Then he disguised himself as the bridegroom, stole the mead, and brought it back to **Asgard.** (Rydberg, No. 123)

Ixcuina *see* **Tlazolteotl.**

Izquitecatl. In Mayan mythology, a **pulque** deity, known as the "two rabbits." (Anderson and Dibble, Pt III, 36; Spence, 1911, 352; Reed, 96)

Japan, Tobacco Origin *see* **Tobacco Origin Story, Japanese**

John Barleycorn. In English and Scottish folklore, the personification of barley malt and alcohol. (Davidson, 108)

Jupiter. The Roman counterpart of the Greek god Zeus. After escaping from the fallen Troy, Aeneas came to Italy where he offered Jupiter all the **wine** of the Italian peninsula. In return, Jupiter sided with Aeneas over an adversary who claimed all the wine for himself and gave his descendants control over the peninsula. In rural Italy, Jupiter was honored as the god of fermentation. During the Vinalia celebrations in late summer when the grapes were harvested, a part of that harvest was offered to him; during the following spring, a portion of the fermented new wine was also offered to him. (Dumezil, 1966, 181–186)

Jurupari. In the mythology of the Uapes Indians of Brazil, a god who was born of a virgin after she drank cachari, a native beer. (Mercantante, 1987)

Kachra-Durwa. In Middle India legend, a culture hero who introduced the rest period for smoking. Kachra-Durwa worked all the time in the fields tilling the earth with a plough pulled by several bullocks, eating only when the sun went down. The bullocks eventually became exhausted and asked **Mahadeo** (the name of Siva in Middle Indian) to help them.

Taking the form of an old man, Mahadeo approached Kachra-Durwa in his field and asked him for some fire. Kachra-Durwa asked what he wanted it for, and the old man replied that he wanted it so that he could smoke his pipe. When Kachra-Durwa said he didn't know what he meant, the old man gave him some of his **tobacco** to smoke, and Kachra-Durwa soon became contented on it. Mahadeo then showed Kachra-Durwa how to sow tobacco seeds and how to pick and dry the leaves and prepare them for smoking. After that Kachra-Durwa regularly took a rest from ploughing to smoke, and in that way the bullocks also got their rest. (Elwin, 1991, 327–328)

Kachui. In South American Ayoreo Indian mythology, the **tobacco** worm from whom tobacco originated.

Kachui was a **shaman** who found a seed in his rib. Curious about what it would turn out to be, he planted it and when it grew into a large plant, he tried it and liked it. When the plant subsequently produced seeds, Kachui collected them and gave some to Hawk to give some to other shamans and to the rest of the world.

In a variant, Kachui was originally a shaman who grew his own tobacco and didn't share it with his neighbors. Envious, they plotted to kill him and take his tobacco. Kachui became aware of their plans but didn't want to leave his plants, so he transformed himself into a worm, but before he changed, he cast a spell over the tobacco plant that required anyone who wanted to become a shaman, to eat or smoke tobacco. (Bormida et al., 190)

Kadru *see* **Garuda.**

Kanabos. In South American Warao Indian mythology, the Supreme Spirits who live in mountains at the end of the world and are dependent on **tobacco** smoke for their nourishment. If they receive their tobacco they give health and abundance; if denied it they send pain and death to humans. (Cox and Banack, 1991; Titcomb, 155; Wilbert, 1970, 66–67)

Kanaloa. In Hawaiian mythology, the evil-smelling god of the under-world who craves awa (**Kava**).

Kanaloa was banished from the heavens for trying to steal awa from **Kane** and became ruler of the Underworld. Sometime later, a boy drank the awa that his father had placed on an altar for Kanaola. When Kanaola saw what he did, he killed the boy and took his spirit to the underworld. Disheartened at the death of his son, the father no longer offered Kanaola any awa. Now without awa, Kanaloa regretted his impetuosity and restored the boy to life. In return, the father once again offered him awa. (Beckwith, 63; Handy and Handy, 190)

Kane. In Hawaiian mythology, the god who planted awa (**Kava**) on earth. Kane lived in an earthly garden paradise where he drank awa. One day, he decided to visit earth and traveled around the islands. When he began to miss his awa, he caused it to grow on the islands so he wouldn't be without his favorite food. (Titcomb, 155)

Kane-Timme. In northern India folklore, the culture heroine who invented rice **beer**.

Kane-Timme was living by herself when a dog came to her home. Kane-Timme had never seen a dog before and asked him who he was and why he had come to see her. The dog told her that he lived among men, but found their company dull, so he had come to her. In return for letting him live with her, the dog told her how to make rice beer. After that both their lives were happier.

A different variant has Kane-Timme living alone with her daughter. One night as she was returning from getting water, she saw an owl flying off with her daughter. Kane-Timme ran after it, but couldn't catch up. When Abo-Tani, the ancestor of the people of northern India, heard Kame-Timme's crying, he appeared to her and asked why she was crying. Kame-Timme told him what had happened and asked if he knew where to find her daughter. Abo-Tani told her the owl was in a tree eating her daughter's dead body that very moment. Abo-Tani then killed the owl and carried what was left of the girl's body to Kame-Timme. As a token of her gratitude, she gave him rice beer to drink. Abo-Tani had never tasted rice beer before and was delighted with it. When he was about to leave, Kane-Timme offered him various gifts as a gesture of thanks, but Abo-Tani said that the only thing he would like was to learn how to make the drink she had given her. Kame-Timme then gave him the ingredients and told him how to mix them, and warned him to make only a little of it at a time because it would grow stronger as it grew older. Abo-tani then taught his children, the people of north India, the secret. (Elwin, 1958, 215–217)

Kani. In Northeast India mythology, a variant of the "girl so ugly no one was attracted to her" motif. Kani cried and prayed to god to have pity on her and he promised he would transform her into something all men would love. After she died, he turned her into a **poppy** plant whose sap was craved by all men. (Elwin, 1958, 218)

Kauyumari. In Central American Huichol mythology, the Creator god and the incarnation of **peyote**. Kauyumari was also known as Deer-Person.

Kauyumari caused life to begin when he found the portway from the Underworld to the Mother Earth in **Wirkuta**, the land of Peyote, so that the gods could emerge into the world and impart their life energy to everything on it. Then he went to back to live in his home on a mountain at the eastern end of the world. Every year when he was needed, Tatewari, the spirit of Fire, shot an arrow at him to tickle him awake from his sleep so that in his manifestation as the Deer-Person, he would guide the quest for the divine Peyote. (Furst, 1972, 97ff; Schaefer and Furst, 15, 155)

Kava (*Piper methysticum*). Also known as awa; a drink made from the roots of a four to six-year-old shrub belonging to the pepper family which grows in the tropical islands of the Pacific Ocean. After the roots are washed and scrubbed free of dirt, they are cut into pieces and then they are either chewed, or finely grated into a pulp. The pulpy mass is then steeped in water to create a strong "tea," or infusion. The thick infusion is then strained or poured directly into containers and drunk, and the bits of root in the mix are chewed. The main psychoactive component is called methysticin. Its effects include euphoria, relaxation, and talkativeness. It is often used to create a context for resolving social disagreements. A common side effect of long term kava use is a dry scaly, yellow skin rash. In several myths about kava, this rash is likened to leprosy. Very heavy kava use is associated with eye irritation, puffy face, shortness of breath and changes in blood pressure. (Rudgley, 143–145; Schultes and Hofmann, 13, 26, 64)

Kava-on-a. In Tonga Polynesian island mythology, the maiden from whose dead body kava originated. (Craig, 110)

Kava Origin Story, Polynesia. Long ago, in this Pentecost Island legend, two orphan twins, a brother and sister, lived happily together. One night, a stranger appeared and asked the sister to marry him, but she declined. Angered, the stranger tried to kidnap her and in the ensuing struggle, he killed her. When her brother found her body, he buried it near their home. A few weeks later an unusual plant, (**Kava**), sprouted from her grave. A year later, the brother, who still grieved over his sister's death and still frequently visited her grave, saw a rat gnaw at the roots of the plant growing over the grave and then suddenly die. In his grief-stricken state, he decided to end his life the same way. But instead of dying, he forgot his grief. After that, he regularly returned to his sister's grave and ate some of the **magic** root which he shared with his neighbors. (Lebot et al., 122–123)

Kebo-Akbo. In Northeast India folklore, a spirit (Wiyu) from whose body **opium** originated.

Kebo-Akbo had the form of a yak and lived in the mountains. One day, he came out of his house and became so frightened at the sight of the sun and the moon that he fled north where he died. As he was dying, his sperm and urine came out of his body. His sperm turned into the poppy and his urine turned into the tea plant, which is why opium eaters in India are partial to tea. (Elwin, 1958, 219)

Keridwen *see* **Ceridwen.**

Kerridwen *see* **Ceridwen.**

Kezer-Tshingis-Kaira-Khan. In Siberian mythology, the counterpart of **Noah.** After a giant turtle who supported the earth moved, the cosmic ocean flooded the earth. Anticipating that something like that would eventually occur, Kezer had built a raft; when the flood came, he gathered his family and plants and animals on it. After the waters subsided, the raft rested on a high wooded mountain. Kezer then let the animals out and sowed the plants and taught his family how to make alcoholic drinks. (Holmber, 366; Jobes, 921)

Khunu (or **Khuno**). In Aymara Indian (southern Peruvian and Bolivian) mythology, the storm god who created coca.

Khunu became angry with people because in clearing the forest for planting, they had polluted the peaks of the mountains where he lived. To punish them, he sent a torrential rain that flooded their homes and caused them to flee to the caves for safety. After the flood, the survivors came out of the caves and although they had not been killed, they were despondent over the destruction that had occurred. Feeling remorse, Khunu caused the coca shrub to grow. When the people chewed its leaves it gave them a new sense of well being and they no longer despaired. (Gagliano, 16)

Kieri Taweakame. Central American Huichol Indian god of **datura** (called "tolache"), and sorcerers.

Kieri Taweakame was an evil god and the bitter enemy of **Kauyumari**, the god of **peyote**. After Kieri taught some sorcerers the black arts, Kauyumari decided that Kieri's evil influence had to end. In their ensuing fight, Kauyumari wounded Kieri with an arrow. The injured Kieri vomited up poisonous things whose strong acrid odors made Kauyumari cough and choke. Kauyumari immediately took some peyote whose power was greater that Kieri's vile emissions, and it suppressed the coughing spells. Kauyumari finally killed Kieri, but before the evil god died, he spewed various maladies into the world. Then his soul returned to the wind and his body was transformed into datura. (Miyahara, 235–263; Meyerhoff, 7–21)

Kinkajou. In South American Yamamomo Indian mythology, the ancestor who discovered **tobacco.** (Albert et al., 168)

Kiri. In South American Campa Indian mythology, the spirit who sacrificed himself to become a palm tree and then taught people how to transform the fruit on the tree into **beer.** (Weiss, 328)

Kitanemuk *see* **Hukaht.**

Kittung. In middle India mythology, the god of sago **wine** and fermentation. (Elwin, 1954, 196)

Kitzihiat. In North American Kickapoo Indian mythology, the god who gave mankind **tobacco.**

Kitzihiat felt sorry for his children, the Kickapoos, and wanted to give them a special gift, so he gave a piece of his heart to one of their dead ancestors who was living in the spirit world and told him to bring it to the Kickapoos.

The elderly Kickapoo swallowed the heart and then went to see his people, but when they saw him, they were frightened at the sight of their dead ancestor. After he reassured them they had nothing to fear, he told them he was bringing them a gift from Kitzihiat. He then vomited tobacco seeds and as soon as he did, rain fell on the seeds and they started to grow. The spirit then instructed them on how to use the plant and then returned to the spirit world. (Latorre and Latorre, 256–257; Winter, 19–20)

Komatari. In Caribbean Arawak folklore, a culture hero who brought **tobacco** to the Arawak.

One day Komatari ran out of tobacco. When he heard there was some growing on another island, he went down to the shore where he met House Master and asked if he would get him some from the island. House Master agreed but the quest took longer than expected because the tobacco field was constantly watched.

When House Master returned, he gave Komatari some of the seeds and said he could also have some of the tobacco leaves. But instead of a few Komatari took as many leaves as he could carry. When the villagers saw him carrying the tobacco, they expected he would give them some in accord with the customs of hospitality. But Komatari did not want to share it. Instead, he hid it in his home and left home very early and came back very late so he would not be there if anyone came by.

One day a neighbor came to visit after Komatari had left and saw some flies in the house. The visitor went home and returned to Komatari's house with some fish, and offered it to the flies if they would tell him where Komatari had hidden his tobacco. When Komatari came home that night, he saw that a lot of his tobacco was gone. Realizing what must have happened, he chased away all the different flies except the black ones and made them his watchmen. Then he planted his tobacco seeds so that he would no longer run out of it. (Radin, 1942, 59–61 Wilbert, 1987, 236–238)

Konda (also known as **Konde** or **Kyomba**). In African Luba mythology, a king whose drunkenness resulted in matrilineal descent among the Luba.

When Konda was the king of the Luba, he became drunk and fell asleep. Reminiscent of what happened to **Noah** and **Woot**, one of his sons, Chinguli, found him lying naked and left him in that condition, but his daughter Lueji covered him. When he woke up, Konda felt ashamed at being seen naked and disinherited his son who had not tried to cover his nakedness, in favor of his daughter who had.

In another version, Konda's sons mistook the milky-colored water he was cleaning his mats with for palm wine and accused him of spoiling it and then beat him. His daughter Lueji found him and took care of him. When he recovered, he disinherited his sons in favor of his daughter.

In a third variant, when Konda became old his sons decided to kill him so they could get his wealth. They dug a hole, planted spears in it, covered it with a mat, got their father drunk on beer, and lured him into the trap. Fatally wounded, Konda called for help. His wife's nephew heard his cries and helped him out of the trap. In return, before he died he passed his authority to his sister's sons instead of his own (De Heusch, 77–78, 147–149)

Kuripowe (or **Nosiriwe**). In South American Yamamomo Indian mythology, the culture hero who spread **tobacco** over the world.

One day a man named Kuripowe (or Nosiriwe) was crying as he walked through the forest, lamenting that there was something he needed but didn't know what it was and his need made him numb to all other feelings. Eventually he encountered the ancestral tobacco god, **Kinkajou,** who knew what it was that Kuripowe needed and gave him tobacco. Kuripowe began chewing it as he walked and wherever he spat its juice, tobacco plants immediately grew and flowered. Hummingbirds then came and sucked honey from the flowers and as a result, tobacco was spread all over. (Albert et al., 168)

Kurusiwari. In South American Warao Indian mythology, a spirit who refused to return to his village unless offered **tobacco**.

A man whose wife was barren took a second wife who subsequently gave birth to a boy named Kurusiwari. One day while he was still a child, Kurusiwari and two of his friends misbehaved and after being disciplined by his stepmother, they ran away. Kurusiwari's parents did not find him until he was fully grown. They wanted Kurusiwari and his friends to go back with them, but Kurusiwari said they would only return if a spirit house was constructed for them and they were offered tobacco. The spirit house was quickly built, but tobacco was not so easily obtained since it grew far away and was guarded by Watch woman. Kurusiwari's father sent several birds to steal it, but they were all killed by Watch woman. Finally Crane, who had endurance but not speed, made the long journey carrying **Hummingbird,** who had speed but not endurance, on his back. When they came to the tobacco field, Hummingbird's speed enabled him to evade Watch woman's arrows, and he was able to steal some tobacco seeds. Hummingbird then sat on Crane's back and they returned home. After the seeds they had stolen grew into tobacco plants, a **shaman** summoned Kurusiwari and his tobacco spirit companions with his rattle, and they returned to the village and continued to come whenever they were summoned by the **shaman's** rattle. (Wilbert, 1970, 223–226)

Kvasir. In Norse mythology, the mysterious being whose blood was turned into **mead**.

Kvasir was created when the two families of Norse gods, the **Aesir** and **Vanir**, spat into a **cauldron** as a symbol of their peace treaty. When the Vanir left, the Aesir kept this symbol of their truce and created Kvasir out of it. Kvasir was a man so wise that he was able to answer any question posed to him. Kvasir then began to wander all over the world imparting his knowledge. In the course of those journeys, he met two dwarfs, Fijarlar and Galar, who murdered him and drained his blood into three vessels, which they then combined with honey and water to create the **Mead of Inspiration and Poetry**, an **elixir** that conferred wisdom and inspired the creation of great poetry in anyone who drank it. When the Aesir noticed Kvasir was missing, they asked the dwarfs what had happened to him. The dwarfs replied that Kvasir had choked on his own knowledge.

Some time later the evil dwarfs invited the giant Gilling and his wife to their home and persuaded Gilling, who couldn't swim, to go out with them in their boat. When they were far from shore, the dwarfs rowed onto a rock and capsized the boat and Gilling drowned. The dwarfs then righted the boat and rowed back and killed Gilling's wife.

When Suttung, their son, heard what had happened to his parents, he found the two dwarfs and tied them to a rock in the sea so that they would die a slow death. To save themselves, the dwarfs told Suttung about the Mead of inspiration and gave it to him in return for their freedom. Suttung took the three vessels of mead back with him to his mountain home, but it was subsequently stolen from him by **Odin**. (Lindow, 206–207; Metzner, 231–232)

Kyomba *see* **Konda.**

Lado. Slavic god of **wine**. (Znayenko, 17)

Latis. In Irish mythology, the goddess of **beer**. (Ross, 180)

Lea. In Polynesian mythology, a goddess who made an inexhaustible amount of **kava** for the demons threatening her village, thereby saving it from destruction. (Craig, 136)

Lefanoga (or Lele'asapai). In Samoan Polynesian mythology, the god who brought **kava** down from heaven.

Lefanoga was the son of **Tagaloa**, the creator god. One day Lefanoga's two brothers went to a council in heaven. Lefanoga secretly followed them but he was discovered and as punishment, was forced to dig kava for them to drink, but instead of giving it to his father and brother, he stole them and brought them to earth. (Beckwith, 438; Craig, 137)

Lele'asapai *see* **Lefanoga.**

Liber. In Roman mythology, the god of fertility and new **wine** (from the latin, "libare," to pour out). Liber was the Roman counterpart of **Dionysus,** although the assimilation was superficial.

Liber was credited with inventing a special Roman wine called Falernian. While he was traveling through southern Italy, a peasant named Falernus invited him to stay at his home and fed him but was so poor, he didn't have any wine to offer. Liber was so appreciative of Falernus' hospitality that he filled all the empty cups with wine. Falernus drank so much he fell asleep. When Falernus awoke, his guest was gone, but the hillsides around his village were covered with grape vines that subsequently produced a wine named after him.

In Rome, Liber did not have his own temple, but shared one with the Roman goddess, Ceres, and his consort, Libera. The temple was located on the **Aventine Hill.** A fertility festival, celebrated on March 17, called the Liberia, honored the two wine deities and their association with fertility. Elderly women wearing crowns of ivy, called "sacerdotes Liberi," sold honey cakes in the street and kept little portable hearths on which they offered those cakes as sacrifices to Liber and Libera in the name of the buyer. In some parts of Italy, revelers celebrated the festival by driving a wagon carrying a large phallus into the countryside and then returning it to the city where the most virtuous matrons publicly crowned it with wreaths, acknowledging that the welfare of the community depended on the fertility of the fields. The festival finally ended when the phallus was returned to its temple site. (Dumezil, 1966, 378; Price and Kearns, 318; Younger, 182, 216)

Liberia *see* **Liber.**

Liberia Festival *see* **Liber.**

Lita. In Middle Indian mythology, a culture hero of the Santals who taught the first man and woman to make rice **beer.** The beer aroused such passion in the couple that they eventually populated the world. (Elwin, 1954, 188)

Lizard. In Aztec mythology, the goddess of the **mushroom.** (Miller and Taube, 91)

Lo'au. In Polynesian Tonga mythology, the god of **kava**.

Lo'au had two servants, a man and his wife, who one day asked him for permission to visit their leprous daughter, Kava-onu, who lived on another island. Lo'au agreed, but when they were gone, he missed them and went looking for them. When Lo'au finally found them, the island where they were visiting was in the grip of famine. Since there was no food except for a single plant to feed Lo'au, the couple cooked it and then killed their daughter and roasted her body together with the plant. Lo'au instantly realized what they had done, and deeply moved by their sacrifice, told the couple to give their daughter a decent burial and watch for and take care of the two plants that would grow from her grave site, and then bring them to him when they were fully grown.

The plant that sprang from the area of the girl's head was kava; the one that sprouted from the area of her feet was sugar cane. One day, the couple saw a rat eating some of the kava leaves and become intoxicated, and then after taking a bite from the sugar cane, recover. He kept repeating the sequences over and over, first eating the kava and then the sugar cane. When the couple returned to Tonga, they brought the kava to Lo'au and told him about the rat. Lo'au then gave the plant to the people of Tonga and told them that, like the rat, they should eat sugar cane after using kava.

Variations of the myth have the same motif of kava sprouting from the dead body of a leprous girl, and differ primarily in how Lo'au came to the island where the couple and the daughter lived. The detail concerning leprosy comes from the scaly skin that many long-term kava users develop. (Bott and Leach, 215–216; Gifford, 71–73)

Lollus. In German mythology, the god of the **opium** poppy. (Metzner, 290)

Lu tung-pin. In Chinese mythology, the god of drunkenness, one of the Chinese Eight Immortals. (Werner, 297–8)

Lycurgus. In Greek mythology, one of several kings who resisted acknowledging the divinity of **Dionysus**, and hence, the possibility of salvation through the **ecstasy** of **altered consciousness**, and paid for his obstinacy by being driven mad. (Dalby, 65–70; Price and Kearns, 322)

Macuiltochtli. In Mayan mythology, "five rabbits," one of the four hundred **Centzon Totochtin** pulque gods. (H. Nicholson, 168)

Mada (also known as Baruni, Madira, Sura, or Varuni). In Hindu mythology, the goddess of intoxication and gambling. She is often depicted as an open-mouthed monster with fearful teeth. Her name is found in "madira" (rice **wine**) and "madya" (brandy). (Dowson, 183, 339; Walker, B., 309)

Madain. In Hindu mythology, the god of distillation. (Briggs, 156; Crooke, 7:643)

Madira *see* **Cyavana, Mada.**

Maebh *see* **Medb.**

Maeldun. In Irish folklore, a seaman who discovered an island where intoxicating fruit grew. The fruit looked like apples but had a rough berry-like rind, and no one in his crew had ever seen anything like it before. The seamen were curious to eat the fruit, but wary that it might kill them. When they cast lots to see who would be the one to try it, Maeldun won.

After he squeezed the juice out of the fruit and drank it, he lapsed into a deep trance in which he didn't move or seem to be breathing. He stayed like that for an entire week, no one being certain he was dead or alive. When he finally awoke, he told everyone of the euphoria he had experienced while in his trance. Assured that the fruit was not poisonous, they gathered as much of it as they could take with them, pressing the juice out of it until their whole ship could hold no more. On their way back to their home they drank some of the juice but it was so powerful they had to dilute it to avoid becoming totally overcome by it. (O'Meara, 46–47)

Maenads. In Greek mythology, female followers of **Dionysus.** They were often portrayed as inspired by him to ecstatic frenzy, through a combination of dancing and drunkenness. During these rituals, they lost all self control, began shouting excitedly, engaged in uncontrolled sexual behavior, and ritualistically tore animals to pieces and ate their parts. During these rites, they dressed in fawn skins and carried the thyrsus, a long stick with ivy or vine-leaves, tipped by a pine cone, and wore ivy-wreaths on their heads. (Guthrie, 148ff)

Maev *see* **Medb.**

Magic. Actions intended to influence supernatural powers to transform what is ordinary into the extraordinary for benevolent or malevolent ends; substances endowed with special properties that enable humans to contact or influence supernatural powers to act on their behalf for good or evil. Magic is generally power performed by humans in contrast to religion, which is power exercised by supernatural beings. **Entheogens** are magical elixirs that enable humans to encounter the supernatural powers that control the vital energies of the world to possibly manipulate them. Magicians or **shamans** are humans whose special knowledge of magic and magical **elixirs** gives them access to the supernatural world. Magical powers are often attributed to the occult regions of the underworld where the energies of life and death are strangely united. (Parry, 1, 17, 20; Price and Kearns, 327–329)

Mahadeo. In Middle India mythology, the Supreme god, who created ganja, **tobacco**, and **wine**. Mahadeo is an avatar of **Siva**.

One day Mahadeo was sitting with his followers when a wind blew some seeds by them that subsequently grew into hemp, tobacco and mahua. Mahadeo told his disciples they should eat whichever of the plants they liked, but no matter which of them they ate, they were still hungry, so Mahadeo showed them what to do to make them more satisfying. He explained how to press the juice out of the mahua to make liquor, how to dry the hemp plant to make ganja, and how to prepare the tobacco plant so that it could be smoked.

In a variant, an elderly childless couple had a favorite cow that they allowed to go wherever it wanted. One day the cow wandered into a field where a tobacco plant was growing and ate it. When the cow returned home, it defecated, passing tobacco seeds in its dung. The old woman spread the dung near her home and eventually, a tobacco plant emerged. Some time later, the man had a pain in his stomach. He took many different plant medicines, but the pain did not go away. Finally, he ate some tobacco leaves which first intoxicated him and then made him fall asleep. When he awoke, he told all his neighbors about the power of tobacco.

In another variant about ganja, Mahadeo, disguised as a boy, came to live with a couple, so that he could marry their daughter. Several years later, they agreed that their daughter was old enough to be married and told the boy he could invite his relatives to the celebration. When tigers, bears, snakes and other animals appeared instead of people, the father was angered because he had collected a lot of liquor and thought it would go to waste. Most of the animals, however, told the father they would drink his liquor, but the snakes and scorpions insisted they had to have ganja. The man then mixed some hemp leaves with water and gave it to the snakes and scorpions who soon became intoxicated from it and began to dance. Before they began to dance, the snakes and scorpions had stood upright, but in this intoxicated condition, they broke their backs, and ever since, they have walked flat on the ground. (Elwin, 1991, 330–333)

Mahalakshmi. In middle India mythology, a vegetation goddess who stayed in the land because of **tobacco**.

When she came down to the plains from the mountains, Mahalkshmi became frightened that she would be entirely consumed when the people began eating all her grain and started to run away. Just before she disappeared, a tobacco plant sprouted under her and pleaded with her to stay, promising that if she would remain, men would eat it first and only when they were satisfied, would they eat her.

Shortly thereafter, a group of men came searching for Mahalaskshmi. They did not find her very attractive standing next to tobacco's beautiful leaves and flowers and they didn't eat as much of her grain as before so that Mahalaskshmi no longer felt she would be destroyed and remained. (Elwin, 1954, 176)

Mahaprabhu. In Middle India mythology, the deity who taught people about **tobacco**, palm **wine**, and distillation.

TOBACCO. There was once a lustful woman whose sexual appetite was unsatisfied because she was married to a snake who was awake for only two days, every six months. The snake was very powerful, however, and when he became angry at his wife's nagging him about her sexual wants, he shouted at her, causing the whole world to tremble. One day Mahaprabhu came to the snake's house, saw his beautiful wife and immediately fell in love with her. He wanted to have sex with her but feared that if the snake woke, he would become so enraged he would kill the whole world. The woman told Mahaprabhu he shouldn't worry because her husband slept for six months and would never know, but Mahaprabhu said that he wanted to be with her always, not just until the snake woke up, and said that they had to kill the snake first.

Mahaprahbuhu then devised a plan about how they could kill him. He told the woman that he was going back to his home and that when the snake woke up, she was to ask him where he kept his soul. When the snake finally awakened, his wife pestered him so relentlessly about his soul, he became very annoyed and killed her. Immediately regretting his impetuosity, he revived her and asked her forgiveness. She said she would forgive him, but in return for what he had done to her, he had to tell her where he kept his soul. The snake said it was in a parrot who lived with a crocodile in the sea. Then the snake went back to sleep.

When he left, his wife immediately sent a messenger to Mahaprabhu to return and she told him where the snake said he kept his soul. Mahaprabhu then took a pig and threw it into the river. When the crocodile came to eat it, his parrot companion was with him. Mahaprabhu was able to catch the bird and killed it and as soon as he did, the snake died. Then Mahaprabhu returned to the wife. But even though he had frequent sex with her, she nagged him to have more, and he too lost his temper and beat her so severely she died. Mahaprabhu then buried her and left. Shortly thereafter, a tobacco plant grew from her head. At first men ate its leaves and felt intoxicated and then discovered that smoking them made them content, so that finally the woman's spirit was satisfied because now the whole world enjoyed her.

In a variant of this story, a merchant had a daughter whom no one wanted to marry because she had no hands or feet and a diseased nose. The girl cried to Mahaprabhu for help but he told her he could do nothing while she was alive. Despondent, she stopped eating and drinking and died. Her family was afraid that her ghost would haunt them since she had died in such misery and they buried her far from their village. After she died, Mahaprabhu caused a tobacco plant to grow from her body so that now she was wanted by all men.

In another variant, after she died, his wife's soul met Mahaprabhu and told him she had no children and therefore there had been no one in the world to care for her. Mahaprabhu felt sorry for her and told her soul that when she returned to earth she would be welcome in every house and everyone would love her. The woman was pleased and returned to earth as a tobacco plant that everyone wanted. (Elwin, 1954, 175–176, 180–181; Elwin, 1991, 324, 327, 329, 338)

WINE. Mahaprabhu was at a party where everyone became very apathetic after all the food was eaten. When he asked why everyone was so lethargic, they told him they no longer had any fire in them. Mahaprabhu then taught them how to make rice beer and how to make wine from palm tree sap. After that people became animated and laughed and danced.

DISTILLATION. After Mahaprabhu showed humans to make palm wine they offered some to their gods, but one of them didn't like it and repaid them by making them all sick. When they told Mahaprabhu that one of the gods hadn't liked the palm wine and had made them sick, Mahaprabhua showed them how to distill the wine so that they would be good-natured when they became intoxicated and would not have any headaches or stomach aches the next day. Many of the gods did not want any to drink, but the god who hadn't liked the wine liked the distillate and after that acted kindly toward humans. (Elwin, 1991, 338; Elwin, 1954, 205–206)

Majahuagy. In Huichol mythology, a culture hero who taught humans about **peyote.**

Majahuagy persuaded many people to adopt a new humane code of laws but this made him many enemies and he decided to lead his followers to a new place. However, before they were able to leave, they were attacked and the gourds in which they were planning to carry water for their journey were smashed. When Tahuehuiakame saw what happened, he took pity on the group and transformed the broken pieces of the gourds into peyote plants. This gave them the ability to withstand thirst and hunger and made them feel energized. After five years of wandering, the group finally reached their destination and Majahuagy promptly died and was transformed into a god. (Lemaistre, 38–39)

Makali'i. An Hawaiian god who stole **Kane's** awa (**kava**) from the heavens. After he escaped, Makali'i hung the awa on a high trellis. However, a rat chewed the rope that held it and the plant fell down to earth spreading its seeds so that humans everywhere could enjoy it. (Handy and Handy, 189; Titcomb, 108)

Makiritare. In South American Baniwa Indian mythology, the spirit who introduced death into the world after drinking poisoned **beer.**

At one of their drinking festivals, the sky people mixed their poisonous hair with fermented beer and produced a venomous drink which they served to their guests. Most of the guests were able to save themselves by drinking an antivenom except for Makiritare, who didn't drink the remedy and died. His death was the beginning of death in the world. (Sullivan, 210–211)

Ma-ku. In Chinese mythology, the goddess of **wine.** (Doolittle, 2: 309)

Mama Coca. The South American Inca Indian goddess of health and happiness who animated the **coca** plant.

Maca Coca was originally a beautiful promiscuous woman who committed adultery and was subsequently killed. Her body was then cut in half and buried. When a coca plant sprouted from her body, men immediately began to gather its leaves but were forbidden to eat them until they had sexual relations with a woman in memory of Mama Coca. (Gagliano, 15; Osborne, 88)

Mana. In South American Amazon Indian mythology, the spirit of intoxication. (Karsten, 1926, 312–213)

Ma'nabush (or **Manabush**). In North American Menomini Indian folklore, a chief who discovered **tobacco**.

One day while Ma'nabush was roaming around a high mountain he smelled an appealing odor emanating from a crevice in the rocks. While he looked through the crevice, he saw a giant who he realized was the rumored guardian of tobacco. Ma'nabush made his way through the crevice and entered a large chamber in the middle of the mountain where the giant asked him very sternly what he wanted. When Ma'nabush answered that he had come for some tobacco, the giant said he would have to come back next year because the spirits had paid him their annual visit and had just left after smoking all his tobacco. Ma'nabush turned to leave, but as he did, he noticed several bags filled with tobacco. He quickly snatched one and began to run, but the giant saw what he had done, and ran after him. Ma'nabush made his way out of the mountain and scrambled to its peak, then leapt to the peak of another mountain, but the giant still followed. When Ma'nabush came to an especially high mountain top which had a very high vertical cliff on its other side, he jumped and landed flat on the rocks. The giant jumped after him but landed on the other side and fell. Badly bruised, the giant climbed back up the mountain. When he was almost at the top, holding on with his fingers, Ma'nabush was able to pry his fingers loose and he fell back to the ground. Ma'nabush then returned home, shared his tobacco with his people, and gave each of them some of its seeds so that from then on, they would always have it for their enjoyment. (Hoffman, 255–256)

Manco Capac. In Inca mythology, the god who gave people **coca**.

One day Manco looked down on earth and saw humans were suffering from famine. Taking pity on them, he sent them a coca plant in the form of a comet and watered it with his tears.

When king Monana saw the blazing comet falling to earth, he ran out of his house and saw it change into a coca plant after it landed in his front yard. When Monana chewed its leaves, he tasted Manco's tears and instantly knew that this was a gift from Manco to his people for them to overcome hunger and fatigue. (Kennedy, 21)

Mani. In Brazilian South American Indian mythology, the spirit that animated manioc **beer**.

Long ago, the daughter of a chief became pregnant. The chief was enraged at the dishonor to his daughter and demanded to know who the father was. His daughter denied she had been with any man, but nine months later, she gave birth to a beautiful girl she named Mani. Word of the baby's beauty spread all over and caused the chief to become reconciled to his daughter and his new granddaughter. However, a year later, the baby died unexpectedly, and her tearful mother buried her near her house. A short time later, a manioc plant sprouted from her grave, eventually flowered, and gave fruit. The Indians had never seen a plant like it before. When they saw some birds eat the fruit and become intoxicated, they were fascinated because they had never seen birds act so peculiarly and they suspected the plant contained a spirit. When the plant finally died, they dug into the grave and saw it had strong white roots shaped in the form of a horn that resembled Mani. They called the plant mandioca (the horn of Mani) and put the roots in water and let it sit and in that way created manioc beer, whose intoxicating effects they attributed to Mani's animating spirit. (Karsten, 1926, 313–314)

Manitou *see* **Gitche Manitou.**

Marijuana *see* **Cannabis.**

Maui. In Fiji, the god of **kava.** (Beckwith, 64; Fison, 148)

Mawari. In South American Waro Indian mythology, the **Tobacco**-spirit. (Wilbert, 1970, 66–67)

Mayahuel. The Aztec goddess of fertility, childbirth, good fortune, and especially the alcoholic **pulque** drink made from the agave plant, which is also known as the maguey plant.

Mayahuel was called the "woman with four hundred breasts," for each of the **Centzon Totochtin,** the 400 pulque gods that nursed on them. She was always depicted in white, the color of the milky white sap, and was often shown with flowers in her hair, or in the process of childbirth. Sometimes she was also depicted with her head falling from her severed throat, an allusion to her mythology (see below) and the cutting of the central stalk of the maguey plant to release the sap.

Mayahuel was a virgin goddess who lived with her grandmother Tzitzimitl, one of the terrifying stellar demons whose malevolence threatened the destruction of the world each day. One day, **Quetzalcoatl** found Mayahuel, seduced her, and eloped with her to earth where they disguised themselves as a forked tree, with Quetzalcoatl as one branch, and Mayahuel, the other.

When Tzitzimitl couldn't find Mayahuel anywhere, she became enraged and went to the night demons to help her find her granddaughter. The demons had no trouble finding the tree where Quetzalcoatl and Mayahuel were hiding. When they showed it to Tzitzimitl, she immediately recognized Mayahuel's branch and angrily broke it off, stripped it to bits, and offered it to the demons and they hungrily ate it. While this was going on no one paid any attention to Quetzalcoatl who was lying on the ground uninjured. When the demons finally returned to their homes in the sky, Quetzalcoatl assumed his normal form and buried what was left of Mayahuel's body. Those remains grew into the first maguey plant from whose fermented juice pulque is made.

There are two other versions of the Mayahuel myth. In one, Mayahuel was a farmer's wife who one day noticed a mouse drinking the sap oozing out of a maguey plant. Mayahuel collected the sap in a gourd and took it back home to share with her husband. The sap made them both feel amorous and content and they decided to share their discovery with the gods who rewarded them by transforming Mayahuel into the goddess of pulque, and her husband into the god known as "Lord of Flowers."

The other version linked the pulque god **Patecatl** and Mayahuel in an unconventional way. In this version, Mayahuel is credited with creating pulque while Patecatl is criticized for interfering with her work. Mayahuel was a farmer's wife and regularly collected the sap from the maguey plant. One morning, when she awoke she noticed that some of the sap was gone and what was left was drooley (i.e., polluted). After noticing the same thing happening over and over, she stayed awake one night to see who was tampering with her sap, and from her hiding place, she saw Patecatl drink her pulque until he became intoxicated, and in the course of drinking, drooling into it. After that, she added garlic and coriander and sometimes chile to the pulque, which Patecatl didn't like, to keep him from spoiling it. (Hunt, 81–82; (H. B. Nicholson, 28–30, 68)

Mead. One of the world's oldest intoxicants. Mead is a type of **wine** made with honey instead of grape or other fruit juice. Its usage and role in European mythology was replaced with wine since wine was easier to produce and bee culture declined with decreasing bee populations and increasing prices for honey. In those areas of Europe such as Scandinavia (where it was Odin's sole source of nourishment), England, and eastern Europe, that were geographically inhospitable to wine, mead continued to be a favorite drink until the Protestant Reformation when the demand for beeswax fell as Catholic churches, which used a lot of it, were replaced by Protestant churches which used much less. In response to lower production, prices for honey rose, and mead was no longer affordable for most people. In Catholic countries, such as Poland and Russia, where wax was still needed, beekeeping, and hence honey making, continued and mead continued to be made.

The classic myth involving mead is the story of the **Mead of Inspiration and Poetry**. The sap running through the trunk of **Yggdrasil**, the world tree in Norse mythology, was mead, mixed with milk from the udders of the goat **Heidrun** and given to the warriors in **Valhalla**. In India's mythology, mead was a favorite drink of the **Asvins** and was also drunk by **Indra**. (Morse, 1ff)

Meadhbh *see* **Medb**.

Mead of Inspiration and Poetry. In Norse mythology, an intoxicating drink brewed from the blood of the murdered sage **Kvasir** which made all who drank it poets or scholars and infused them with ecstatic inspiration and divine wisdom.

When the constantly warring **Aesir** and **Vanir** finally made peace, they sealed their treaty by spitting into the same **cauldron**. The spittle fermented into Kvasir, who became so wise he could answer any question. Kvasir traveled around the world disseminating his wisdom to all, but two dwarfs named **Fjalar** and Galar subsequently murdered him for no apparent reason, drained his blood into three cauldrons, and brewed it with honey (which was frequently added to fermented drinks for taste or was mixed with water and itself fermented) to make an intoxicating drink that came to be called the **Mead of Inspiration and Poetry**, or Kvasir's blood.

After they created the Mead of Inspiration, the dwarves invited the giant, Gilling, and his wife to their home and then killed them. Gilling's son Suttung caught them and to avenge his parents, tied the dwarves to a rock in the middle of the sea so that they would drown when it became submerged by the tide. To save themselves, the dwarves bartered their lives for the mead they had created. Suttung then took the mead to his mountain home where he entrusted its safekeeping to his daughter Gunnloo.

When **Odin** learned of the theft, his all-seeing eye showed him where Suttung had taken the mead of poetry, and he devised a plan to steal it for the gods. First he disguised himself. Calling himself Bolverk, he made friends with a group of serfs who were mowing hay for Suttung's brother, the giant Baugi, by offering to sharpen their scythes. The whetstone made their scythes so sharp the serfs all wanted it and began to fight over it. Bolverk then threw it into the air and as they all swiped at it to get it they cut each other's throats with their own scythes. Still disguised as Bolverk, Odin then went to visit Baugi and told him his serfs had killed one another and he didn't have any workmen left. When he finished lamenting his loss, Odin/Bolverk offered to do their work in return for one drink of his brother Suttung's mead. Baugi said he couldn't speak to his brother, but promised to arrange a meeting with Suttung so Odin could ask for some of the mead. After Odin finished his work, he demanded payment from Baugi. Baugi then took Odin to meet with Suttung but Suttung refused to let Odin have even a single drop, and they left.

When Suttung refused to give him any of his mead, Odin turned himself into a drill and began to bore a tunnel through the mountain to get into Suttung's home. After the tunnel was finished, Odin turned himself into a snake and crept through it and he entered Gunnloo, Suttung's daughter's room, whom he then seduced. Odin slept with her for three nights, and on the fourth day persuaded Gunnloo to give him a sip of the mead from the three cauldrons containing the mead. When she did, Odin took an immense sip from each and drained them. Then he transformed himself into an eagle, and with the mead in his beak, flew off to **Asgard**.

As soon as he took off, Suttung discovered Odin's theft and also turned himself into an eagle to get the mead back. But Odin had too much of a head start. As Odin neared Asgard, the Aesir saw him coming and put a large barrel out in front for Odin to regurgitate into. Odin spat nearly all the mead into the barrel, but a few drops spilled to earth and those humans who drank it (the apoettaster's share) gained wisdom, the creativity to compose poetry and the ability to speak eloquently. Unlike **soma** or **ambrosia**, however, the Mead of Poetry/Inspiration did not confer immortality or eternal youth. Those divine endowments were conferred by eating the golden apples that were tended by the goddess Idunn. (Fee and Leeming, 17–18; Lindow, 224–225; Metzner, 231; Simek, 208)

Meave *see* **Medb**.

Medb (also known as **Maebh, Maev, Meadhbh, Meave** or **Medba**). In Celtic/Irish legend, a triune goddess who in one of her avatars assumed a human form, and lived among mortals as a warrior queen, the most famous queen in Irish literature. She was often portrayed as a pale, long-faced woman, with long flowing hair, wearing a red cloak, and carrying a spear, a raven and a squirrel, perched on her shoulder.

Medb's name literally means, "she who intoxicates." The word is related to the Greek, and Latin, medus, meaning "**wine**," Welsh "meddw" meaning "drunken" and "mead" in English. In keeping with her eponym, Medb had a reputation for arbitrary, destructive, and wanton behavior; she incited men to fight and fought alongside them.

Medb was the dominant partner in all her sexual relationships. She was both sexually promiscuous and insatiable, boasting that she was never without a suitor and that it took many men to satisfy her sexually. She was also the apotheosis of fertility, but her primary attribute was sovereignty, the power to confer kingship on her husbands, of which there were many. No king could assume that title unless she offered him the "Cup of Sovereignty." To symbolize her bestowing it, newly crowned kings drank the Adergfhlaith, the red "ale of sovereignty," at their inauguration feasts.

Medb's reign on earth finally came to an end as a result of her murdering her pregnant sister, Clothra. The baby survived by being cut from her sister's womb before her death, and when he grew up, he revenged his mother's death by killing Medb, like the biblical David, with a slingshot, only in her case, the missile was a piece of hard cheese. (MacKilllop, 288)

Medba *see* **Medb.**

Meng Po. In Chinese mythology, the goddess of **wine** and the afterworld. Meng Po stood at the exit of the underworld and gave the souls of those about to be reincarnated the "broth of oblivion," a wine potion that made them forget everything that happened to them in their previous existence, except for pain. Souls that refused to drink it voluntarily were made to drink it by her two ferocious demon attendants. (Werner, 312)

Menqet. An Egyptian **beer**-goddess. (Lutz, 113)

Merope *see* **Orion.**

Methe. In Greek mythology, the goddess of drunkenness. Methe was one of **Dionysus's** companions. (Nonnos, 20.123)

Mimir *see* **Mimir's Well.**

Mimir's Well. Also known as well of Urd. In Norse mythology, a mead-filled well at the base of one of the roots of the world ash tree, **Yggdrasil**, containing a **magic** mead that imparted wisdom. The well was owned by Mimir, who drank from it every day. **Odin** was so desirous of wisdom or mystic vision, that he exchanged one of his eyes for a drink from the well. (Lindow, 231–232)

Min Kyawzwa. The Burmeses god of **wine** (Jobes, 1106; Scott, 354)

Minyas's daughters. In Greek mythology, daughters of King Minyas of Orchomenus, who refused to participate in revels honoring **Diony-sus**. Not wishing to punish them without giving them a chance to reconsider, Dionysus disguised himself as a young girl and came to their home to persuade them not to disregard his sacred rites. When they still refused, he turned himself into a bull, a lion, and a leopard, to frighten them, and when that didn't work he caused **wine** to flow out of their spindles and vines to sprout from their looms. After they still refused, Dionysus was so frustrated by their obstinacy he drove them mad and caused one of the sisters to kill her own son; then the three of them tore the boy's body to pieces. In one version of the myth, the sisters then ran off to join the rites, but were rejected by the **Maenads** who killed them, unworthy Dionysus turned them into. (Gantz, 736–737)

Miru. In Polynesian mythology, the goddess of the underworld who ate the spirits of the dead after they were drugged with **kava**.

Miru was an ugly hag who lived in Avaiki (Underworld) where she raised a huge, constantly growing, kava plant, from which all the different kava plants in the world originated. In contrast to her ugliness, she had two beautiful daughters who numbed the senses of the newly deceased who had come to the underworld, with bowls of their mother's strong kava. Once they become stupefied, Miru's daughters baked their spirits in an oven and then ate them.

Miru was especially desirous of eating Ngaru's spirit because of his great fame, and was too impatient to wait for him to die so she devised a plan to decoy him to her realm by sending her daughters to the upperworld to seduce him and entice him to their home in the netherworld.

When the girls came to Ngaru's home he was suspicious and pretended to be asleep while his grandfather talked to them trying to find the real reason for their visit. They told him their mother Miru had sent them to invite Ngaru to visit Avaiki, saying that she had heard of his virtue and that she wanted to give him her two daughters, whose beauty exceeded that of any mortal, to marry.

Suspecting deceit, Ngaru showed the girls the utmost hospitality and while they were visiting, sent his servants, little lizards, to go to the underworld to see what dangerous weapons Miru possessed. When they got there, they saw that she had a house full of kava that she kept for the express purpose of stupefying her victims before baking their souls. The lizards returned to the upperworld and told Ngaru what they had seen.

When evening came, Ngaru and the two daughters started out for Avaiki. On the way, they gave him some kava to chew. Ngaru chewed it all and to their amazement, instead of having its usual stupefying effects, he didn't fall asleep and remained alert when Miru called to her daughters to bring Ngaru to her underworld home. When he saw the oven he asked Miru what she intended, and she told him that she was going to cook him. But as Ngaru came closer to the oven, a great rain fell and extinguished the fire in the oven and swept Miru and her daughters away. (Andersen, 322–324; Williamson, II, 19)

Mohsek Eis. In the mythology of the Choroti Indians of Brazil, the good spirit that animated plants and caused fermentation. (Karsten, 1926, 125–126)

Moirai *see* **Fates.**

Momoy. In Northern American (California) Chumash Indian mythology, the goddess of **datura.**

Momoy was an old woman with the power of clairvoyance. Although she could see into the future she couldn't directly affect it or frustrate the plans of evildoers. However, those who drank water in which she had washed her hands, fell into a deep sleep in which they were able to see the future and subsequently could try to avoid evil. After the great flood, Momoy was transformed into the Datura plant and in that way she continued to inspire visionary dreams. (Blackburn, 36)

Moon. Universal symbol of water, rain, plant life, including intoxicating plant substances, female fertility, birth, initiation, death, and regeneration, because of its monthly renewal and because of the control it exerts over the ebb and flow of water, the source of all life. The association between female fertility, represented by the Great Goddess, and the moon was universal and stemmed from the similarity between their common cycles and the similarity between the moon's silvery white color and the white color of a woman's milk.

In many myths, the early Mother Goddess, and the moon she represented, were depicted as a bowl or container. The idea then developed into the idea that the moon was the storehouse of intoxicating substances like **soma**. The moon's waning and waxing was variously attributed to the gods who drank its contents. The moon was also commonly associated with the prolifically fertile rabbit, and in many myths, a rabbit lives on the moon; as a result of that association, in many myths rabbits are incarnations of soma and other intoxicants. The ancient Chinese depicted the rabbit pounding medicinal herbs in the moon, symbolized by a mortar. In ancient Mexico, the rabbit pounded the agave plant to make pulque in a bowl, symbolizing the moon. In Aztec mythology, the rabbit's association with the moon and intoxicants resulted in the rabbit becoming deified as a **pulque** god called Ometochtli as well as a group of four hundred rabbit pulque gods known as the Cetzontotochtin, each rabbit representing a different aspect of intoxication.Lunar gods such as Siva in India, Hathor in Egypt, and their consorts represented the life cycle and especially regeneration.

Iconically, moon gods, e.g., Egyptian Hathor, Isis, Ishar, Mesopotamian Sin, and India's Siva/Rudra, were depicted with a crescent or with horns on their heads. In Aztec mythology, the association between the moon and pulque gods was represented by a bony semicircular ring they wore in their nose.

The moon's influence over plant life extended to the transformation of substances derived from plants that resulted in those substances becoming imbued with the moon's **magic** and prophetic powers. When ingesting a plant or its components resulted in intoxication, the plant was said to contain a divine essence, and the condition was attributed to the divine madness that essence induced. (Briffault, 1ff)

Morfran *see* **Afagddu.**

Morning Glory *see* **Ololiuqui.**

Morpheus. In Greek mythology, the god of dreams. Morpheus was the son of Hypnos, the God of sleep, but was never worshiped as a god since he only showed himself in dreams. His counterparts were **Somnus**, in Roman mythology, Nepthys in Egyptian mythology, and Nodens, Bormanus, Borbo or Bormo in Celtic mythology. The word morphine comes from his name. (Grimal, 296; Price and Kearns, 358)

Mother Peyote *see* **Peyote.**

Mt. Hara *see* **Divine Banquet.**

Mt. Olympus *see* **Divine Banquet.**

Mukat. The North American Cahuilla Indian god who created **tobacco** from his heart. (Bean and Saubel, 90)

Mwatiktiki. In Polynesian Tanna island mythology, the god of **kava**.

Mwatiktiki brought a kava plant to Tanna where he buried it in a hole in the rocks near the seashore. It remained there for a long time until one day two women chanced to sit there while they were scraping peels from some yams. As the two women squatted, shoots from the plant suddenly sprouted and entered the vagina of one of the women. The woman felt a pleasurable sensation and when she saw what caused it, she pulled the plant out and brought it back to her village where she secretly put it in the ground where it thrived. After it was fully grown, two women dug it up and made it into a drink which they brought to the men in their village telling them that it would make them feel very unusual, and they began drinking kava. (Lebot et al. 127–128)

Myrrha. In Greek mythology, a girl who committed incest with her father after getting him drunk, and subsequently gave birth to Adonis.

Myrrha, the daughter of Theias, the king of the Assyrians, neglected her duty to **Aphrodite**, the goddess of love. Angry at being slighted, Aphrodite punished her by giving her incestuous feelings for her father. Myrrha had her nurse tell her father that there was girl who was in love with him and several nights later, she arranged to get her father drunk and then disguised herself and came to her father's bedroom. The king later became curious about who the girl was, and when he discovered his daughter's deception, he became furious and tried to kill her. Myrrha ran into the forest to escape and begged Aphrodite for mercy. Aphrodite relented and turned her into a myrrh tree. Ten months later, the trunk of the myrrh tree burst open and a beautiful baby boy, Adonis, was born.

Aphrodite was immediately smitten with the baby's appearance but since she was unable to take care of him on a full time basis, she asked **Persephone**, the Queen of the Underworld, to look after him until he was older. But when Aphrodite came back to reclaim him, Persephone wouldn't let him go. Aphrodite appealed to Zeus to mediate and Zeus appointed the muse, Calliope, to arbitrate the dispute. She decided that each of the goddesses should have Adonis' company for six months. Aphrodite was angered by the decision since she felt Adonis should be her constant companion, and she vented her anger by enraging the Thracian **Maenads** against Calliope's son, **Orpheus**, and they killed him and tore him apart. (Gantz, 730)

Mystery Religion. The word "mystery" comes from Greek, *musteria*, a purification ritual in which an initiate experiences a symbolic descent into the underworld or ascent to the upperworld where the secrets of existence are revealed. The initiate then returns to earth to a life of enlightenment and the promise of spiritual life after death. A common motif and ritual in the mystery religions is **entheogen** consumption, as a communion, a way of eating the god. In agricultural communities, many myths featured the devouring of a hero or a god, e.g., Zagreus, by monsters (e.g., Titans). The god was identified with the plant which died at the end of the growing season and was subsequently resurrected in the spring. By eating it or drinking its sap (the "blood" of the god) the devotee hoped to achieve divine inspiration, and a resurrection of his or her own spirit after death. In many of these myths, the number three figures prominently in the story (e.g., **Kvasir's** blood is collected into three bowls), or ritual associated with a myth, e.g., in **soma** ceremony took three days and soma was poured into three bowls; participants drank from a different bowl on each day. The three-day period, or three bowls, refers to the time required for fermentation. By eating or drinking the earthly counterparts of these gods or their plant incarnations, their powers could be absorbed. This belief provided the basis for sacrificial ritual meals in various religions. (Price and Kearns, 361–363)

Myth. A traditional narrative describing or explaining the origins or reasons for universal questions and issues such as how or why the world was created, why people speak different languages, origins of social customs, etc. Usually the main characters in myths are gods or superheroes. Myths are often connected with religions, especially religious rituals, but are often remembered long after their original associations have been forgotten. Myths have several levels of interpretation. The surface layer is often some adventure story or conflict between adversaries; beneath this surface layer are psychological questions. Regularly occurring images, symbols, patterns, etc., are often attributed to a universally inherited "collective unconscious" part of the brain rather than specific experiences. (Oosten, 1–11; Price and Kearns, 364–366)

Mythology. A collection of myths within a tradition. (Price and Kearns, 363)

Nagyasszony. In Transylvanian mythology, the goddess of **belladonna.** (Donotor, 127)

Nakwone *see* **Namona.**

Namona (or **Nakwone**). In South American Cuiva Indian folklore, the supreme Creator, who created the first **yopo** plant, and was the first to inhale the intoxicating snuff made from it. (Arcand et al., 230)

Namuci. In Hindu mythology, a demon (Asura) who stole **Indra's soma** and was eventually destroyed by him in revenge.

Although Indra defeated most of the cloud demons who were keeping the rain from falling to earth, he was eventually overpowered by the demon, Namuci. Namuci promised to release Indra in return for Indra's promise never to kill him by day or night, by staff or bow, with palm or fist, or anything dry or wet. Indra agreed and the two rivals became friends for a while. But Namuci took advantage of their friendship and got Indra drunk on **wine** and then stole his soma. Indra appealed to the heavenly doctors, the **Asvins** and Sarasvati, the goddess of wisdom, for advice on how to regain his soma, and promised to share it with them if they would tell him how to revenge himself on Namuci in such a way that he would not break his promise. The Asvins and Sarasvati created a thunderbolt that was neither wet nor dry from the foam of water and Indra used it to cut off Namuci's head. But by then Namuci had drunk all Indra's soma and it began flowing out of his severed body. Since it was mixed with Namuci's blood, it was impure and Indra couldn't drink it. Realizing Indra's problem, the Asvins drank the mixture and purified it in their divine bodies and then they returned it to Indra in its pure form. (Bloomfield, 1893, 143ff; Fowler, 36–40; MacDonell, 161–162)

Nanbush *see* **Four Manido.**

Nan-capue. In Polynesian mythology, a god of **kava** and feasting. (Christian, 382)

Nanga Baiga. In middle India mythology, the god who gave mankind **tobacco.**

Nanga Baiga was told that a certain cobra had seeds in his head that would grow into special plants. When he found the snake he killed it and planted the seeds that spilled out of its head. The seeds grew into the tobacco plant which just like the snake's poison, made people drunk. (Elwin, 1991, 325)

Nanibozo. North American Ojibway Indian god who brought **tobacco** to humans. (Quinn, 112)

Narcotic. A psychoactive substance that induces tranquility, sleep and stupor. (Rudgley, 172; Schultes and Hofmann, 10, 26, 31, 72–75)

Nawat. In South American Toba mythology, the spirit who taught the Toba how to make alcoholic beverages.

Long ago, before anyone knew anything about alcohol, a group of women went out to gather honey and took an old **shaman** with them for protection. During the search, the shaman wandered off and met Nawat, who invited him to his house which was full of spirits drinking fermented honey. Nawat showed the shaman how it was made and when Nawat returned to earth, he showed the Toba women how to ferment honey into **mead**. (Cordeau et al., 187–188)

Nectar. In Greek mythology, the drink of the gods. The Olympian counterpart to **wine**, it was brought to them by divine cup-bearers, first **Hebe**, and then **Ganymede**. Like **ambrosia**, it conferred immortality and lasting beauty on those who drank it. Plato wrote that the honey drink, viz. **mead**, came to Greece before wine and was called nectar. (Plato, 203b)

Neurotransmitters. The chemicals that enable nerves to communicate with one another. Nerves are specialized cells. There are an estimated 15 billion nerve cells in the brain. These nerve cells are separated from one another by tiny gaps called synapses. The cells bridge these gaps through their neurotransmitters. Psychoactive substances mimic the actions of these neurotransmitters or cause nerves to either reduce or enhance their secretion of them. The primary neurotransmitters are, in alphabetical order, acetylcholine, anandamide, dopamine, epinephrine, endorphins, GABA, glutamate, norepinephrine, and serotonin. The effects of all psychoactive drugs are the final results of changes in the stimulation or inhibition of neurotransmitters. Psychoactive drugs thus do not create experiences, but instead affect combinations of nerve interactions that are interpreted by other nerve cells according to the user's expectations (a prior condition referred to as "set") and the environment in which they are taken (referred to as "setting"). (Abel, 1974, 106)

Ninkasi. Sumerian goddess of beer. Ninkasi was the consort of Pagestin, the "lord of the vine," and her home was Mt. Sabu, not a mountain, but literally, the "mount of the tavern." She was known as "the intoxicating beverage which decreed life." Ninkasi had nine children whose names described the effects of intoxication, such as Mehus, "he of frightening speech," "the brawler," Meazag, "he of clear speech," Emetere, "he of eloquent speech," Kidurkazal, "he of the abode of mirth," Nusiligga, "the braggard," and Ninmada, "the lord of the land." (Lutz, 132)

Ninurta. A Sumerian **wine** god. (Lutz, 133)

Nirantali. In middle India mythology, the culture heroine who gave **tobacco** to the Kond.

In the days before there was any tobacco, the Kond had no excuse for rest and worked all day without stopping. Nirantali saw their plight and to give them some respite, she plucked a white bug from her hair and threw it into her garden. When the rains fell, the bug became a tobacco plant. After its leaves were fully grown Nirantali showed the Kond how to make them into cigarettes to smoke which gave them a reason to rest periodically from work during the day. (Elwin, 1954, 179–180)

Noah. In Hebrew mythology, the man who saved himself and his family and two of each species of animal and plant from disappearing in a world flood. After the flood abated, Noah planted a vineyard and was the first person to make **wine** and become drunk.

Various myths subsequently evolved to explain how Noah discovered wine. One discovery motif, common to many intoxicants, is that Noah became a viticulturist after seeing a male goat becoming drunk and cheerful after eating grapes.

A Hebrew tradition held that the grape was the forbidden fruit on the Tree of Knowledge in the Garden of Eden. The flood washed it out of Paradise and Noah found it after the flood waters receded but was troubled in his mind as to whether he should plant it and prayed to God to ask what he should do. God sent him an angel, Sarasael, telling him he should.

Many of the myths relating to Noah as a viticulturist explain the different characteristics or different degrees of drunkenness. One such myth relates that Noah found the juice of the first wild grapes bitter and to sweeten them he took blood from four animals, the lion, lamb, pig and the ape, mixed it with earth, and then used the mixture as a fertilizer for his grapevines. The resulting wine tasted much better so that Noah drank much more than he should have and became drunk. Different characteristics of drunkenness were related to the characteristics of the four animals whose blood he had used—irritability came from the lion's blood, gentleness from the lamb, gross behavior from the pig, and curiosity and happiness from the ape.

A variant of this story has the devil sprinkling blood from the four animals on Noah's vines; the subsequent effects were explained in terms of degrees rather than varieties of drunkenness. Those who did not drink were as peaceful as a lamb; those who drank moderately felt as if they had the strength of a lion; those who drank immoderately behaved like a pig; whereas those who became completely inebriated, and behaved foolishly and irrationally, were like the ape. The different animals were variously replaced by the goat (lechery), the stag (symbolic of the cuckold), the bear, dog, cat, wolf, ass, goose, etc.

Animals in the Noah legend also found their way into the doctrine of the four humors that determine temperament and personality. The "wine of the lion" flowed through the blood of the Choleric; when he drank too much he wanted to make noise and fight. The "wine of the singer" coursed through the blood of the Sanguine; the more he drank, the gayer and more lecherous he became. The Phlegmatic had the "wine of the lamb" in his blood; when he became drunk he appeared wiser and more focused on his business than before, while the Melancholic had the "wine of the pig" in his veins; when he became inebriated, he only wanted to sleep and dream. (Janson, 241–243; Lutz, 141–143; Ginsberg, 79)

Nosiriwe *see* **Kuripowe.**

No Vitals. In the mythology of the North American Crow Indians, the culture hero who introduced **tobacco** to his people.

When No Vitals and his brother were on a vision quest they both experienced visitations from Corn. However, No Vitals also saw a vision of another plant growing far away. His brother, who became chief of the Hidatsas, went no farther but No Vitals, who became chief of the Crows, continued his vision quest in search of the plant. Finally he found it growing in the foothills of the Bighorn mountains and Yellowstone River and brought it back to the Crow. From thereon, the Crow believed their destiny was tied to tobacco, and that as long as they cultivated it they would retain their identity. (Frey, 8, 11)

Numli-nyou. In Himalayan mythology, the goddess of fermentation.

One day an insect came to Numli-nyou's house and said he would help her in return for some millet, but his real intention was to see how she turned millet into **beer**. Numli-nyou agreed to let him live with her but put him in a tightly woven box when the time came for her to make her beer. However, one of the baskets she put him into was loosely woven and the insect was able to see her mixing yeast with the millet and then heating it. Two days later when the millet had fermented, Numli-nyou put it into an earthen pot. When she let him out, the insect tried to steal the pot with the yeast in it but couldn't so he concocted another plan. He told Numli-nyou there were lice in her hair and told her he could remove them if she wanted. She agreed, and while he was delousing her, she fell asleep. The insect then stole the pot and ran away. When Numli-ynou woke up she immediately noticed her pot was gone. Realizing that the insect would tell her secret to everyone, she cursed the beer so that everyone who drank it would become drunk and quarrelsome. (Gorer, 483–484)

Nungui. The South American Jivaro Indian fertility goddess who created plant life including **tobacco**, and manioc **beer**.

Before they knew about manioc, the Jivaro survived on other plants and many died of hunger. One day a Jibaro woman named Ungucha and her companions were wandering along the bank of the river looking for food and they found some manioc shells. They followed the bank looking for more and came to an open place where they found Nungui washing dirt from manioc and other plants. Ungucha asked Nungui for some food and she gave her a fat little baby girl, named Ciki, who, she said, was manioc. The baby would give the Jivaro women whatever they asked, but she warned them not to abuse the baby or leave it in the house, or everything would disappear.

When the Jivaro women returned home they asked Ciki to give them manioc. Ciki commanded it to appear and it immediately filled their houses. When they asked her to give them a garden she showed them how to sow seeds, and all kinds of food immediately came into being. Next they demanded a large beer brewing jar and it instantly appeared. Then they asked for jars to be filled with manioc beer and she showed them how to make it.

One day they forgot Nungui's warning not to leave Ciki alone. While they were gone, some Jivaro children came to Ciki and told her they wanted to see snakes and a demon, and they immediately appeared. Then one of the children derided the baby for bringing the snakes and demons and abused her by throwing ashes in Ciki's eyes, which made her cry.

When Nungui heard Ciki's cries, she took Ciki back and returned with her home into the interior of the earth. However, the Jivaros were no longer in danger of starving because Ciki had taught them how to sow seeds so that they would have food for themselves, and how to make beer. (Harner, 73; Karsten, 1926, 300–301; 1935, 125)

Obatala. In African Yoruba mythology, a Creator god who created deformed humans while he was intoxicated.

Obatala was unhappy that there was nothing in the world, so he asked Olorun (or Olodumare), the ruler of the gods, for permission to create dry land and plants and animals to live on it. Many months later, after he had made the plants and animals, he became bored and decided to create beings like himself out of clay to keep him company. The work made him thirsty and to relieve his thirst he began drinking palm **wine**. Obatala drank so much he became drunk, but not realizing how drunk he was, he continued making people. As a result, many imperfect beings were created. The next day after he recovered from his drunkenness he saw what he had done and swore never to drink again and to take care of all those who were deformed. (Courlander, 189)

Octli. Aztec term for an alcoholic drink, made from the sap of the maguey plant, Agave Americana. Also the collective name for gods of intoxicating drinks. The Spanish, and better-known term for octli, is **pulque**. The word pulque comes from "poliqui" meaning "decomposed" in Aztec. The Spaniards corrupted poliqui to pulcre and later to pulque. (H. Nicolson, 172–174; Reed, 110)

Odherir *see* **Odraerir.**

Odhroerir *see* **Odraerir.**

Odin (also known as **Voden, Votan, Wodan, Woden, Wotan,** or **Wuotan**). In Norse and German mythology, the supreme head of the godly pantheon, known as the "All Father."

Although a shape-shifter, Odin was usually pictured as a tall, one-eyed giant with a long flowing white beard. When he traveled on earth, he dressed in a blue cloak and broad-brimmed hat to hide his missing eye.

Odin's favorite weapon was a magic spear called Gungnir. Fashioned by dwarfs, it never missed its mark. He also had two ravens perched on his shoulders. One of the ravens was called Hugin, "thought," and the other, Munin, "memory." Every day the two birds flew through the world and told him what the gods, giants, dwarfs, and humans were doing. This enabled Odin to know everything that was going on in the world. Odin was married to Frigga, but like Zeus, he was not faithful and had many sexual liaisons, and many children, among them Baldur, the epitome of goodness who was murdered (see below) and **Thor** (Donar), who succeeded Odin as the head of the pantheon.

Odin was a multifaceted god. Although the Creator and the wisest of all deities, he was also the god of war, fertility, ecstatic wisdom, poetry and eloquence. As a war god, he inspired men to fight like wild animals. Those whom he frenzied with his battlefield intoxication were called **berserks**. The spirits of brave warriors killed in battle were taken by the Valkyries to **Valhalla**, Odin's banquet hall in **Asgard**, where they fought each other all day and drank **mead** and **beer** all night. Odin himself did not eat and survived solely on ale or mead. As a fertility god, he resembled other fertility gods in dying and being resurrected annually. His German name, Wodan, is the root of Wednesday, a day believed favorable for sowing seeds.

In a variation of the god who sacrificed himself or was sacrificed for the benefit of mankind to gain wisdom, Odin hanged himself (a sacrifice of himself to himself) from the world tree, **Yggdrasil**. Odin remained there without food and water for nine days until in a shamanic trance, his spirit journeyed to the land of the dead where he obtained a drink of the precious mead of wisdom that he subsequently gave to the gods and men.

A variant of the sacrifice motif has Odin plucking out one of his eyes for a drink of the wisdom-conferring mead after his son, Baldur, who represented goodness in the world, was killed through the treachery of the malevolent god, Loki. Odin's wife, Frigga, knew that her son's life was in danger because of his goodness, and asked all the living things in the world to take an oath not to harm her son, but overlooked the mistletoe. Loki realized her oversight and had an arrow made from it. During one of their **divine banquets**, the gods made a game of shooting at Baldur, knowing he couldn't be harmed. Hodur, Baldur's blind brother, also took aim, but didn't know that Loki had surreptitiously slipped the deadly mistletoe arrow into his quiver. When Hodur shot the arrow, Baldur fell to his death. Although it was a duty to avenge murder, none of the gods was willing to kill Hodur and end the life of another of Odin's sons. With no one able to fulfill the sacred duty of revenge, the end of the world seemed imminent. Odin did not know what to do, so he journeyed to the Underworld to the Kingdom of

Mimir to ask him if Baldur's death meant the end of the world. Mimir told him that the answer lay at the bottom of his well of knowledge. To learn it, Odin would have to rip out one of his eyes and throw it into the well. Then, if he took a drink from the well, he would learn what his eye saw. When he did, Odin saw that there would eventually be a cataclysmic end of the world, called Ragnarok, when the gods and giants would fight to the death.

Some of Odin's exploits portray him as a **shaman**-like shape-shifter. One of his best-known shape-shifting adventures involved his theft of the **Mead of Inspiration and Poetry** which the giant Suttung had concealed in his mountain fortress. In that adventure, Odin took the form of a snake so that he could pass through a narrow opening in the mountain to where Suttung lived, then took the form of a handsome giant so that he could seduce Gunaloo, Suttung's daughter, to whom Suttung had entrusted the mead, then assumed the form of an eagle and flew with the stolen mead in its mouth to Asgard.

In a variant of this story, Odin journeyed to Jotunheims, the land of the giants where Suttung was hosting a wedding banquet for Gunnloo and **Ivaldi**, his son-in-law to be. Ivaldi had discovered a secret well of mead but had had it stolen from him by Nepur, the moon god, who had then shared some of that mead with the gods. Ivaldi subsequently killed Nepur and took his mead back. Then he allied himself with the giants for protection and asked to marry Suttung's daughter, Gunnloo, to seal the bargain. On the night of the wedding, Odin killed and disguised himself as Ivaldi. When the banquet finally came to an end, Odin was left alone with Gunnaloo. Although she finally realized who he was, Odin by then had so charmed her that she helped him escape with the mead through a hole in the palace walls. Odin then transformed himself into an eagle and carried the mead back to Asgard.

In southern German folklore, the fly agaric mushroom, *Amanita muscaria*, is said to have originated from Wotan's (Odin's) horses. One Christmas Eve while Wotan was riding his horses, he was suddenly pursued by devils. He put his horses to a fast gallop to escape, and as he sped away, a red-flecked foam dripped from their mouths. The following year, the white-spotted red caps of the fly agaric appeared wherever the horses' foam fell on earth. (Davidson, 70, 147; Lindow, 249–251)

Odraerir (also known as **Odherir, Odhroerir, Odrorir,** or **Othrorir**). In Norse mythology, one of the three vessels in which the dwarfs who murdered **Kvasir** drained his blood and mixed it with honey. Odraerir was a **cauldron**, whereas the other two vessels, called Son and Boden, were crocks. (Metzner, 231)

Odrorir *see* **Odraerir.**

Oedipus. In Greek mythology, the man who killed his father, King Laius of Thebes, and married his mother.

The oracle at Delphi had warned Laius not to beget a son because that son would kill him. However, one night Laius drank too much and had intercourse with his wife in violation of the oracle's warning. Oedipus was subsequently born and when he grew up he fulfilled the oracle's prediction. (Grimal, 323–324; Price and Kearns, 384–385)

Oeneus (also known as **Oineus** or **Oinos**). In Greek mythology, a king of Aetolia who invented viticulture.

When **Dionysus** came to visit Oeneus, he sent him away to discover vines and winemaking. While Oeneus was gone, Dionysus seduced his wife. In another myth a shepherd, Staphylus, one of Oeneus' shepherds, discovered **wine** after noticing the playful behavior of a goat who had eaten some strange fruit. Staphylus told Oeneus about the incident and gave Oeneus the idea of pressing grapes to make wine, which was subsequently described by his name (Oinos is the Greek word for "wine"). (Grimal, 125; Price and Kearns, 385)

Oeno. In Greek mythology, one of three female *oinotrophoi*, or "wine-growers," who, along with her sisters Elias and Spermo, their father dedicated to **Dionysus.** In return Dionysos granted each of them the power, after invoking his name, to turn whatever they touched into **wine**, oil or corn. During the Trojan War, they were kidnapped by the Greeks and forced to provide **wine** for them. Just as they were about to be chained to prevent their escape they cried out to Dionysus for help and he restored their freedom by turning them into white doves. (Graves, 1992, 645; Gantz, 578)

Oenopion *see* **Orion.**

Oenotrophoi or **Oinotrophoi** *see* **Oeno.**

Oilikukaheana. In Hawaiian mythology, a god who brought awa (**kava**) to Maui for the priests to use in making offerings to the sharks.

When he came to the island, he saw a beautiful woman, Kamaile, whom he married and gave her his kava plants to care for. But Kamaile didn't know what they were for and threw them away. Some were found by Moikeha who also didn't know what they were used for, but brought some of them to the island of Oahu and planted them. After the plants grew, he took some to Ewa who said she would eat some of the plant, and if she subsequently died, Moikha was not to plant it, but if she didn't die, they would be rich. After eating the plant, Ewa became intoxicated the whole day, and when she awoke, she called the plant awa. (Handy and Handy, 189)

Oineus *see* **Oeneus.**

Oinos *see* **Oeneus.**

Oinotrophoi *see* **Oeno.**

Okabewis. In North American Ojibwa Indian mythology, a young girl sent to teach the first humans basic skills such as making fire and how to use **tobacco.** (Gill and Sullivan, 222)

Okuninushi. In Japanese mythology, the god of fertility, the moon, and sake. (Yamamuro, 270)

Ololiuqui. In Aztec mythology, the goddess of morning glory seeds (Rovea corymbosa) and the drug infusion made from them. Sometimes identified with the Mother, fertility and water goddess, Chalchiutlicue. The primary psychoactive ingredient is very similar to lysergic acid amide, closely related to LSD. Effects include vivid visual hallucinations. Side effects include nausea, vomiting and abdominal pain. The common morning glory growing in the United States does not contain any of the hallucinogenic substance. (Furst, 1976, 67–72; Rudgley, 180; Schultes and Hofmann, 171–174)

Omacatl. Mayan god of banqueting. If not properly honored, he became angered and appeared in the neglectful person's dreams asking why he had been affronted. If totally ignored, he could become enraged and cause the banqueters to choke on their drinks. (Anderson and Dibble, 2:33).

Ome Tochtli. In Mayan mythology, "Two Rabbits," the head of the **pulque** gods (there is no "One Rabbit"). Like all Mayan pulque gods, he wore a golden crescent-shaped nose ornament, symbolizing the moon. His face was red in the middle and black or dark green on the side, and he wore a headdress of white feathers, a long necklace and earrings. He carried a stone ax in his right hand, and a bicolored red and black colored shield in his left.

Ome Tochtli was responsible for gathering all the other pulque gods and giving them each a drinking tube through which they could drink the ceremonial pulque. However, only one of the tubes was hollow so that only one could drink and become intoxicated. After he alone drank, everyone dispersed.

Ome Tochtli was killed by **Tezcatlipoca**, the supreme god, with his consent, so that by his sacrifice, he alone would die from drinking pulque, sparing everyone else who drank it. (Anderson and Dibble, 3:194; H. Nicholson, 160, 172–174; Spence, 1911, 105)

Opium. Opium comes from the poppy plant (*Papver somniferum*) which is indigenous to Asia Minor. Six thousand years ago, the Sumerians, the first of the ancient Mesopotamian civilizations, called it "the joy plant." The Greek god of sleep, Hypnos, and his Roman counterpart, Somnos, were often depicted wearing or carrying poppies. Initially, the entire plant was ground and used and called meconium by the Greeks. Subsequently, the pods were cut to cause the thick milky fluid to come to the surface after which it was scraped off. The extract, called opios, Greek for "little juices," was boiled to concentrate it, and then mixed with **wine** or honey or heated and inhaled or chewed. In the 19th century, its active ingredient was purified and called morphine (from Morpheus, the Roman god of dreams). Effects include euphoria, lassitude, analgesia and tranquility. Side effects include nausea, vomiting, constipation, flushing, narrowing of the pupils, heaviness of limbs, and respiratory depression which can result in death. Frequent use results in addiction and severe withdrawal when usage ends. Psychoactive effects are due to the similarity in chemical structure between morphine and naturally occurring **neurotransmitters** in the brain called endorphins. (Rudgley, 181–184; Schultes and Hofmann, 12–13, 20–21)

Opium Origin Myth, Northeastern India. One day after being neglected and badly beaten by her husband, a woman ran away and hanged herself. Her husband subsequently found her body and brought it back to his home and burned it nearby. Sometime later, a seedling sprouted from the dead wife's ashes and turned into a beautiful poppy flower. Curious, the husband cut it open and collected the white juice that came out of it on a piece of cloth and put it in his pipe and smoked it. It gave him so much pleasure, he couldn't stop smoking it, and when other people in his village noticed his contentment, they began growing poppies and smoking the juice they collected from them. (Elwin, 1958, 218–219)

Orestheus. In Greek mythology, the son of **Deucalion** (the Greek Noah) who planted the first vine.

Orestheus was a hunter who traveled to Aetolia, the western part of the Greek mainland, looking for a place to create a kingdom. During the journey his dog gave birth to a vine stalk which Orestheus buried, because it was not yet grown. Almost immediately, a vine with many clusters of grapes grew out of the ground at the place. When Orestheus' son was born he called him Phytius the vine grower, and Phytius, in turn, called his son **Oeneus**, "wine." (Grimal, 330)

Orion. In Greek mythology, the bee-keeping son of Poseidon and the daughter of Minos, king of Crete. One day Zeus, Poseidon and Hermes came to Hyrieus' house in disguise and he entertained them. In return for his hospitality, they offered to grant him whatever he wanted. Hyrieus said that he was a widower and childless and what he wanted most was to have a son, but that it wasn't possible because of his age. Zeus told him to urinate on a bull hide and bury it in his dead wife's grave (in some variants the gods did it themselves). Nine months later Orion was born from the grave site. Hyrieus named his son Orion from the strange manner of his conception (*orourein*, meaning, "urination").

When Orion was older he became a giant hunter and a gatherer of hides (a likely connection with his birth), but was impetuous. He met and fell in love with Merope, the daughter of **Oenopion**, the King of Chios, who was one of **Dionysus's** mortal sons (his mother was **Ariadne**). Although Oenopion agreed to their marriage, he kept putting off the wedding day. Finally overcome with frustration, one night Orion broke into Merope's bedroom and forced himself on his bride-to-be. Oenopion was outraged. Following Dionysos's advice, he got Orion drunk and then blinded and abandoned him by the seashore while he was still insensible. When Orion regained consciousness, he was mysteriously told that he could regain his sight if he journeyed to the east and let the sun shine on him as it first rose. (In a variant, the goddess of Dawn fell in love with him and persuaded her brother, Apollo, the sun god, to restore his sight.)

When his sight was restored, Orion returned to Chios to avenge himself on Oenopion. But the king learned of his impending return and hid until he left. Apollo subsequently became concerned that his sister Artemis would fall in love with Orion so he tricked her into killing him by telling her that Orion had seduced one of her priestesses.

Orion's birth from a leather sack and his father's occupation as a bee-keeper have been interpreted as an allusion to a time when honey preceded grapes as the main source for wine, since hides were used for storing **mead** and **wine**. Because of his unfamiliarity with wine, Orion fell victim to its effects, and as punishment for his uncivilized behavior, which he acted out while in a drunken state, he was blinded by Oenopion. (The transition from mead to wine was identified with **Aristaeus**, another of Apollo's sons). (Gantz, 271–273; Kerenyi, 178, 202; Oosten, 101–103; Price and Kearns, 393)

Orpheus. In Greek mythology, a Thracian poet, musician, and **shaman**, who was punished by **Dionysus** for no longer worshipping him and whose persona became the basis for a rival cult emphasizing asceticism rather than Dionysian excesses.

Orpheus came from Thrace and was initially a devotee of Dionysus. In various accounts he was the son of a local king, Oiagros, or Apollo. His mother was Calliope, the Muse of epic poetry. Orpheus became a gifted musician who was invited to be a member of the Argonauts when they went to retrieve the Golden Fleece. He proved his value to the expedition by drowning out the song of the Sirens whose music would otherwise have lured the crew to their deaths.

Orpheus subsequently married Eurydice, but soon after his marriage **Aristaeus** tired to rape her. In trying to escape, Eurydice was bitten by a snake and died. With the **shaman**'s power to visit the Underworld, Orpheus set out to rescue her from death and succeeded in charming Hades and **Persephone**, the rulers of the Underworld, with his music, so that they granted him permission to take Eurydice back on condition that he not turn back to look at his wife before she had crossed the edge of the Underworld. However, curiosity got the better of him. At the edge of the Underworld, Orpheus turned back to see if Eurydice was behind him. After he caught a brief glimpse of her, she returned to the dead and Orpheus returned to the upper world, so despondent he withdrew from all society and became an ascetic, worshipping Apollo instead of Dionysus. In retaliation for his apostasy, Dionysus sent the **Maenads** to punish him, and they killed him and tore him apart.

A variant of this story has Orpheus attacked by the Maenads because his asceticism was antithetical to their Dionysian excesses. A third variant says that after losing Eurydice, Orpheus hated all women and refused to let them participate in certain of Dionysus' rites.

In all variants, the Maenads tore Orpheus to bits and threw his head into the river. The head, which continued to sing, floated to the shore of the Island of Lesbos where the inhabitants buried it and created an oracle which later became the center of an ascetic cult called the Orphics. The Orphics claimed Orpheus as their founder, and denounced the *omophagia*, the Dionysian rite of tearing animals apart, as a sin which originated in the **Zagreus** myth, even though the myth became the basis for their belief in death and resurrection. (Gantz, 721–725; Grimal, 331–333; Price and Kearns, 394–397)

Oseema. In South American Yupa folklore, the god who showed the Yupa how to make **chicha** beer.

Oseema first made two humans by carving them out of a tree. These humans had many children and he lived among them for a time. On the last day of his stay on earth, he showed them how to brew chicha **beer**, and promised that after they died, he would bring all the dead Yupa to live with him. (Wilbert, 1974, 43, 75)

Osiris. In Egyptian mythology, the god who discovered the vine and taught men how to make **wine**. (Budge, 1:39, 45; Lutz, 113–114)

Osmo's Daughter *see* **Osmotar.**

Osmotar. In Finnish mythology, the **shaman** or goddess who invented brewing. At first Osmotar did not know how to make **beer** and experimented with various substances to see if they would ferment grain. First she created a squirrel by rubbing her palms and then told the squirrel to fetch some spruce cones. When she couldn't create ale with the cones, she created a fox and told it to bring her some legumes. When the brew wouldn't ferment from them, she created a marten and told it to gather the saliva of wild boars. Using this saliva, she was finally able to ferment grain into ale. (Davidson, 139)

Othrorir *see* **Odraerir.**

Pa-gestin-dug. In Sumerian mythology, a **wine** god, literally "the good vine stalk." His wife, **Ninkasi**, was the Sumerian goddess of **beer**. (Albright, 267; Hyams, 39; Lutz, 132)

Pamashiut *see* **Hukaht.**

Pamuri-gahsiru. In South American Desana Indian mythology, the god of fermentation. (Reichel-Dolmatoff, 1971, 55)

Pamuri-mahse. In South American Desana Indian mythology, the first one to make **chicha beer.** (Reichel-Dolmatoff, 1971, 36)

Pan. In Greek mythology, one of **Dionysus'** entourage who symbolized the lustful side of Dionysian drunkenness.

Pan was one of the **satyrs**, with the legs, horns, beard, tail, and the feet of a goat. He is often portrayed wearing a loincloth and carrying a shepherd's crook or leading Dionysus' chariot, playing a pipe and dancing as if inebriated. Pan roamed the forests at will, often frightening the nymphs, whom he often tried to engage sexually. Our word "panic" comes from his eponymous name. (Barthell, 264; Price and Kearns, 401–403)

Pandual. In middle India mythology, underworld spirits who distilled liquor and were constantly drunk (Elwin, 1954, 204).

Papa-iea. In Polynesian Marquesa mythology, the god of feasting and **kava** drinking. (Christian, 190)

Papaztec. One of the four hundred Mayan **pulque** gods. (Bancroft, 1886, 3:418; Boone, 203; I. Nicholson, 168)

Parvati. A female culture hero who introduced **tobacco** to Middle India.

Parvati married when she was a young girl. When she came to her husband's home, he immediately began to yell at her. Parvati mistook his yelling for desire, but her husband's only interest in her was as someone to prepare and serve him his dinner. This went on for ten years. Parvati finally despaired of his impatience and neglect and ran off into the jungle where she found an unusual plant and begged him to help her make her husband treat her better. The plant told her to roll one of its leaves into a pipe and to light and give it to her husband the next time he started yelling for his food.

After her husband smoked the pipe, he became intoxicated and forgot everything, including his hunger. After that, as long as he got his pipe, her husband no longer demanded to be served immediately. Parati then returned to the jungle and took seeds from the plant and sowed them in her garden, and eventually, the tobacco plant became known to all the people of India. (Elwin, 1954, 177–178)

Patecatl. One of the four hundred Mayan **pulque** gods; in some Mayan myths, the husband of **Mayahuel.** (Anderson and Dibble, 3:194; Boone, 204; H. Nicholson, 167)

Pava. Polynesian culture hero associated with the island of Samoa, who stole the secret of **kava** making from the Creator, Tangaloa-le-Mana.

One day Tangaloa-le-Mana came down from heaven to visit earth, and became thirsty for kava which he drank regularly. Believing no one was about, he sent for his attendants and told them to bring him his bowl, strainer, cup and a kava plant. But in their hurry, they tore the kava plant up by its roots instead of just tearing off its leaves. Tangaloa-le-Mana chewed the stem of the plant and threw the rest into the bushes where Pava was watching. Tangaloa-le-Mana then spat the chewed kava into the strainer and then caused a heavy rain to fall to help him brew the kava. After Tangaloa-le-Mana left, Pava planted the roots. After that, humans were able to enjoy the drink of the gods.

In a variant myth, Tagaloalagi came down to earth and taught Pava, the first man, about kava and how to use it, cautioning him that as part of the rite, no one was allowed to enter the space between them. While they were drinking the kava, Pava's young son ran between them. Because he had violated the code, Tagaloalagi tore him limb from limb. When Pava began weeping uncontrollably for his dead son, who was his only chance to populate the world, Tagaloalagi felt remorse and poured a few drops of kava on Pava's son's dismembered body and it was restored to life. (Craig, 206; Lebot et al., 124–125)

Peaches of Immortality *see* **Queen Mother of the West.**

P'eng-Lai. In Taoist mythology, a paradise island where a magic mushroom grew that conferred wisdom and immortality. (Pas, 252, 254)

Pentecost Island *see* **Kava Origin Story, Polynesia.**

Pentheus. In Greek mythology, a king of Thebes who refused to recognize **Dionysus**' divinity and was torn apart for his obstinacy.

Pentheus was a grandson of Cadmus, and a cousin of Dionysus, but when Dionysus appeared at Thebes and invited the women there to join in his celebration, Pentheus discouraged such participation. But when he arrested the celebrants, the ropes he bound the women with unwound of their own accord and their prison doors opened. Pentheus then decided to make Dionysus a prisoner, but no prison could hold him either. Although warned by a prophet that he would be torn apart if he continued to deny Dionysus' divinity, and though Dionysus himself tried to convince him to recognize his divinity, Pentheus persisted in his denial. Frustrated by Pentheus' obstinacy, Dionysus made him mad, and in his demented state he persuaded Pentheus to disguise himself as a woman and spy on the women celebrating his rites in the hills. When the revelers, among them Pentheus' own mother, Agave, noticed

Pentheus watching them in their religious **ecstasy** they mistook him for a wild animal and seized and tore him apart. Agave, still feeling the ecstatic spell, took his head and carried it back to the palace where she exhibited it as the head of a lion that she had overcome. (Grimal, 356–357; Price and Kearns, 415)

Persephone *see* **Demeter.**

Peyak Noin. In the mythology of the South American Tobas Indians, a good spirit that animated plants and caused fermentation. (Karsten, 1926, 125–126)

Peyote. (*Lophophora Williamsii*). A small, grayish green spineless cactus that grows predominantly in the deserts of northern Mexico and southern Texas. It is also known as mescal, mescal bean, and mescal button (but is not the same as the alcoholic mescal, made from the agave plant). It is eaten either directly while it is still a green plant, or more commonly as the dried button or top of the cactus. The main psychoactive component is mescaline.

Intoxication begins with feelings of nausea, headache, general discomfort in the area of the stomach, and perspiration that lasts for about one to two hours, followed by a dream-like state of weightlessness where time and space perception are altered, and what is often described as a kaleidoscope of brilliantly colored visual images, sounds and smells. These hallucinations are believed to forge a communion with the spirit world.

Peyote is used primarily by descendants of the Aztecs known as Huichol, the Cora and Tarahumara, another Central American native group, and by Plains Indians in North America, each of whom have their own name for the god within the plant. Once a year, the Huichol come together in the sacred desert north of the Sierre Madre called the Wirikuta, and about 15 of them go on a sacred peyote hunt while the others wait their return. The hunt is led by a **shaman** who communicates with the Peyote god, through visions. The hunters share some of their peyote with those who remain behind and send some to the Tarahumara Indians who do not have a quest. Several months after the annual quest, the Huichol ingest peyote during their planting ceremony and while intoxicated, dance, chant and pray to the gods for a good crop in the next year.

In many North and Central American Indian mythologies, peyote is both a plant and the god within it. In the Plains and Southwestern

Indian traditions the supernatural element takes the form of a revelation, and the focus of the story is on its discovery which is told with several different motifs, including the following:

1) Peyote reveals itself to someone in distress and teaches that person about peyote and how to use it.

One day a Comanche raiding party went into Mexico and was closely pursued. One of the elderly women accompanying the raiders became ill and exhausted and told the rest to go on without her. Knowing their pursuers would not harm an old woman or a little boy in those conditions, the Comanches gave her food and left a little boy to take care of her, promising they would come back for them as soon as they evaded their pursuers. The little boy, however, didn't want to be left behind. When it was dark, he slipped away from the sick woman and tried to catch up to the fleeing war party but soon grew tired and fell asleep. When the woman noticed he was gone, even though she was sick, she went after him, fearful he might get lost.

She did not go far, however, before she collapsed and fell into a coma. In this condition, an unknown spirit appeared and told her that the child was safe and that if she didn't do what he was about to tell her, she would not live much longer. When he left, he told her she would find an herb where he was standing, and if she ate it she would be cured and the Great Spirit would appear and teach her the songs and rituals of a new Indian religion. She ate as many of the plants as she could and immediately recovered her strength. After a while, the plant took the form of a thief and medicine man. Then he told her his name was Peyote and led her to the boy and then to the rest of her party.

2) Peyote is acquired from an enemy, after which enemies become friends.

A Comanche warrior who believed he was the only survivor of a battle decided to stop fighting and lay down on the ground. When he heard the sound of someone coming from the east he thought it was an enemy and waited to be killed. But instead of an enemy, Peyote appeared and told him there were others who had survived the battle and were no longer in danger, including his own children. Then he told him that if he used him properly, no trouble would come to him or his people anymore. When the man opened his eyes, the spirit was gone, but a peyote plant was in his hand. The man found his people, and they began to use peyote.

3) Peyote is found in the course of a quest.

A young boy decided to prove he was a man and went off on his own to hunt (In some versions of this story, he lives with his father and mother and sister in a desert area, in others he and his sister are orphans). When he didn't come back to camp, a search party (or his father) went to look for him, but didn't find him and returned to camp. His sister, however, continued the search. After several days without eating or drinking, she became too weak to walk any farther and lay down and prayed to god to let her see her brother one more time before she died.

While she was praying, the voice of Peyote told her that there was a plant behind her that when eaten, would take away her hunger and thirst and revive her strength. After she ate some of it, she immediately felt better. Then Peyote told her that her brother had returned to their camp and she should also go back. When she returned she told her family about her vision and the plant, and that was how the Comanches discovered it.

In a variant, a man became lost while he was hunting. About to die of hunger and thirst, he lay down under the shade of a tree, and as he stretched out, his hand touched a plant and he ate it. A spirit immediately entered his body and took him to a region above where a spirit told him that he had caused him to go through all this suffering because without having done so, he would never have learned of the spirit's religion. The spirit said that his own father, **Earthmaker**, had given the peyote plant to him and he was permitted to put it on earth and give some to the Indians. The spirit then said that the religion existed at the present in the south and he wanted it to come to the north so that the Indians would stop fighting.

Central American tribes, such as Huichol, have an entirely different origin tradition for peyote. In Huichol mythology, peyote is called **Hikori**, and is considered to be an incarnation of the divine deer, called **Deer Person** or Elder Brother Deer. (Anderson, 2–23; Furst, 113–114; Hultkrantz, 197; Petrullo, 34–41; Rudgley, 189–193; Schultes and Hofmann, 144–155)

Peyote Woman. In North American Kiowa Indian mythology, the girl to whom Peyote, called Aseni, first appeared and taught the Kiowa how to use it.

When two of her brothers did not return from a war the Kiowas had fought far to the south, their sister believed they were dead and went into the hills to mourn them. Worn out with grief and crying, she was too tired to return to the camp that night, and she lay down to sleep.

In her dreams, Aseni, the peyote spirit, came to her and told her that her brothers were still alive, and that in the morning when she awoke, she would find a plant underneath her head that would restore them to her. When morning came, she got up and looked where she had been sleeping and found peyote. She took the peyote back to camp, showed it to the tribal **shamans**, and told them of her vision and the instructions Peyote had given her. The shamans then said prayers and sang songs and ate the peyote which had miraculously increased. After they took it, they saw a vision in which the two young warriors were wandering on foot in the Sierra Madre. A search party was immediately organized and after searching for many days through enemy territory, the young men were found and brought back to their people. (O. Stewart, 36)

Phan Ningsan. In northeastern India mythology, the god who created the **opium** poppy.

Phan Ningsan created a girl by rubbing dirt in his hands together. Although she was very beautiful, she smelled so badly of the dirt from which she was created that the other gods and men avoided her and she remained unmarried. When she was older, she complained to Phan Ningsan about her loneliness. He told her that her fate was only temporary, and that when she died, a plant called opium would grow from her grave that men would find so desirable they all would love her. (Elwin, 218–219)

Pichurey *see* **Hukaht.**

Pima North American Indian origin myth for cactus **wine.**

A pumpkin baby disappeared into the ground and reappeared as a giant cactus far away. When the Pima couldn't find him, they asked **Coyote** for help. Using his sense of smell, Coyote searched and finally came to the giant cactus, but wasn't sure it was the baby and told the Pima he hadn't found it. The Pima then asked Buzzard for help. Coyote told Buzzard about the cactus and said he wasn't sure about it. Buzzard flew around the giant cactus and then told the people he had found a fully grown cactus and that something good would come from it.

After the cactus bore fruit the people collected it and made it into cactus wine and spread the seeds to dry in the sun. Badger stole the seeds and the people sent Coyote to get them back. When Coyote saw Badger he asked him what he had in his hand. Badger was reluctant to show him what he had, but was reassured when Coyote said that he would be satisfied if he would just open his hand so that he could see what he had. When Badger opened his hand, Coyote slapped it and knocked the seeds into the air, scattering them everywhere. (Bahr et al., 105–106)

Piskisum. In middle India mythology, the god of **tobacco**.

Long ago four brothers and their wives lived in the jungle. In those early times men did not make any sound when they walked, so that their wives never knew when they were coming home. Because they couldn't hear them, the women were sometimes naked when the men returned, and they felt ashamed. When they asked Piskisum to help them, he gave them a tobacco leaf and told them to grind it up and throw it at their husbands the next time they came home. When the men breathed the tobacco, they began to cough and sneeze. After that, the women always knew when their husbands were returning. (Elwin, 1954, 182)

Priapus. In Greek mythology, the son of **Dionysus** and **Aphrodite**. Hera disapproved of Aphrodite's promiscuity and caused Priapus to be an ugly child with a very large and constantly erect phallus. His images were often placed in vineyards to encourage their growth. (Grimal, 391–392)

Psilocybin. From the Greek, *psilo*, meaning "bald," and *cybe*, meaning "head"; the active psychoactive ingredient in over 75 species of mushrooms belonging to the three genera of mushrooms, *Psilocybe*, *Panaeolus*, and *Conocybe* that have about 100 different species. The most common species in the United States are *Psilocybe mexicana*, *Psilocybe cyanescens*, and *Psilocybe cubensis*. In Central America, these mushrooms were called "teonanactl," the "flesh of the gods," by the Aztecs.

Psilocybin (4-phosphoryloxy-DMT) has a chemical structure similar to LSD but is about 100 times less potent on a milligram basis than LSD. When mushrooms containing it are eaten, the psilocybin is converted to psilocin. Onset of activity after chewing these mushrooms occurs within 10 minutes. Initial effects include yawning, malaise, stomach aches, and nausea. After about two hours, these effects are replaced with vivid auditory and visual imagery for another four to six hours. Symptoms of overdosing include fever, increased pulse rate, stiffening of the muscles, difficulty walking, anxiety, paranoia, and an inability to speak. (Rudgley, 206–2101; Schultes and Hofmann, 23, 69, 73, 79, 159, 185–189)

Psychopomp. An envoy who guides departed souls to the land of the dead. Psychopomps are usually gods but in some myths, they are **shamans**, their mortal counterparts, who are able to traverse the boundary between life and death (Parry, 17).

Pu'a. In Tahitian mythology, the god of awa (**kava**).

One day Pu'a's five older brothers went to Hawaii to court an underworld princess and refused to take him with them. Undaunted, Pu'a built a canoe and went on his own. When the brothers came to the island, they were told by the girl's father that if they wanted to marry his daughter, they would have to pull up the roots of a kava plant that was possessed by a demon who killed everyone who disturbed him. Pu'a arrived after all his brothers had been killed, but succeeded in uprooting the plant. He then restored his brothers to life and turned them into porpoises. After that he married the princess, but almost immediately deserted her and returned to Tahiti with the kava. (Beckwith, 251; Henry, 561)

Pufafine. In Polynesian Tonga mythology, the goddess of the **kava** plant.

A fleet of canoes beached on the island and found a kava plant whose leaves and stem the men plucked and brought back to their king. The king made a drink from it and liked it and told the men to bring him more. However, there was only one plant on the island and it contained the spirit of Pufafine. When the first man to find it dug it up, Pufaine developed a sexual desire for him, but did not have sex with him. However, when he fell asleep, she had intercourse spiritually with him. When he awoke, Pufafine told the man she was pregnant, and that while he might leave, he should return in five nights. However, the man didn't come back, but on the fifth night, he became unconscious (i.e., died) and his spirit returned to stay with Pufafine. (Firth, 216; Lebot et al., 124)

Pulekukewerek. In North American Yurok Indian mythology, the creator god who grew from a **tobacco** plant and then gave it to humans.

When Pulekukewerk was still a small humanlike immortal, the Yurok smoked the leaves of the pepperwood plant, but it was so strong it killed many of them. When Pulekukwerek saw its effects were too strong, he decided to see what he could do. During his search for a substitute, he met the ten Earthquake brothers who smoked a tobacco that was so strong it also killed people. The brothers offered Pulekukewerek some of their tobacco to smoke, and continued offering him more until Pulekukewerek smoked as much as ten pipes, and fell over. Thinking he was dead, the brothers threw him into the bush and left him. When he revived, Pulekukwerek found a way to make the tobacco weaker and gave it to the Yurok.

In a variant, Pulekukwerek made a fire and offered tobacco smoke to the Sky Possessor who had never had tobacco before and was grateful for the gift. When Sky Possessor told Pulekukwerek he wanted to make the world better, Pulekukwerek offered to live with him so that he would always have tobacco, and then told him to blow the smoke out after inhaling it. When he did, the fog that came out of his mouth became the sky. Then as he blew out more fog it turned into clouds and stars. (Kroeber, 126–127, 366–368)

Pulque. A milky, slightly foamy, viscous alcoholic drink made by fermenting the sap of certain types of maguey (agave). The goddess incarnating the sap was depicted as a heavily-breasted woman and the sap was called "mother's milk."

The maguey plant has very fibrous roots and thick shoots that enable it to withstand prolonged drought. It does not produce enough sap to be extracted until it is four to six years old. It flowers only once, and then dies soon afterward. The plant was a mainstay of many Central American households since its fibers could be twisted into threads for making clothes or containers or into rope for tying. Its leaves were used as roofs to cover huts, and its thorns were made into needles and were also used as devices for inflicting penitential pain during religious ceremonies.

Among the Central American Indians, the sap was fermented to make pulque which was not only used as a ceremonial intoxicant, but also as a primary food since it provided vitamins that would otherwise have come from green vegetables that could not be raised in the desert climate.

Pulque was also used as a ritual intoxicant by priests in performing sacrifices and was given to those being sacrificed to numb their senses. The word comes from "octli" meaning "decomposed" in Aztec. The Spaniards corrupted poliqui to pulcre and later to pulque. The word maguey is also of Spanish origin; the Aztecs called the plant metl.

After the maize was harvested, large amounts of pulque were drunk and more of the **pulque gods** were invoked to give strength, courage, and virtue. Those who drank it were said to come under the influence of one of the **Centzon Totochtin**, the four hundred pulque gods or spirits, among whom **Ome Totchtli** was the most powerful. This was one of the few times drunkenness was permitted. Otherwise, except for the aged, and priests, drunkenness was proscribed by the "fifth cup," the rule that no one was permitted to drink more than four cups of pulque. (Reed, 110)

Pulque Gods. In Aztec and Mayan mythology, the gods or spirits personifying **pulque**. While **Mayahuel** was the female spirit animating the sap from which pulque was made, the pulque gods were almost all male. Among the Aztecs, these pulque gods were collectively called the **Centzon Totochtin**, the "400 Rabbits," because the rabbit was deemed to be totally devoid of sense. The myriad effects of drinking were attributed to the influence of one of the four hundred different spirits that animated pulque.

All the pulque gods were closely linked to the earth and the earth goddess. They all wore a crescent-shaped nose ornament (representing the **moon**) and carried a square shield in one hand and a stone axe in the other. They wore headdresses of white feathers, and their faces were typically painted red in the middle and black or dark green on either side, as were their blankets and shields. (H. Nicholson, 172–174; Miller and Taube, 138; Spence, 1911, 105)

Pumenerru. In South American Warao Indian mythology, the culture heroine who gave the Warao **tobacco**.

Pumenerru and her brothers were constantly trying to ascend to heaven by dancing. One day, during their dance, they saw a hummingbird. At first they didn't pay any attention to the bird, but then noticed smoke coming from its beak, and then when they looked at it longer, they saw a man in the sky looking down at them. Pumenerru's brothers shot arrows at him, and eventually killed him. When the man fell to earth, they burned his body and buried his ashes. A little later, tobacco plants grew from his grave. Pumenerru made cigars from the plants' leaves and showed her brothers how to smoke them, and also warned her brothers not to tell anyone else about their discovery. However, a stranger saw them smoking and when one of the brothers threw away his butt, the stranger picked it up and smoked it. Then he told others about the plant. (Wilbert, 1970, 238–243)

Puopie. In South American Ayoreo Indian mythology, the **tobacco**-god whose spirit gave power to **shamans**.

One day the Ayoreo were collecting honey, when they came upon a stranger who was also collecting honey. When they tried to kill him he took refuge in a tree. Cornered, his pursuers shot arrows at him and fatally wounded him. Just before he died his blood flowed on the bodies of his pursuers, and his magic power entered their bodies and made them shamans. (Bormida et al., 186)

Pythia. In Greek mythology, the priestess of Apollo's temple at **Delphi**. She entered a prophetic trance after inhaling a potent smoke (variously said to be **henbane** or **cannabis**), during which she was able to contact Apollo and learn the future from him. (Ratsch, 29)

Quatlapanqui. In Mayan mythology, the god of headache that came from drinking **pulque**. (Spence, 1912, 82)

Queen Mother of the West (or **Hsi Wang Mu**). In Chinese mythology, variously a fairy queen, or a monster goddess with the face of a woman, the teeth of a tiger, and the tail of a leopard, who lived in a mountain where she entertained the Eight Immortals in her palace gardens and introduced them to "celestial **wine**," an **elixir** of immortality and wisdom, which she made from peaches that grew on a giant cosmic tree in her orchard. The tree measured three thousand miles around, and its peaches ripened only once every three thousand years. (Knapp, 188–189; Pas, 254; Sanders, 29)

Quetzalcoatl. Aztec god of civilization who restored human life and introduced agriculture, part of which included establishing **pulque** brewing and ceremonial drunkenness.

Quetzalcoatl, whose name means "the feathered serpent," is usually a god, the son of the fertility goddess, Coatlicue, in Aztec mythology, but in some myths, he is a king or a priest. As a god, he represented the forces of good and light, in contrast to his arch enemy, **Tezcatlipoca**, who represented evil and darkness.

In Aztec mythology, there were five creations or "Suns," each of which ended with a cataclysm. The first Sun was ruled over by Tezcatlipoca who was dethroned by Quetzalcoatl prior to its end. The second was ruled by Quetzalcoatl who in turn was overthrown by Tezcatlipoca. The third was ruled by Tlaloc, the rain god and was extinguished by Quetzalcoatl. The fourth was ruled by a water goddess and ended with a flood in which all humans were destroyed.

After the end of the Fourth Sun the gods convened to discuss the next sun, and decided to repopulate it with the humans who had been destroyed during the Fourth Sun. The restoration job was delegated to Quetzalcoatl who descended into the underworld and after performing many seemingly impossible tasks given him by Mictlanteculti, the god of death, retrieved the bones and ashes of the previous humanity and created a new race of people by splashing his own blood on them.

After humans were created, the gods discussed how they would keep them alive. To provide nourishment, Quetzalcoatl brought pulque to mankind. To do this, he first seduced and kidnapped **Mayahuel,** a young goddess, from the home of her grandmother and carried her to earth. To escape her grandmother's detection, Quetzalcoatl and Mayahuel transformed themselves into a tree with each of them a large branch. The disguise didn't fool the grandmother, and she attacked the tree which split in two. Mayahuel's branch was torn to pieces by the grandmother and her entourage. Quetzalcoatl, however, was unharmed and when they left, he gathered up what was left of Mayahuel and buried her. From her grave the maguey plant grew, which not only provided humans with nutrients and intoxicating pulque from its sap, but also the fibers to make their clothes from its leaves.

Sometime later, Quetzalcoatl once again came into conflict with his arch rival, Tezcatlipoca, this time over human sacrifice. The current era of The Fifth Sun, in which humans were permanently created, was attributed to Quetzalcoatl's self-sacrifice when his blood gave birth to mankind. The Aztecs believed that their preeminence was predicated on regular blood sacrifices to Quetzalcoatl, but Tezcatlipoca believed he was also entitled to blood sacrifice, and hatched a plan to discredit Quetzalcoatl so that he would have to leave his home, allowing Tezcatlipoca to inherit the blood sacrifice.

For the first part of the plan, Tezcatlipoca disguised himself as a young man. Appearing at Quetzalcoatl's house with a mirror, he told the servants guarding Quetzalcoatl that he had come to show the god what he looked like physically. Curious, Quetzalcoatl agreed to see the visitor. When he saw his own image, Quetzalcoatl became completely despondent at how old he looked and resolved to keep himself hidden. The disguised Tezcatlipoca then left but soon returned in the form of two avatars who persuaded Quetzalcoatl to meet with them after sending him a message telling him they had a potion that could make him young again. Quetzalcoatl was excited at the prospect of being rejuvenated. He took the potion they offered him, which was pulque, and after drinking five cups, became drunk (which was a taboo in Aztec culture). Inebriated, Quetzalcoatl summoned his sister Quetzalpetlatl, and she drank five cups as well. In their debauched condition, they engaged in incest. When Quetzaloatl awoke the next day, he realized he had violated the taboos against drunkenness and incest and felt he had to leave his home, which at that time was located in the Aztec city of Tulla.

Tormented with remorse, Quetzalcoatl wandered in self-imposed exile for many years until he came to the east coast of Mexico, from which he sailed away, promising someday to return. (Graulich, 110ff)

Rabbit. In many North American Indian mythologies, a dual-sided character, on one hand a **trickster** buffoon, on the other a cultural benefactor hero. In other world mythologies, he is often associated with the **moon** and his image was said to appear in the full moon.

In Mayan mythology, the rabbit was regarded as being completely lacking in sense, and was therefore the personification of **pulque,** and the drunkenness that came from drinking it. Different numbers of rabbits represent different degrees of intoxication. Four hundred rabbits stood for complete drunkenness, 15 or 20 implied conviviality. Since the pulque gods were also lunar gods, the rabbit was also associated with the moon and its image was said to appear in the full moon. (Vaillant, 1ff)

Ramma and Bimma. In Middle India mythology, two estranged brothers who were reconciled by **tobacco.**

One day, Ramma and Bimma discovered some tobacco seeds and sowed them in their garden and then when the plant grew, they smoked its leaves. Sometime later, they quarreled and separated. When the village elder wasn't able to persuade them to reconcile, he ordered the villagers to uproot all Ramma's tobacco plants. Although he no longer had anything to smoke, Ramma was too proud to ask his brother for some of his tobacco. Then the elder gave some cigarettes to Bimma and told him to smoke them in front of his brother's house. When Ramma saw his brother smoking, he became discomfited and asked his brother for some. Once they began to talk again, the brothers were reconciled. Since then, the gift of tobacco has made men friendly toward one another. (Elwin, 1954, 181)

Raven. In North American Haida Indian mythology, the transformer who created **tobacco.**

During one of his travels, Raven encountered a group of people shooting arrows at the leaves of a tall tree and eating those that fell. When

Raven asked them the name of the tree, they told him it was tobacco. Raven then shot the tree near its base, so that when it fell, they were able to get the leaves more easily. The Raven told them to plant its eggs (seeds) so that they would have the plant forever. (Winter, 27)

Rbhus. In Hindu mythology, three divine carpenters and cupmakers who worked for the gods and because of their help, were allowed to take part in the **Soma** offering. (Belier, 62, 141)

Ritual (or **Rite**). A formalized series of symbolic activities, such as singing, dancing, recitation of texts, sacrifice, eating certain foods, or consuming special, usually intoxicating drinks, that are regularly performed as a demonstration of worship or as a way of preparing oneself to achieve consciousness of a deity. The association with reverence for a god distinguishes religious rituals from civic rituals such as oaths of allegiance and coronations, and repetitive behaviors that have no social associations such as those regularly performed as part of psychological disorders.

Many rituals are orgiastic. Drinking and sexual orgies are often ritualistic harvest festivals or spring festivals connected with sowing seeds, representing a central belief in many cultures that there is a sympathetic link between human and agricultural fertility. The orgy is the collective counterpart of the ancient Near Eastern hierogamy, an annual ritualized sexual intercourse between a ruler and a priestess of a fertility goddess believed to persuade the goddess to bestow her power on the new growing season. In cultures where there is a belief that humans are copies of their gods, intoxication is deliberate because what is enjoyable for humans is thought to be approved of by the gods. The Lacandon, descendants of the Mayas, believe that the gods gave them balche after becoming intoxicated with it themselves. For the Lancandos, drinking **balche** to the point of inebriation is a means of achieving a state of ritual purity essential for interacting with the gods. It is through balche-induced intoxication that the transcendental state of mind is induced enabling communication with the gods. (Goodman, 6, 16, 31–33; Price and Kearns, 471–473)

Ruksey. In Malay mythology, the god of intoxicating drinks and distillation. (Crooke, 344)

Sabazius. An Anatolian **wine** and vegetation god, who was head of the Thracian pantheon. Later identified with **Dionysus**. (Albright, 270; Farnell, 96; Jobes, 1356)

Sacrifice. A gift to a god in expectation of a favorable return. Items that are sacrificed are believed to be desired by the god to whom the sacrifice is made. A common theme in **tobacco** myths is that tobacco is a spiritual food that creates an interdependent relationship between the gods and humans. In return for providing them with food and protection, humans provide the gods with tobacco smoke. (Price and Kearns, 486–489)

Saguaro (Carnegiea gigantean; Cereus giganteus). A large cactus that grows in the desert regions of Arizona and northern Mexico. Its sap was fermented into a potent alcoholic drink by the Pima and Papago Indians. (Schultes and Hofmann, 39, 6–77).

Salvation. The promise of life after death or a change in perspective during life on earth. In the **Mystery Religions**, salvation comes following initiation into the sacred rites, including the feeling of **entheogen**-induced **ecstasy** and **enthusiasm**. In Christianity, salvation is attained through belief and is ritualized in some denominations through a communion called the Eucharist. The Bacchic Mystery Religion ritualized its promise of salvation through the communal eating of an animal's flesh and drinking of its blood. (Smart, 40, 63, 80, 91–94, 114, 140; Worthen, 77–81, 194–196, 203, 205)

Samael. In Hebrew mythology, the angel who planted a vinestalk in the Garden of Eden, the fruit of which was used by Satan to seduce Adam. The vine was swept out of Paradise at the time of the great flood and was discovered by **Noah**, who replanted it. (Lutz, 141)

Samudra. In Indian mythology, the home of the god **Soma**, and also the name for the terrestrial ocean that was churned to obtain the **amrta**. Samudra is also the name for the vessel used to press soma in sacrifices. (Dange, I:239)

Sarasvati (or Vac). In Hindu mythology, the goddess of wisdom. Sarasvati sprang from Brahma's forehead. As soon as he saw her, Brahma became enamored of her even though she was his daughter, and married her. Whereas Brahma was the source of knowledge and intelligence, Sarasvati was the source of life's energy and creativity. Together, they created the earth and its human inhabitants.

Sarasvati, who was also called Vac ("speech"), offered herself to the **Gandharas** in exchange for **soma**. In another adventure, she helped **Indra** defeat the demon, **Namuci**, enabling Indra to regain the soma that Namuci had stolen from him. (Mahony, 38–39)

Satyrs. In Greek mythology, naked woodland creatures, also known as silens. Like the **centaurs**, they were human-like in the upper part of their bodies, and horse-like in the lower half, but unlike the centaurs, they only had two feet and they were not contentious. They were often found with **Dionysus**, and were known for their mischievousness, cowardliness, and insatiable sexuality and love of **wine**. The best known of the satyrs was Silenus. (Price and Kearns, 497)

Saura. Persian god of drunkenness. (Hinnels, 12)

Semele. In Greek mythology, the daughter of Cadmus, the king of Thebes, and the mother of **Dionysus.**
  Zeus fell in love with her and she subsequently became pregnant with Dionysus. Hera was jealous and tricked her into asking Zeus to appear to her as he did to Hera. When Zeus did, Semele was consumed by his firey presence. But before she died, Zeus snatched the unborn Dionysus from her womb and placed him in his thigh, and subsequently gave birth to Dionysus himself. Later on, Dionysus went down to the underworld and brought Semele back, named her Thyone, and ascended with her to heaven where Zeus made her immortal. (Grimal, 415–416; Price and Kearns, 504)

Seme-peyaru-pora. In South American Desana Indian mythology, a **chicha** beer deity. (Reichel-Dolmatoff, 1871, 196)

Set. An individual's expectations and personality traits that influence the way he or she perceives the effects of an intoxicant. (Fuller, 158–159)

Setting. The influence of the surroundings in which intoxicants are taken on the experience produced by those intoxicants. (Fuller, 159)

Shaman. In many cultures, the mediator, usually male, between humans and the supernatural powers who control the world and reside in the heavens and beneath the earth. These supernatural powers, however, depend on humans for their food whereas humans depend on the protection of these powers for their health and lives. Both groups rely on the shaman to maintain harmony between them.
  The shaman's spiritual journey has three components. First, he has to leave the reality of the natural world which is known through the ordinary senses and travel to the supernatural world, a world that can only be perceived through an altered state of consciousness. The shaman's ability to make these spiritual journeys is very much a result of his ability to enter a trance state, often drug-induced, which sends

him on his **ecstatic** journey. Not everyone is able to enter this trance state. In South America, those wanting to be shamans are required to drink **tobacco** juice or chew a lot of tobacco leaves. Those who do not vomit can then become shamans because the spirit of the tobacco, which gives the shaman his power, remained within their bodies. During the initial phase of the spirit journey, the shaman travels to the realm of the Supernaturals, and is often guided or protected by an animal spirit, or he becomes an animal spirit himself. Myths in which a god or hero flies or sails to some distant island, descends to the underworld, or undergoes some kind of shape-shifting metamorphosis in which he changes his physical appearance and becomes an animal or vice versa, represent shamanic spirit journeys and many myths describing quests are thought to have been created or interpreted and preserved by shamans.

Once he arrives in the spirit world, he interacts with the Supernatural beings, bringing them gifts from his people, and gaining from them the information for restoring health, controlling the weather, successfully hunting animals, or restoring the delicate balance between mankind and these spirits. The third phase of the shaman's journey involves his return to the natural world where he tells his people what he has learned. (Fuller, 11, 22, 24–31, 49, 168; Ripinsky-Naxon, 1ff; Stutley, 1ff; Torrance, 137ff)

Shesmu. The Egyptian goddess of the **wine** press. (Lutz, 114)

Shiva *see* **Siva.**

Shojo. In Japanese mythology, Shojo was the counterpart of the Norse god, **Aegir**, the god of brewing. He was typically depicted with long hair, a boyish face reddened from drinking sake (rice **wine**), and carrying a sake ladle.

One day, a man who lived near Mount Fuji became very ill. Thinking he was about to die, he asked his son to bring him one last cup of sake. Since there was no sake in the house, his son went out to get him some. Wandering along the seashore, he encountered a strange-looking creature with long red hair and a cherry-colored face, and seaweed around his groins, who was drinking sake from a large cup that never emptied. The boy told the stranger, who was Shojo, that his father was dying and that he wanted a last cup of sake, but he was too poor to buy some. Shojo then poured some of his sake into the boy's gourd and he took it back to his father. As soon as his father drank it, he felt stronger and asked his son to get more. After drinking more of Shojo's sake, the boy's father completely recovered.

Shojo kept giving the boy more sake. When his neighbor, who was very fond of sake, heard that the father had an endless supply of it, he sneaked into his house and drank some, but it tasted like filthy water. He then beat the boy and ordered him to take him to the place he had gotten it. The boy led the neighbor to Shojo and told him that the neighbor had tasted some of the sake and had spat it out, imagining the boy had played a trick on him. The neighbor then asked Shojo for some sake, and he gave him some. When he tasted it, he became sick.

Shojo then told him that he had given the sake to the boy's father because he was a good man, and therefore, it was able to exert its beneficial effects on him. But because the neighbor was greedy and selfish, sake was a poison to him. The neighbor then became very ashamed and pleaded with Shojo not to let him die. Seeing his contrition, Shojo gave the neighbor an antidote to overcome the poison. After he took the antidote, the neighbor became a new person, made friends with the boy's father, and was once again able to enjoy sake. (Davis, 359–363; Dorson, 1962, 86; Jobes, 144)

Sibia-pora. In South American Desana Indian mythology, the god of drunkenness and sexual excitement. (Reichel-Dolmatoff, 1971, 196)

Siduri. Babylonian guardian of the vineyard of the gods, an avatar of **Inanna**.

During his search for the elixir of immortality, the semi-mortal Gilgamesh came to a wonderful garden whose fruits were the purple color of lapis-lazuli (grapes on the vine). The garden belonged to Siduri, who didn't allow him to enter and urged him to give up his quest and go back to his home. (Lutz, 130–131)

Silenus. In Greek and Roman mythology, an old and cheerfully drunken **satyr**, usually depicted as bald, snub-nosed, pot-bellied and carrying a cup in his hand. Silenus was **Dionysus'** or Bacchus' tutor during his childhood and watched over him to keep him from being discovered by Hera. Although he was habitually drunk, Silenus had a reputation for great wisdom and the gift of being able to tell the future. (Grimal, 419; Price and Kearns, 497)

Sing Bonga. In Indian mythology, the Creator god who taught the first man and woman how to make rice **beer**; after drinking it, they developed sensations that made them come together and populate the world. (Elwin, 1954, 188)

Siris. In Sumerian (Mesopotamian) mythology, a **beer** goddess who lived on a mountain; sometimes identified with **Ninkasi.** (Albright, 260)

Siuuhu. In North American Pima-papago Indian mythology, alternatively the culture heroine, from whose body **tobacco** grew, or the goddess or god who created saguaro cactus from which the Pimas made **wine.**

A powerful medicine man had a daughter named Siuuhu who was so discouraged that no one had asked to marry her. Frustrated, she asked her father to end her life and bury her. When a tobacco plant subsequently sprouted from her grave, her father took some of its leaves and smoked them. When the people smelled it, they all wanted some.

In the other variant, Siuuhu decided to show the Pima the benefits of eating the fruit of the saguaro cactus. However, the man and his brother-in-law that he chose to bring the fruit of the cactus to the Pima when it was ripe, kept it for four days and it fermented. When the Pima ate the fermented fruit, they became intoxicated. When Siuuhu saw their drunkenness, he was annoyed because the Pima weren't using the fruit as he had wanted, and he modified the cactus so that it took a long time before it gave any fruit, and when it did, it only ripened once a year. (Bahr et al., 125–130)

Siva. In Indian mythology, one of the Hindu triumvirate (the other two being **Brahma** and **Vishnu**).

Siva is a multidimensional god. In addition to being the god of intoxication, **ecstasy**, eroticism, and consciousness, he is also an ascetic, a benevolent guardian, a loving husband, a dancer whose cosmic "Dance of Bliss" maintains the rhythms of the universe, and a malevolent god who takes pleasure in creating havoc and destruction. Siva had four arms, and four faces with three eyes in each. The third eye, located in the middle of each of his foreheads, is the fire of consciousness and has the ability to create as well as destroy. His skin is white, symbolizing enlightenment, except for his throat which is blue, a consequence of his saving the world from destruction during the **Churning of the Ocean** to recover the **amrta**, by swallowing a poisonous vapor that emerged from the deep. Before it could harm the **Asuras** and **Devas**, Siva held the vapor in his throat, not swallowing it because it would have killed him. But it turned his throat permanently blue. Siva wears a garland of skulls around his neck symbolizing the constant reoccurrence of human reincarnation, and a crescent moon on his head which contains **soma.**

Siva is an androgynous god with many similarities to **Dionysus,** but in place of wine, Siva is the god of **cannabis.** Siva discovered cannabis after quarreling with some family members. Upset, he went off to be by himself in the mountains. The sun, however, was so hot that he took refuge under a cannabis plant. As he sat and cooled off, he became curious about it and ate some of its leaves. He enjoyed its effects so much that it immediately became his favorite food, and he brought bhang (cannabis) from the Himalayas for the people of India. Siva continues to be associated with bhang in parts of present-day India, especially in connection with his being India's god of eroticism. As such, he is symbolized, as was Dionysus, by a lingam, representing his erotic and regenerative powers. Bhang (cannabis), his favorite drug, is poured over his symbol as an offering, in hopes that it will bring fertility. In middle India myths, Siva appeared as **Mahadeo,** and was credited with bringing **tobacco** to the people. (Oosten, 29–30; Walker, B., 2: 406–409; Worthen, 19, 64, 66–67, 159–160)

Skeleton Man. In North American Seneca Indian mythology, a fasting **shaman,** who sat in the midst of human bones and craved tobacco. He sent young men to the spirit world to outwit the malevolent spirits who guarded the **tobacco** and bring it back to him. Whenever they were successful and Skeleton Man smoked the tobacco in his pipe, the bones of the dead took on flesh and returned to life. (Furst, 1995, 545).

Sky Father. In North American Navajo Indian mythology, the god who initiated creation after he and Earth mother smoked **tobacco.** (Reichard, 432)

Sky Maiden. In North American Susquehannah Indian mythology, the spirit who gave humans **tobacco.**

One day Sky Maiden came into a camp where two hunters were cooking a deer and told them she was hungry. They offered her some of their meat and she sat down with them to eat it. After she finished, she thanked them and told them to come back to that place thirteen moons later. When they returned, maize and kidney beans were growing where her hands had touched the ground, and tobacco was growing from where she had sat. (Penn, 11; Quinn, 112; Setchell, 402).

Soma. In Hindu mythology, simultaneously a plant, a sacred, intoxicating drink brewed from the sap of the plant, and a god personifying the inspiration obtained from drinking it.

SACRED DRINK. Like the Greek **ambrosia**, soma gave the gods immortality and wisdom, cured disease, and enabled them to overcome all obstacles. Soma also produced **ecstasy**, stimulated poetry, and was a catalyst for mystical contact with the gods. While sometimes described as interchangeable with the **amrta** that arose from the **Churning of the Ocean**, they are not the same. Amrta is a celestial **elixir** possessed solely by the gods; soma is derived from a plant, is offered to the gods, and is taken by officiating priests in whom it induces a new consciousness of reality.

The myths about soma represent the earliest idea that ultimate reality is not accessible through the ordinary senses, but can only be attained through special methods, in soma's case, through ingestion of drugs.

PLANT. In a variant of the world tree motif, soma grew in heaven and spread its branches all over the world. The soma tree bore fruits and seeds of every kind in the world and was nourished by a river which renewed the youth of everything that bathed in it. Two birds sat on top of the tree, one of them eating figs while the other pressed soma juice from the tree's branches that fell to the earth.

In another variant, soma originated in the mountains (or heavens) and was obtained from a plant by crushing its stalks with stones and collecting and straining its yellowish brown sap. Priests offered the sap to the gods and then ingested it themselves either undiluted, or mixed with milk, honey or barley water. It was always taken immediately and never allowed to ferment. Humans who drank it experienced an intoxication, inspiration and **ecstasy** that made them conscious of the divine, and that consciousness was the bridge spanning the world between humans and the gods.

When the priest poured soma onto a ritual fire, the smoke that rose from it was carried by the god **Agni** to the **moon** where it was stored, making the moon full again. The moon's waning resulted from the gods' consumption of it; and its waxing reflected its replenishment. When the gods drank it, it reinvigorated their immortality enabling them to maintain rta, the cosmic order, in their ongoing battle with the demonic forces that were always trying to create chaos.

Despite extensive scholarly attention, there is no agreement about soma's identity. Among the plants most frequently mentioned are **amanita muscaria, cannabis,** and **mead.** Soma in fact may not be the name of a specific plant, but a general term for plants whose ingestion produced the visionary or ecstatic experiences associated with **entheogen** use.

GOD. Soma was a god who was simultaneously the spirit of soma and a god who existed on his own. Although Soma was never depicted in a human form, the myths about him are anthropomorphic.

Before the gods had Soma, Soma lived in the mountains where he was protected by the **Gandharas,** a tribe of demigods who kept such close watch over him that the Deva gods could only get Soma by cunning.

In one variant, the Devas were aware of Soma's attributes and they wanted him with them, but they didn't know how to get him. They finally hit on a plan that relied on the fondness of the Gandharas for women and they sent Vac (also called Vash and **Sarasvati**), the goddess of speech, to them. She managed to seduce them and when they were not watching, brought Soma to the gods. The Gandharas pursued Vac, but when they came to the realm of the Devas, they told them they could keep Soma, but they wanted Vac. The gods agreed to let Vac decide and each side competed to win her over. The Gandharas tried to seduce her by reciting the Vedas, while the Devas invented the lute and made music. Vac preferred the latter and stayed with the gods.

In another variant, Soma was already on his way to the camp of the Devas when he was abducted by the Gandharas who demanded a ransom for his return. The Devas asked the Gandharas what they wanted in return for Soma, and they answered that they wanted the power of speech. When Vac heard this, she volunteered to ransom herself for Soma, and the trade was made.

A third variant has the Devas, who at the time were living on earth, sending Gayatri, who is **Brahma**'s wife or daughter, to fetch Soma. She flew into the heavens in the form of a bird but was captured by the Gandharas who released her and Soma in return for Vac.

Yet another variant has **Indra**, mounted on an eagle, flying to Soma's home and grasping him in his talons. As he flew away, Soma's archer guardian shot an arrow at the eagle which dislodged one of its feathers, but otherwise left him unharmed. The feather drifted to earth and became the soma plant on earth. Indra was particularly fond of soma, and it inspired him to perform many of his most notable deeds. Before battling a dreadful dragon name Vritra, Indra drank rivers of soma to gain the strength he needed to overcome the dragon.

Soma was also honored as the god who gave **wine** to earth. One of soma's synonyms was madhu, "mixed drink," which became the word for honey wine, "methu" in Greek, and later "**mead**" in various Indo-European languages. (Brough, 331–362; MacDonell, 104–115; Wasson, 1971, 1ff)

Somnus. In Roman mythology, the god of sleep and the **opium** poppy. His eponymous name occurs in the Latin term for poppy, *Papaver somniferous*, "Bringer of Sleep." Somnus was a small boy who wore a crown of poppies and carried an opium horn in which farmers collected opium sap. Somnus was often depicted leaning over a woman and pouring opium juice into her closed eyes. (Booth, 20)

Soonjalhai. In South American Nivakle Indian folklore, the woman from whose body **tobacco** originated.

Soonjalhai was a cannibal monster who castrated, then killed and ate her husband. When her children saw her eating his testicles they believed she would eat them too, and they killed and cremated her and then buried her ashes. A few days later, when they visited her grave, they saw a plant which gave off a very intense aroma, growing over her grave. When they smoked its leaves they became dizzy, but eventually they became accustomed to its effects. The next day they took some of the leaves to their village and showed all the men where the plant was growing so they would have it when they wanted. (Chase-Sardi et al., 421–426)

Spenta Armaiti. In Persian mythology, the goddess of vineyards. (Ananikian, 35)

Staphylus. In Greek mythology, a shepherd who looked after the flocks of King **Oeneus**. One myth has him telling Oeneus about the playful behavior of a goat who ate grapes. Oeneus then came up with the idea of pressing the juice out of grapes and making **wine**.

A different myth makes Staphylus the son of **Silenus** and the individual who introduced the custom of mixing water and wine. (Grimal, 425–426)

Star Boy. In North American Crow Indian mythology, a son of one of the heavenly stars who was transformed into **tobacco**.

Long ago, before there were any separate tribes, a woman gave birth to twin boys, but she didn't know who the father was. When the boys became young men, one of them became fascinated with plants, while the other became interested in exploring the land. One day, as Star Boy was climbing a mountain, he met a stranger who told him he was Star, his father, and that as a token of his love, he was giving him a tobacco plant that he should sow wherever he journeyed and should share with everyone he met. When Star Boy came down from the mountain, he met his brother and offered to share his tobacco with him. His twin said he didn't need to climb mountains to have visions, and that he too had met his father, Earth, who had given him a special pipe. The two agreed to remain friends and they never quarreled. While one of the boys had been given tobacco, the other had been given the medicine pipe in which to smoke it. Shortly thereafter the people separated, some going with one of the boys, some with the other. Those who went with Star's son called themselves the Crow, while those who went with Earth's son became farmers and called themselves Hidatsa.

A variant of this myth has Star Boy transformed into tobacco by Transformer, the Creator god, who decreed that tobacco was to be the means of living for the Crow. (Lowie, 274–296)

Suasamiavaava. In Polynesian Samoan mythology, the culture hero from whose body **kava** grew. When Suasamiavaava was a young boy living in Fiji, he became fatally ill. As he lay dying, he told his mother not to weed his grave and to take whatever grew over it with them when they visited their relatives in Samoa. When his mother visited Suasamiavaava's grave, after his death, she saw two plants, kava and sugarcane, growing from it. When she visited it again, she saw a rat eating the kava and becoming giddy. Then after a short time, the rat ate some of the sugar cane and recovered. Suasamiavaava's mother then plucked the plants from her son's grave and took them with her to Samoa as he had asked. (Steubel and Herman, 104–105)

Sukracarya. In middle India mythology, a guru who placed a curse over **wine** because his daughter's lover was killed by drunken demons. (Mahapatra, 130).

Sundimari Deota. In middle India mythology, a culture hero who invented distillation.

When the gods smelled Sundimari Deota's liquor, they visited him and asked to taste it, but he refused to give them any. Enraged at his disrespect, they cut off his head. After that, whenever people distilled alcohol they offered some to the gods in his name. (Elwin, 1954, 202)

Sun Father. In South American Desana Indian mythology, the god who placed **viho-mahse**, the spirit of snuff, in the **tobacco** plant. (Reichel-Dolmatoff, 1971, 36)

Sura *see* **Mada.**

Susano *see* **Susa-no-ono.**

Susa-no-ono. In Japanese mythology, the storm god, god of the oceans and earth, and god of sake and drunkenness.

Susa-no-ono was resentful over the powers of his sister, Amaterasu, the sun goddess, and decided to prove to her that he was more powerful. After he caused a great storm on earth that destroyed all the rice plants, he threw excrement at all the temples devoted to his sister. Susa-no-ono's behavior frightened Amaterasu and she hid herself in a cave which confined her radiance so that the earth was in darkness. She was finally coaxed out by the other gods who then blocked the entrance to her cave.

Susa-no-ono was banished from heaven by his father for his behavior and was forced to live on earth. One day as he was roaming about, he met an earth spirit and his wife and their daughter who were all crying. He asked them why they were so despondent; they told him that every year an eight-headed dragon came to devour one of their daughters. Susa-no-ono offered to help them. When it was time for the girl to be taken to the dragon, Susa-no-ono told the earth spirit and his wife to brew some sake and put it into eight separate vats. Then each of the dragon's heads drank from each vat, they each became drunk, and Susa-no-ono chopped them all off. After that he married the girl himself. (Anesaki, 249; Mason, 128–131; Yamamuro, 271)

Suttung *see* **Odin.**

Svantovit. In Slav mythology, the god of wine. (Dixon-Kennedy, 325)

Tafa'i *see* **Pua.**

Tagaloa (or **Tagaroa**). In Polynesian mythology, the Creator god who gave the islanders awa (**kava**).

In the Samoan variant of the myth, Tagaloa had two sons, Ava'ali'i and Sa'a'sa'ali'i. After Awaiali'i died, Tagaloa told Sa'a'sa'ali'i that a plant would grow from his brother's grave that would be highly esteemed. Sa'a'sa'ali'i and his children kept close watch over the grave and three days later, two plants sprouted from it. Then they saw a rat come over and eat the first plant and then go over to the second. The second caused him to stagger away in intoxication. Tagaloa then told his son to call the first plant sugar cane, and the second awa (kava) in honor of his dead brother.

In a variant of this myth, the gods in heaven drank awa which at that time was unknown on earth. One day, Tagaloa and his two attendants came down from heaven to go fishing. After they were done, Tagaloa wanted some kava to drink. Since there was none to be had on earth, his attendants returned to heaven and uprooted a kava plant and brought it down to earth. Tagaloa then scattered its parts all over the land so he would have it whenever he visited earth. (Lebot et al., 125)

Tagaroa *see* **Tagaloa.**

Tahuehuiakame. In Central American Huichol mythology, the sky god and creator who gave the Huichol peyote.

Tahuehuiakame sent Majahuagy to earth to teach humans the arts and agriculture, a new code of laws, and a more humane religion to live by. Majahuagy convinced many people that they should change their ways, but he also made many enemies and decided that he and his followers should leave and find some new land where they could live in peace. However, when he assembled his followers, they were attacked and the gourds in which they had planned to carry the water that they needed for their journey were smashed, along with everything else they needed for their migration. Seeing their misfortune, Tahuehuiakame took pity on them and transformed the broken pieces into **peyote** plants that had the **magic** power to stave off thirst and hunger and give energy, enabling the group to set out without having to be overly concerned about food and water. After five years of walking, Majahuagy and his followers finally reached their destination. (Schaeffer and Furst, 38–39)

Taliesin. In Celtic mythology, a wizard and poet created when three drops from a magic brew from **Ceridwen's cauldron** fell on **Gwion Bach**, Taliesin's earlier incarnation. (Stewart, R., 88–90)

Tallur Muttai. In Middle India mythology, the woman who created sago **wine**.

Tallur Muttai and her husband were the first humans. Tallur Muttai loved her husband, but he had no passion for her. To excite him, she created the sago palm. When her husband drank the fermented juice from the plant, he was filled with passion for her. (Elwin, 1954, 188)

Tanna. A Polynesian myth explaining the origin of **kava** and why only men are permitted to use it.

One day a woman from a nearby island was squatting by the seashore peeling yams when a spirit slipped a slender stone covered with knots and buds into her vagina. When she felt something inside her, she immediately pulled it out, brought it to the village and showed it to the chief who immediately claimed it. That night, as he was showing it to the men of the village a spirit appeared and turned the object into an enormous kava plant and said that the stone was sacred and had to treated with respect. The people immediately put the stone into a canoe-shaped bowl and dripped some water onto it. The next day, the canoe was filled with thousands of similar stones. People came from all over the island and took the stones back with them to their villages and planted them and they turned into kava plants. After that, men had all the kava they wanted, but women were not allowed to have any, because it had once been in contact with a part of their body considered to be unclean. (Lebot et al., 127)

Tantalus. In Greek mythology, a minor god who stole **ambrosia** and was punished eternally for his misdeed.

Tantalus was an invited guest at Olympus, the home of the gods, but abused his privilege by stealing some of the gods' ambrosia and giving it to some mortal. Other variants related that he wanted to test how perceptive the gods were and killed and cooked his own son, Pelops, to see if they could detect the forbidden food. As punishment for his misdeed, Tantalus was banished to the Underworld where he was forced to experience eternal thirst and hunger by being made to stand in a pool of water up to his neck, over which there was a fruit tree. Whenever he tried to sip some of the water, it drained away, and whenever he reached for the fruit, the branches sprang upward. (Grimal, 431)

Tatewari. In Central American Huichol mythology, the first **shaman**.

Shortly after creation, the gods became sick because the rain givers were unable to make rain and masters of the animals couldn't find prey. Tatewari told them their illness was the result of failing to visit Wirikua, the sacred home of **peyote**. When they did, their health was restored. (Myerhoff 148, 186–8)

Tenemet. An ancient Egyptian goddess of intoxicating drinks. (Muller, 66)

Tepoztecatl. One of four hundred Mayan **pulque** gods. He was depicted as a warrior, with feather and plant ornaments, wearing a nose ring with the shape of the moon, a shield and a copper ax. Tepoztecatl was associated with the town of Tepoztlan in the mountains of Central Mexico. When someone there died from drunkenness, a celebration was held in his name. (Boone, 183, 203; Spence, 1911, 105; I. Nicholson, 165)

Tereteth. In Yap (Polynesian) mythology, the goddess of coconut **wine**. (Christian, 385)

Tezcatlipoca. Malevolent Aztec **pulque** god of sorcerers, thieves, misfortune, discord and drunkenness; his name means "smoking mirror," from the mirror he used to cause **Quetzalcoatl's** demise after getting him drunk. Tezcatlipoca was responsible for accidents associated with drunkenness such as dying as a result of a fall, suicide due to hanging, and homicide. Like all pulque gods, he wore a crescent-shaped nose ornament. He also wore a white feathered headdress, a fan of red feathers, a necklace, and a shield. (Alexander, 77; Anderson and Dibble 2:51 Boone, 204; Guerra, 248)

Thor (or **Donar**). In Norse mythology, the god of thunder and son of **Odin** whom he succeeded as supreme ruler of the gods. Among the early Germans, he was venerated as Donar; the Anglo-Saxons called him Thunor.

Thor was a hard drinker and very potent beers were brewed in his honor; to make them even more potent, they were spiked with **henbane**, his sacred plant.

Thor was the champion of the gods in their ongoing battle with their enemies, the giants. Anytime the giants threatened the gods or mankind, Thor, who was renown for his enormous strength, could be called upon for help and he would immediately appear with his powerful axe-hammer, called Mjolnir, which magically returned to his hand after he threw it.

Thor was a prodigious drinker of ale, but was a central character in only a few myths involving it. In one of these he journeyed to the home of the giant **Hymir** for a **cauldron** big enough to brew enough ale to satisfy all the gods.

Another myth referring to his prodigious drinking begins with his hammer being stolen by the frost giant, Thrymir. When Thor demanded its return, Thrymir said he would only return it on condition that the goddess Freya become his wife. When Freya refused the god, Loki persuaded Thor to disguise himself as Freya and accompanied him to the wedding banquet. Thor drank so much ale and ate so much food at the banquet that Thrymir became suspicious, but was placated by Loki, who told him that Freya had been so excited about her forthcoming wedding that she had not been able to eat or drink until then. When Thrymir finally produced the stolen hammer, Thor shed his disguise, snatched the hammer and used it to slaughter all the giants.

In another myth involving a drinking competition, Loki, who was also a **trickster**, gave Thor a special drinking horn and told him that whoever was able to drink its full contents in one draught was a mighty warrior. Most who drank from it, he said, had to take two draughts, and no one was so poor a drinker as to need three. Thor didn't think the horn was that big but it did look very long. He began to drink from it taking great gulps. When he ran out of breath, he stood up and looked inside the horn, but it didn't seem like he had drunk very much. Loki told Thor that although he had taken a large drink, it was not excessive. He wouldn't have believed it, he chided, if someone had told him that Thor, the leader of the gods, wouldn't have been able to drain it in one draught, but said he was sure Thor would do so in a second draught. Challenged, Thor took a second drink, determined he would finish it all this time. When he finally could not hold his breath anymore and looked inside the horn, it didn't look as if it had gone down much below its previous level, although it had gone done far enough so that the horn could be carried without spilling its contents. Loki then taunted Thor again, saying that he was undoubtedly intending his last draught to be his biggest, and that if he didn't, he would no longer be able to be considered as great as the gods boasted him to be. Angered, Thor took one more draught, but though he drained most of it, there was still some left. After Thor admitted he hadn't been able to drain the horn completely, Loki showed him that the far end of the horn had been in the sea and that the level of the sea had become very low as a result of Thor's having drunk so much of it. (DuBois, 60–61; Fee and Leeming, 42–43; Metzner, 286)

Thrita (or **Trita**). In Iranian mythology, the first doctor. He received ten thousand healing plants from Ahura Mazda, the Zoroastrian supreme god, from which he prepared **haoma** (the Iranian counterpart of **soma**) for the world. Trita, his counterpart in India, prepared **soma** for **Indra** in the cosmic battle with Vrtra. (MacDonell, 67–68)

Tlacolteotl *see* **Tlazolteotl.**

Tlaelquani *see* **Tlazolteotl.**

Tlaltecayohua. One of the four hundred Mayan **pulque** gods belonging to the **Centzon totochtin** complex. (Boone, 204; H. Nicholson, 168)

Tlazolteotl (also known as **Tlacolteotl, Tlaelquani,** or **Ixcuina**). In Mayan mythology, the triune goddess of pleasure, drunkenness and death. Literally, her name means "A Dirty Lady." Tlazolteotl was especially associated with uncleanliness, witchcraft, and lust. Those asking the gods for favors were often sent to Tlazolteotl to test their virtue. Those who succumbed to her intoxicating charms were killed and turned into scorpions. Penitents who confessed their sins to her priests were told they had to pierce their tongues with thorns from the maguey plant (from which **pulque** was made) to earn her forgiveness. (Alexander, 78; Anderson and Dibble, 23)

Tlilhuatzin. A Mayan **pulque** god. (Boone, 204)

Tobacco (*Nicotinana tabacum*). Tobacco belongs to the nightshade family of plants that includes **belladonna, datura, henbane** and mandrake. It is native to the Americas and was unknown to the rest of the world until Europeans discovered the continent. The word comes from the Spanish "tobacco," the name the Spanish gave to pipe in which it was smoked.

Prehistoric traces of tobacco use in South America have been traced back three thousand years. Tobacco was used by Amerindians, either by smoking, chewing, or snuffing, for its own sake and as an offering to their gods or as an enema to induce altered states of consciousness.

The main psychoactive substance in tobacco is nicotine (from the last name of Jean Nicot de Villemain, who brought it from the Americas to France in 16th century. The nicotine content in native tobaccos is much higher than in industrial cigarettes (about 0.5–2.0 %) and there are also several varieties of tobacco such as *Nicotina rustica*, that contain much greater concentrations of nicotine than others, such as *Nicotina tabacum*.

Implicit in many of the myths involving tobacco is a recognition of tobacco's addictive properties primarily due to nicotine. A common motif in tobacco origin myths is that the spirits all craved tobacco as their sacred food and that it was given to humans as a gift without their keeping enough for their own use, or was given to humans by the Great Spirit as a way to seal the bond between humans and the spirit world.

Nicotine, however, is only one of several hundred other chemical constituents in tobacco. Another important group is the harmala alkaloids, such as harman, norharman, harmine and harmaline which have known hallucinogenic effects. Indigenous cultures generally use the much more potent rustica variety of tobacco which, because of these **alkaloid** properties, can induce trance states. A **shaman** will often smoke as many as 30 cigars in ecstatic journeys to the supernatural. (Rudgley, 240–255; Schultes and Hofmann, 10, 17, 29, 63–64, 73, 79, 108, 116–117; Wilbert, 1987, xvii).

Tobacco Origin Story, Apache *see* **Coyote.**

Tobacco Origin Story, Japanese. After a mother lost her only daughter she wept over her grave for several days. One day, an unusual plant sprouted from the grave that her tears had watered. The mother tasted it but it was not good to eat. She also boiled it, roasted it and steamed it, but it was still not tasty. Meanwhile, some of the leaves dried. She put them into the end of a bamboo shoot and lighted and smoked them. The flavor was delicious and no matter how unhappy she remained, smoking the leaves comforted her. (Mayer, 238)

Tobacco Origin Story, Yaqui. According to this North American Indian legend, long ago there was a very ugly woman whom no man wanted. No longer able to stand being alone, she went to a **shaman** and asked what she could do to be liked. He offered to transform her into tobacco, and she agreed. After that everyone liked her, and she was caressed by men every time they smoked a tobacco cigarette. (Moises et al., 95)

Tobacco Origin Story, Yuchi. In this North American Indian myth, a man and a woman went into the woods where they had sexual relations and some of the man's semen fell on the ground. The two then departed. Sometime later, the woman happened by the place where they had been and noticed some unusual plants growing there. When she later saw the man she had been with, she took him to see the unusual plants and asked him what they should call them. Neither of them could come up with a name for the plants and they left. Sometime after that the woman gave birth to a son and when he was older, she took him to see the plants. The boy studied them for a while and then said he was going to name the plant "tobacco." Then he dug the plants up and took them home and replanted them. The plants smelled good and the boy decided to see what the leaves tasted like. He liked the taste and showed his people the plants and how to use them. He then saved the seeds when they were ripe and planted them. After that, the

Yuchi had tobacco whenever they wanted it. (Speck, 146–147; Swanton, 87–88)

Tobacco-spirit. In many American Indian mythologies, the spirit of tobacco.

In South American Cashinaua Indian mythology, Tobacco Spirit created mankind out of tobacco. When the ancestors of the Cashinaua took tobacco for the first time, they were transformed into game animals. However, one woman did not take any and retained her human form. Tobacco-spirit then ordered her to dry some tobacco leaves. When she did, she became pregnant and mankind was created from her pregnancy.

In Acawaio, Warao, and other South American Indian mythologies, Tobacco-spirit was an old man with the power to influence all other spirits because none of them could resist tobacco.

In North American Indian Papago mythology, Tobacco spirit was originally human. One day, he and Corn, who was also originally human, were competing with one another to see who was the best archer. The two couldn't agree and quarreled and were ostracized from their tribe for their disturbances. As they left, they kept looking back hoping that they would be called back. When no one came, they each took a piece from their hearts and planted it in a field. Years later, the Papago began to miss them and sent some men to bring them back. After searching for a long time, the search party found the plants, but neither Tobacco nor Corn would return and the searchers returned with seeds from the plants that were now growing in the field where they planted them.

In North American Pima Indian mythology, Tobacco and Corn are also rivals. This time, only Tobacco left and traveled to the west but was missed and invited back. Tobacco refused, but gave the emissaries tobacco seeds. Another Pima tobacco myth has the universal motif of the plant growing from a dead body. In this variant, a powerful **shaman's** unmarried daughter despaired of being single and asked her father to bury her. Shortly thereafter, tobacco sprouted from her grave and her father took some of its leaves and smoked them. When the people smelled the smoke, they wanted some, and now the girl who was previously ignored was wanted by all men. (Bahr et al., 87–88, 94–95; Underhill, 83; Wilbert, 1987, 153)

Tokhuah. In South American Mataco Indian mythology, the god who taught humans how to make mead. (Del Campana et al., 120–121)

Tomiauhtecutli. In Aztec mythology, a **pulque** god. (Spence, 1911, 299)

Tomi-riwe. In South American Yanomanmo Indian mythology, the ancestral spirit who gave the Yanomanmo **tobacco** seeds and showed them how to cultivate the plant. (Albert et al., 171)

Totoltecatl. In Mayan mythology, one of the four hundred **pulque** gods belonging to the **Centzon totochtin** complex. Totoltecatl was especially associated with the settlement of Tollan. (Boone, 203–4; H. Nicholson, 168)

Trickster. A cunning character, seemingly foolish and sometimes malevolent, who uses his guile to resist tyrannical forces in the world. By tricking these forces, often by stealing magical substances that belong to them and giving them to humans, he modifies the physical or social world and makes culture possible. The trickster is responsible for order coming out of disorder, wisdom arising from confusion, and life coming from death. By constantly violating social rules and challenging the status quo, the trickster initiates progress.

In many myths, the trickster is not an individual but a substance that induces intoxication which brings about change. In the Near Eastern story of **Inanna** and Enki, for example, drunkenness leads to a relaxation of social codes whose violation results in loss of power by divine powers and attainment of culture by humans. The intoxication trickster is also the agent that enables humans to overcome cultural inhibitions that stand in the way of their survival. In the Bible, for example, Lot's daughters get him drunk to overcome the incest taboo whose observance would mean the end of mankind. (Radin, 1972, 1ff; Worthen, 11–12, 49 64, 67, 82, 86)

Trita *see* **Thrita.**

Tsango (or Tsangu). In South American Jibaro Indian mythology, the male spirit of **tobacco** who enabled **shamans** to communicate with the Supernaturals. (Karsten, 1926, 323; Naranjo, 132)

Tsukit Ukut *see* **Hukaht.**

Tu K'ang. In Chinese mythology, the god who invented **wine.** (Werner, 526)

Tultecatl. In Mayan mythology, a **pulque** god. (Bancroft, 3:418)

Tupa. In Polynesian Island Marquesas mythology, the god from whose body **kava** originated.

Tupa died in heaven, and his body fell to earth and was eaten by a mortal named Kaukau who subsequently died. The kava plant grew from his grave. (Craig, 301)

Tvastr. In Indian mythology, the god who created the world. He was also a great craftsman, the counterpart of the Greek Hephaistos and Roman Vulcan, who gave **Indra** his thunderbolt, and the gods the bowl from which they drank **soma**. Indra is said to have either stolen soma from Tvastr's house (i.e. the earth) or found it on his mother's (i.e. Earth's) breasts (i.e. in the mountains), and drank it.

Tvastr and Indra sometimes quarreled. On one occasion, Tvastr's son, Visvarupa, a being with three heads, called the soma-drinker, the wine-drinker, and the food eater, was overheard to say that the demon **Asuras** should be allowed to share in the sacrifices made to the **Deva** gods. When Indra was told what he had said, he became alarmed that if the Asuras were allowed to have a portion of the sacrifices, they might become so powerful they would overthrow Indra and the other Deva gods. To keep that from happening, Indra cut off each of Visvarupa's heads with his thunderbolt. When Tvastr learned that Indra had killed his son he became enraged and in his next soma offering to the gods he didn't invite Indra. Seeing the sight, Indra grabbed the soma vessel and drank from it. Tvastra was able to grab the vessel back and cursed Indra. However, he didn't emphasize the right words when he uttered the curse and before he could kill Indra, Indra killed him instead. (Brown, 86; MacCulloch, 31, 117–119; Nagar, 2:48–49)

Tzocaca. In Mayan mythology, one of the four hundred **pulque** gods of the **Centzon Totochtin** complex. (H. Nicholson, 168)

Ua-ogrere. In Papua New Guinea mythology, the first woman in the world and the one who showed her descendents, the Masingle, how to make a drink from the **kava** plant.

A long time ago, Ua-ogrere killed a kangaroo and then roasted it on a fire to singe away its hair. But the kangaroo wasn't dead yet, and when it cried out, Ua-ogrere became frightened and threw its body away. The kangaroo subsequently died and worms that had been in its body emerged as the Masingle people, while a kava plant grew from the region of the kangaroo's navel. Ua-ogrere then showed the Masingle how to make a special drink from the plant.

A variant of this myth begins with the semen from a male kangaroo dropping on the earth while it was playing. The semen quickly dried in the hot sun and from its dried remains, a boy and a kava plant appeared. Sometime later, the kangaroo appeared to the boy in a dream and showed him how to grow and make a drink out of the kava plant. The boy then told his people, the Masingle, what he had learned. (Lebot et al., 124)

Ukat (or **Hukaht**). In North American Yokut Indian mythology, the god of **datura**. (Hudson and Underhay, 57)

Uncle. In Central American Indian Tarahumare mythology, the spiritual force of peyote. Uncle sang in the fields to enable the Tarahumare to find **peyote**. (Bonnefoy, 1186; Petrullo, 17)

Une. In Polynesian Marquesan mythology, a goddess who gave birth to the **kava** plant. (Craig, 17)

Vac (or Vak). See **Sarasvati**.

Vahiyinin *see* **Great Raven.**

Vai-mahse. In South American Desana Indian mythology, the Master of Animals who watched over animals. One of his daughters owned the **yage** (*Banisteriopsis caapi*) plant and another owned the **coca** plant. While each of the girls was separately in pain from childbirth, an old woman took each of their hands to comfort them, but the girls twisted so hard, they broke one of her fingers off in the old woman's hand. She kept the fingers in her house. One day a young man stole the fingers from the old woman's house and planted them; the yage plant sprouted from one of the fingers and the coca plant from the other. (Reichel-Dolmatoff, 1971, 36–37)

Vak *see* **Sarasvati.**

Valhalla. In Norse mythology, **Odin's** home where the einherjar, the great warriors who were killed on the battlefield, were taken by the Valkyries. In Valhalla, the einjerjar spent their days practicing their fighting skills so that when Ragnarok, the end of the world came, they would fight skillfully alongside the gods against the giants. At the end of each day's fighting, the dead were revived and all the warriors spent their evenings feasting and drinking endless gallons of **mead** from the teats of the goat **Heidrun** who lived on Valhalla's roof. (Fee and Leeming, 23–24)

Vanir. In Norse mythology, agricultural earth deities who after constantly warring with the **Aesir** sky gods reconciled with them and sealed their truce by spitting into a **cauldron** that created **Kvasir**, the wisest being in the world.

The Vanir were lustful and intoxicating forces, who represented the triumph of fertility over the frigidity of the giants who represented winter, mountains, and death. (DuBois, 54–55; Fee and Leeming, 16–18, 4–47)

Varuni *see* **Mada.**

Vash *see* **Sarasvati.**

Viho-mahse. In South American Desana mythology, the divine personification of the hallucinogenic snuff, "viho" (*Piptadenia*), who lived in the Milky Way. Viho powder originally belonged to Father Sun who kept it in his navel. One day after he engaged in incest with his daughter it fell to earth from his navel where he had hidden it (or alternatively from his semen which fell to earth). Father Sun then created Viho-mahse, "snuff person," gave him the power of good and evil, and put his spirit into the snuff plant so that when **shamans** went into a trance, they could contact Viho-mahse, and through his help, they could contact the other Supernaturals. (Reichel-Dolmatoff, 1971, 27–28, 77)

Vishnu. In Indian mythology, one of the three gods in the Hindu pantheon (the other two are **Brahma** and **Siva**). Vishnu is concerned with maintaining harmony and balance in the universe. His wife is Lakshmi, the goddess of success and failure. Vishnu wears a garland of flowers around his throat, representing the five senses. He has four arms, representing the four stages of life, and wears a dazzling jewel on his chest, representing the consciousness embedded in the heart.

Since Vishnu is concerned with preserving order in the universe, he often appeared with many Avatars, among them Mohini, a beautiful girl who distracted the demon **Asuras** when they were fighting with the **Deva** gods to see who would get the **amrta** after it had been released during the **Churning of the Ocean.** (Walker, B., 2: 574–576)

Visvakarma. In Hindu mythology, a **trickster** who made humans immortal for a time until drunkenness caused him to reveal what he had done, and death returned to the world.

Visvakarma was a skilled, aging carpenter. Fretting about his eventual end, he decided to do something to prevent it, so he carved a cave in a large tree and a door that blended so well with the rest of the tree that the hollow inside could not be detected when the door was closed. One day, Death came for Visvakarma as expected. Visvakarma told Death about the cave he had carved into a tree and Death said he would like to see it. When Death stepped inside, Visvakarama slammed the door shut; once the door was closed, Death was imprisoned inside the tree.

Sometime later, Death's relatives went to Bhagwan, the Almighty, and told him Death had disappeared. Bhagwan went looking for him, but eventually gave up and returned to his home. Death's relatives, however, continued grieving over his disappearance and complained to Bhagwan that humans were committing crimes because they were becoming desperate from the overcrowding that had occurred following Death's disappearance.

Baffled, Bhagwan decided he had to find some other way of finding Death. For his new plan, he boiled some Mahua flowers in a pot and created an intoxicating drink. Then he went to earth and offered it to everyone he could find. When Visvakarma heard about the drink, he asked for some too. Like everyone else who drank the intoxicating brew, he began talking without thinking, and began bragging about his cave, and Bhagwan asked to see it. As soon as Visavakarma opened the door to show him the cave, Death escaped; as he did, he took Visvakarma off to the land of the dead. Before he went back to his home, Bhagwan taught people how to prepare his special drink that would enable them to prepare for death better. (Beck et al., 283–285)

Voden See Odin.

Votan *see* **Odin.**

Wanade. In South American Indian mythology, the creator god who brought everything into existence by thinking it while smoking **tobacco**.

Wanade visited earth many times after he created it. On one of those visits, he created Odosha as an incarnation of earthly evil, including death. He subsequently regretted what he had done and returned to earth to undermine Odosha by showing him that he was only an illusion. To do this, he smoked some tobacco and dreamed his own mother, fully grown, into existence. Then he immediately dreamt of her death, demonstrating that Odosha's power was illusory. (Guss, 55)

Wapaq. In Siberian Koryak mythology, the spirits in the **fly agaric mushroom** that empowered **Great Raven** and enabled him to lift a heavy bag containing the food Whale needed to sustain himself on his long journey. (Furst, 1976, 89)

Wenebojo. In North American Indian Chippewa mythology, the spirit who gave the Chippewa **tobacco**. (Barnouw, 77)

White Buffalo Woman *see* **Wohpe.**

Wine. A large class of alcoholic drinks made by fermentation. Although most wines are made by fermentation of grapes, any fruits can be fermented. Although wines were once distinguished from **beer** in that wine was made from fruit and beer from grain, barley-wines and rice-wines (e.g., sake) blur this distinction. Viticulture, the growing of grapes for wine, was regarded as the symbol of civilization because vineyards required many years of tending, which required remaining in one place.

Wine figures prominently in many world mythologies. In the **Gilgamesh** epic, dating from about the second millennium B.C., but undoubtedly much older, Gilgamesh's friend Enkidu becomes "civilized" after drinking wine. In the Bible, **Noah** is credited with being the first viticulturist and the first drunkard. In Greek mythology, **Dionysus** is the god of wine. Wine is also a prominent symbol in Christianity. (Unwin, 1–165; Younger, 1ff)

Wirikuta. In Central American Huichol mythology, the desert area in northern Mexico where the mythical past and the ancestral gods, including **Peyote**, originated. (Furst, 1976, 113–119)

Wodan *see* **Odin.**

Woden *see* **Odin.**

Wohpe. Also known as White Buffalo Woman. In North American Dakota Indian mythology, a shape-changing woman who introduced the Dakota to **tobacco** and showed them how to smoke it.

One day, while two Dakota men were searching for food, they saw a naked woman coming toward them who had such long hair it covered her body like a robe. One of the men was filled with lust for her, but when he tried to grasp her, a bolt of lighting struck him and he burned to death. The woman then turned to the other man and told him she was Wohpe, the White Buffalo Woman, and that if he did as she told him, he would be able to get any woman he wanted for his wife, but if he disobeyed, he too would be destroyed. Then she told him to return to his camp and prepare a feast for her and said she would reappear. After all the preparations were done, she appeared and told the Dakota that she would serve them always, and that since they had first seen her as smoke, they would always see her as smoke. Then she took a pipe she was carrying and filled it with tobacco and showed them how to smoke it, and to offer prayers with it. (DeMallie and Jahner, 109–112; Leeming and Page, 36–37)

Woot. In African Kuba mythology, a culture hero who caused the separation of animals and humans after some animals drank his **wine** and smoked his **tobacco**, and whose own drunkenness resulted in establishing matrilinear inheritance of kingship.

Woot had sexual relations with his sister, Mweel. When the incest was discovered, Woot ran away, but Mweel didn't want him to leave and sent some men to bring him back. When they weren't able to find him, she sent a dog, a fly and a turtle to search for him. The animals found Woot hiding in a cave, but when they told him Mweel wanted him to come back, Woot wouldn't listen, and left them in his cave. While he was gone, the animals began looking inside Woot's cave. The dog discovered some meat and ate it, the fly found a pot of palm wine and drank it, and the turtle found a pipe full of tobacco and smoked it. The next day, when Woot returned and saw that the animals had stolen his food and drink, he took away their power of speech and sent them back home.

In another myth, Woot, like **Noah**, became drunk on palm wine, fell asleep, and was discovered lying naked by his sons, who mocked him. When they told their sister about what they had seen, she approached Noah with her back turned and covered him. When Woot woke up and was told what had happened, he disinherited his sons in favor of his daughter, so that from then on, only her sons would inherit kingship. (De Heusch, 1982, 112–115; Josephsson, 4)

Wotan *see* **Odin.**

Wuotan *see* **Odin.**

Xochitl. In Aztec mythology, the goddess of **pulque** before **Mayahuel.**

Xochitl, who was also the goddess of early sexuality, prostitutes, embroiderers, and flower arrangers, accidentally discovered the honey-like sap in the maguey and against her father's wishes, took some to the king of Tula, who became drunk from drinking it, and raped Xochitl. After that, young people were forbidden to drink pulque and could be put to death for violating the restriction while older people were allowed to drink it provided they did not become drunk. (Vaillant, 109)

Xolotl. In Aztec mythology, the messenger of the gods who nurtured the first humans on **pulque**.

In the Aztec creation myth, the mother goddess, Citlalcue, gave birth to a flint knife. When her sons saw it, they became fearful that it might be used to harm them and they threw the knife to earth. When it landed, 1600 gods came into existence. These new gods felt alone and sent a messenger to ask their mother to empower them to create humans so that they would have servants. Citalcue agreed and told them to send someone to the realm of Mictlanteuctli, the God of Hell, and steal a bone from the dead, and when he returned to earth, they were to sprinkle some of their own blood over the bone.

When Xolotl, who was chosen for the quest, returned, he put the pieces of bone that he had stolen into a basin and all the gods sprinkled some of their blood into the pot as directed. Four days later, something inside the pot began to stir, and a boy appeared. The gods took him out and then sprinkled some more of their blood into the pot. Four days later, a girl appeared. The gods entrusted the children to Xolotl to bring up, and he nurtured them on the milk of the maguey, i.e., pulque. The two pulque-fed children grew to adulthood, and from their pulque-fed bodies all the people of the present world were created. (Bancroft, 3:59)

Xowalaci. In North American Joshua Indian mythology, a deity known as "the Giver" who created land out of **tobacco** smoke.

In the beginning there was only sky, fog, and water. The water was still and a sweat lodge rested on it in which Xowalaci and a companion lived and smoked tobacco. One day they saw something approaching in the distance. The strange object was land, which continued to come nearer until it bumped into their lodge and stretched out from there to the north and south. Xowalaci went out and blew tobacco smoke over the land and it became motionless and trees and grass began to grow on it. Then Xowalaci made people and houses and animals to live on the land. (Farrand and Frachenberg, 224–225; Gill and Sullivan, 351)

Yage *see* **Ayahuasca.**

Yage (or **Yaje**) **Woman.** In South American Tukano Indian mythology, the first woman whose first child was Yage.

Yage woman was impregnated by the Sun through her eye and gave birth to a child who became the Yage plant *(Baniseriopsis Caapi)*. When the child was born, he radiated brilliant yellow and red flashes of light (like those experienced by its users). After she cut the child's umbilical cord, she rubbed the Yage-child with **magic** plants and shaped its body. Although she was its mother, Yage woman didn't know who the father was; when she asked who he might be, all the men fought each other claiming fatherhood. Unable to settle the dispute, the men turned on the child and ripped him apart, each taking a piece. Then they went their own separate ways, planted the pieces, and each of the people of the Amazon then had his own yage which differed slightly from everyone else's. (Reichel-Dolmatoff, 1971, 37)

Yama. In Persian mythology, the first man to make **haoma**. (Herzfeld, 544)

Yaqui Indians, Tobacco Origin *see* **Tobacco Origin Story, Yaqui.**

Yasi. In South American Siriono Indian mythology, the Moon god who transformed animals into their present shapes as a result of their drunkenness.

One day while the animals were carousing at a drinking festival, Jaguar killed Yasi's child. Enraged, Yasi twisted the necks of the drunken animals into their present shapes. (Sullivan, 197–198)

Yaya. In Caribbean Taino mythology, the Creator sky god from whose spittle cahoba was created.

When Yaya's grandsons broke a gourd containing Yaya's fish, he became enraged and spat at him. The spittle turned to cahoba which the shamans subsequently used to visit the spirit world. (Stevens-Arroyo, 117–118)

Yggdrasil. In Norse mythology, the World Tree that passed through Midgard, the realm of mankind, and bridged the realms of good and evil. Made of ash, at the center of the world, the "axis mundi," its sap was transformed into a wisdom-conferring **mead** tree. **Odin** hanged himself on Yggdrasil and then was reborn as a way of gaining knowledge and wisdom through self sacrifice.

The tree had three roots, each of which penetrated to a well located in a different part of the world. One of those roots extended into the home of the gods in the heavens, one to the home of the frost giants, and one to the Underworld, and each root was watered by a sacred fountain.

The fountain in the Heavens where **Asgard**, the realm of the gods was located, was called Urd. This is where the Norns or Fates and the gods had their judgment-seats.

The second root extended into Jotunnheim, the realm of the frost giants, and was nourished by a well filled with mead. This mead was so charged with wisdom that Odin traded one of his eyes for a single drink from it.

The third root was watered by a frightful dragon who constantly nibbled on its root while a squirrel ran up and down the trunk trying to stir up enmity between the dragon and an eagle who perched at its top.

Some of Yggdrasil's branches hung over **Valhalla**, the banquet hall in Asgard where the brave warriors that fell in battle dined. The sap rising through Yggdrasil's trunk entered its leaves and were eaten by Odin's goat, **Heidrun**, in whose body it fermented into an endless amount of mead instead of milk from her teats.

Yggdrasil also produced a morning dew which fell to Midgard, where it was captured by flowers. Bees extracted it from flowers and produced the honey which humans transformed into mead. (Davidson, 195; Kelly, 140–141; Lindow, 319–322; Metzner, 192)

Yi *see* **Chang'o.**

Yopo. A potent hallucinogenic snuff made from beans of the Anadenanthera peregrina tree. In the West Indies, it is called Cohoba; in Guyana, **Epena.**

The Anadenanthera peregrine tree grows as high as 65 feet with a diameter of 2 feet. Three to 10 glossy black round seeds from which the snuff is made develop in each of its woody pods.

The primary hallucinogenic ingredient is Dimethyl-tryptamine (DMT). (Rudgley, 12–14; Schultes and Hofmann, 27, 30, 35, 65–66, 116–119)

Yopo Woman. In South American Cuiva Indian mythology, the woman from whose body **yopo** originated.

While a man was away hunting, his son-in-law and the man's wife stayed behind. Alone together, the son-in-law asked his mother-in-law why her husband was drunk nearly all the time. The woman said she was too bashful to tell him. The son-in-law eventually seduced his mother-in-law, who confessed to him that her vagina was yopo, and that her husband was drunk so often because he made love to her for a long time. The son-in-law then had sexual relations with his mother-in-law but she warned him to make love to her briefly so as not to become very drunk. The son-in-law, however, didn't listen and when the father-in-law returned he saw his wife and son-in-law together. The husband beat his wife so hard her body was transformed into yopo beans which he then threw out of his house. The next day the forest was filled with yopo trees that sprouted from those beans. (Arcand et al., 110)

Ytopul. A Mayan **pulque** god. (Boone, 68)

Yuchi Indians, Tobacco Origin *see* **Tobacco Origin Story, Yuchi.**

Yupa. In South American Yupa Indian folklore, the culture hero who gave the Yupa **tobacco**.

One day while hunting, Yupa encountered the son of the Sun who invited him to his father's house where he offered him some tobacco juice to drink. Yupa, however, declined because he thought Sun might have mistaken him for a deer and would want to kill and eat him. Meanwhile, **Moon**, who had seen what was happening, came to Sun's house and assured Sun that Yupa wasn't a deer. Moon then brought Yupa to his own house, fed him, and gave him some tobacco seeds to take back with him, telling him that while he and Sun ate and drank tobacco, Yupa and his people were to smoke it. Yupa then returned home and planted the seeds and after that, the Yupa had tobacco. (Wilbert, 1974, 45–46)

Zagreus. In Greek mythology, the first incarnation of **Dionysus**.

Before he met **Semele**, Zeus fell in love with **Persephone** who was being hidden in a cave by his mother, **Demeter**, to protect her from the advances of gods like him. Nevertheless, Zeus saw her, and disguising himself as a snake, entered her cave and impregnated her. Zeus wanted to make his son, named Zagreus, his heir, but **Hera**, his wife, was outraged at being betrayed, and plotted to kill Zagreus. But before she could carry out her plan, Zeus brought Zagreus to some nymphs who hid him in the forests of Parnassus. Hera was not deterred, however, and eventually discovered where Zeus had hidden him and persuaded the Titans to kill him. Just as the Titans were about to attack him, Zagreus transformed himself into a bull. But the Titans still were able to subdue him, and they killed and tore Dionysus to pieces, and began to eat his bodily parts. When his grandmother Rhea (or in some versions, Athene) saw what was happening, she immediately came to see if she could save Zagreus. All that was left of him were some scattered parts of his body, one of which was his heart which was still beating. Rhea managed to snatch it away and brought it to Zeus who swallowed and regenerated Dionysus in three different mythical traditions. In the more common tradition, Zeus placed Dionysus in Semele's body when he impregnated her. In the other tradition, associated with the **mystery religion** at **Eleusis**, Zagreus was reincarnated as **Iacchus**, who led the procession of those being initiated in the mystery religion.

In the third tradition, Zeus buried Zagreus' remains in the sacred omphalos at **Delphi**. The omphalos was both a tomb and a temple, in the shape of a beehive. From here, Zagreus was resurrected as the god of fertility. Zagreus' internment in a beehive-shaped coffin was subsequently adopted by devotees who had themselves buried in beehive-shaped tombs in the hope of achieving rebirth.

The sacred character attributed to the beehive stemmed from the intoxicating **mead** drink, made by fermenting honey in water, which was first associated with Dionysus before mead was replaced by **wine** as Greece's favorite alcoholic drink. (Grimal, 466; Zafiropulo, 40)

Zame y Mebege. In Gabon, Africa, mythology, the Creator who gave the Bwiti, **iboga**.

When Zame y Mebege saw the Pygmy, Bitumu, in a tree gathering fruit, he caused him to fall and had his body brought to him. Zame then cut off the Pygmy's little fingers and little toes and planted them in various parts of the forest where they sprouted into iboga bushes.

When Bitumu didn't return, his wife married Bitumu's brother, in accord with levirate law, but she continued searching for him until one day, she found some bones in a stream in the forest she thought might be the remains of her husband. Before taking their bath, she washed the bones and left them to dry. When Bitumu's wife returned, an animal had taken the bones, and the women headed back to her village but lost her way. As she wandered through the forest, a man chasing some animals ran by and then suddenly disappeared. She followed in that direction and soon found a cave. When she went inside, she saw the missing bones, and then heard a voice that sounded like her husband's, asking who she was and what she wanted. When she answered, the voice told her to look to her left. When she did, she saw an iboga plant. The voice told her to dig it up and eat its roots. Then the voice told her to look to her right where she saw a mushroom and the voice told her to eat it, too. Then the voice told her to look back to the entrance of the cave. When she did, a fly flew into her eyes and made her tears flow so hard that she wasn't able to see. Then the voice told her to turn around again. When she turned back, her husband and other dead relatives were standing where the bones had been and they told her that the iboga plant that she had found would enable her people to see and communicate with the dead, and that from then on, her name would be Disomba.

When Disomba came back to her village with the iboga, her new husband killed her for leaving, and she was then reunited with her first husband. (Dorson, 1972, 353–354; Fernandez, 1972, 245; Furst, 1976, 41)

Appendix 1

Subject Categories

ARCHETYPAL MYTHS

Churning of the Ocean
Destruction of Mankind

Girl That Nobody Loved

CULTIC PLACES, RITES AND PARTICIPANTS

Aventine Hill
Bacchae
Bacchanalia
Bacchantes
Bakkhai

Delphi
Dionysia
Eleusis
Eleutherai
Liberia festival

Maenads
P'eng-Lai
Wirikuta

CULTURE HEROES AND TRICKSTERS

Animal

Coyote
Fum Mbombo
Great Raven
Kachui
Rabbit
Raven
Vahiyinin

Human

Alofi
Amphictyon
Apikunni
Aseni

Bandzioku
Bege
Beleke Belei
Bonde Ilonga
Bran
Bunyi
Cashinaua
Coca Mama
Cohiba
Cyavana
Daspajka
Deucalion
Doini-Botte
Du Kang
Duraosha

Eurypylos
Ewa
Frashmi
Gadaba Brothers
Gama Sennin
Gilgamesh
Gobind Singh
Hashoriwe
Haydar
Icarius
Kachra-Durwa
Kane-Timme
Kani
Kava-on-a
Kebo-Akbo

Kezer-Tshingis-
Kaira-Khan
Kinkajou
Komatari
Konda
Kuripowe
Lita
Majahuagy
Ma'nabush
Nirantali
Noah

Nosiriwe
No Vitals
Okabewis
Orestheus
Pamuri-mahse
Parvati
Pava
Pemenerru
Peyote Woman
Soonjalhai
Star Boy

Suasamiavaava
Sundimari Deota
Tallur Muttai
Tomi-riwe
Ua-ogrere
Visvakarma
Woot
Yage/Yaje Woman
Yama
Yopo Woman
Yupa

CUP BEARERS

Catamitus
Ganymede

Goibineau
Hebe

Rbhus

GODS, GODDESSES AND SUPERNATURAL POWERS DIRECTLY ASSOCIATED WITH INTOXICANTS

Acan
Acetes
Acolhua
Aegir
Aesir
Aethra
Agathos Daimon
Agni
Ahura Mazda
Aic-Ahau Quiche
Aittah Slahsa
Aittah Tavakai
Aitvaras
Alonkok
Alwiss
Amasanga
Amphictyonis
A'neglakya

Anura
Aphrodite
Aristaeus
Arutama
Asuras
Asvins
Atlacoaya
Ava'ali'i
Awa-iku
Awe-n-ha'i
Bacchus
Baitogogo
Balams
Baldev
Ba-Maguje
Bar Allei Toyon
Baruni
Baugi

Bes
Beyla
Bhanganath
Bhimo Raja
Bol
Bona Dea
Boram Burha
Braciaca
Bragi
Buffalo Spirit
Byggvir
Byrgir
Cannibal Woman
Caterpillar
Centzon Totochtin
Ceres
Ceridwen
Chandu

Chang'o
Cherri-choulang
Chi
Chimalpanecatl
Chiu Hsien
Chu'ang Mu
Chuckit
Cihuacoatl
Coadidop
Colhuatzincatl
Comus
Corn Goddess
Dagda
Deagahgweoses
Deer Person
Demeter
Devas
Dionysus
Donar
Dumuzi
Dusares
Earthmaker
Earth Mother
Elder Brother
Elder Sister
Enki
Fates
Fauna
Fjalar
Four Hundred Rab-
    bits
Four Manido
Galar
Gandharas
Garuda
Geirhild
Geshtinanna
Gitche Manitou
Goibniu
Grandfather

Tobacco
Great Spirit
Gymir
Hathor
Hikori
Hinon
Hiro
Hler
Ho
Ho Hsien Ku
Hsi Wang Mu
Huitaca
Hukaht
Hyas
Iacchus
Ilako
Inanna
Indra
Ino
I-ti
Ivaldi
Ixcuina
Izquitecatl
Jupiter
Jurupari
Kanabos
Kanaloa
Kane
Kauyumari
Khunu
Kieri Taweakame
Kiri
Kitanemuk
Kittung
Kitzihiat
Kurusiwari
Kvasir
Kyomba
Lado
Latis

Lea
Lefanoga
Lele'asapai
Liber
Liberia
Lizard
Lo'au
Lollus
Lu tung-pin
Luxus
Macuilotchtli
Mada
Madain
Maeve
Magyasszony
Mahadeo
Mahalakshmi
Mahaprabhu
Makiritare
Ma-ku
Mama Coca
Mana
Mani
Manitou
Manoc Capac
Manqet
Maui
Mawari
Mayahuel
Meadhbh
Meav
Medb
Meng Po
Methe
Mimir
Min Kyawzwa
Miru
Mohsek eis
Moirai
Momoy

Morpheus

Mother Peyote

Mukat

Mwatiktiki

Nakwone

Namona

Namuci

Nanga Baiga

Nan-capue

Nanibozo

Nawat

Ninkasi

Ninurta

Nisaba

Numli-nyou

Nungui

Obatala

Odin

Oeneus

Oeno

Oenotrohoi

Oilikukahaena

Oineus

Oinos

Okuninushi

Ololiuqui

Omacatl

Ome Tochtli

Orpheus

Oseema

Osiris

Osmo's Daughter

Osmotar

Pa-gestin-dug

Pamashiut

Pamuri-gahsiru

Pan

Pandual

Papaztec

Pap-iea

Patecatl

Peyak noin

Phan Ningsan

Piskisum

Pu'a

Pufafine

Pulekukewerek

Pulque Gods

Puopie

Pythia

Quatlapanqui

Queen Mother of
   the West

Quetzacoatl

Ruksey

Sabazius

Samael

Sarasvati

Saura

Seme-peyaru-pora

Shesmu

Shiva

Shojo

Sibia-pora

Siduri

Sing Bonga

Sirius

Siuuhu

Siva

Skeleton Man

Sky Father

Soma

Somnus

Spenta Armaiti

Staphylus

Sun Father

Sura

Sureswari

Susano

Susa-no-ono

Suttung

Svantovit

Tafa'i

Tagaloa

Tahuehuiakame

Tantalus

Tatewari

Tenemet

Tepoztecatl

Tereteth

Tezcatlipoca

Thor

Thrita

Tlacolteotl

Tlaelquani

Tlalecayohua

Tlazolteotl

Tlilhuatzin

Tobacco Spirit

Tomiauhtecutli

Totoltecatl

Trita

Tsango

Tsukit

Tu K'ang

Tultecatl

Tupa

Tvastr

Tzocaca

Ukat

Uncle

Une

Vac

Vai-mahse

Vanir

Varuni

Viho-mahse

Voden

Votan

Wanade

Wapaq
Wenebojo White
Buffalo Woman
Wodan
Woden
Wohpe

Wotan
Wuotan
Xochitl
Xolotl
Xowalaci
Yasi

Yauhtecatl
Yaya
Yi
Ytopul
Zagreus
Zame y Mebege

GODS, MORTALS, ANIMALS, AND PLACES INDIRECTLY RELATED TO INTOXICATION THEME

Admetus
Adonis
Adrastia
Aegeus
Afagddu
Agave
Alrek
Amalthea
Amethyst
Ampelos
Ariadne
Ask
Atropos
Aturarodo
Aura
Autonoe
Avagdu
Berserks
Bragafull
Brahma

Butoriku
Cachui
Callirrhoe
Centaur
Charops
Chyavana
Cronos
Cusna
Drunkard Boy
Einherjar
Embla
Erigone
False Faces
Hera
Hero Twins
Hou Ki
Hrungnir
Hymir
Ino
John Barleycorn

Lycurgus
Madira
Maeldun
Makali'i
Minyas's Daughters
Morfran
Myrrha
Oedipus
Oenopion
Orion
Pentheus
Persephone
Priapus
Ramma and Bimma
Semele
Silenus
Sukracarya
Taliesin

INTOXICANTS

Amanita muscaria
Ambrosia
Amrta
Awa
Ayahuasca

Balche
Belladonna
Brew of Inspiration
Caapi
Cannabis

Chicha
Coca
Cohoba
Datura
Deadly Nightshade

Epena
Ergot
Fly Agaric
Haoma
Hashish
Henbane
Hoasca
Iboga
Kava
Marijuana

Mead
Mead of Inspiration
    /Poetry
Morning Glory
Nectar
Ololiuqui
Opium
Peaches of Immor-
    tality
Peyote

Psilocybin
Pulque
Saguaro
Soma
Tobacco
Wine
Yage
Yopo

MAGICAL CONTAINERS

Amen
Cauldron of Bran
Cauldron of Cerid-
    wen
Cauldron of
    Daghda
Cauldron of Rebirth

Cauldron of Wis-
    dom and Inspira-
    tion
Celestial Wine
Heidrun
Holy Grail
Mimir's Well

Odherir
Odhroerir
Odraerir
Odrorir
Othrorir

MYTHICAL PLACES ASSOCIATED WITH SUPERNATURAL POWERS

Asgard
Mt. Hara

Mt. Olympus
Samudra

Valhalla
Yggdrasil

SHAMANIC ANIMAL MESSENGERS AND INTERMEDIARIES

Dagul'ku
Eagle

Hummingbird
Im-dugud

Intshanga
Kadru

TERMS, CONCEPTS AND SYMBOLS

Alcohol
Alkaloid
Allegory

Altered State of
    Consciousness
Ambrosia Cycle

Animal Tales
Archetype
Cauldron

Culture Hero
Divine Banquet
Divine Smiths
Ecstasy
Eleusian Mysteries
Elixir
Entheogen
Enthusiasm
Ephiphany
Forbidden Fruit

Hallucinogen
Hierophant
Magic/Magical
Moon
Mystery Religion
Myth
Mythology
Narcotic
Neurotransmitter
Norse

Psychopomp
Ritual/Rite
Sacrifice
Salvation
Satyrs
Set
Setting
Shaman
Trickster

TRIBAL AND NATIONAL ORIGIN STORIES
NOT INCLUDED ELSEWHERE

Apache
Arawak
Hitchiti

Japan
Pentecost Polynesia
Pima

Tana
Yaqui
Yuchi

Appendix 2

Geography of Mythologies

AFRICA

Gabon

Zame y Mebege

Hausa (Nigeria)

Ba-Maguje

Kuba

Bunyi
Woot

Luba

Fum Mbombo

Pygmy

Alonkok
Bandzioku
Beleke

Yoruba

Obatala
Uganda

ASIA

Burma

Min Kyawzwa

China

Celestial Wine
Chang'o
Chiu Hsien
Chu'ang Mu
Du Kang
Ho Hsien Ku
Hsi Wang Mu
I-ti
Lu tung-pin
Ma-ku

Meng Po
Peaches of Immor-
    tality
Queen Mother of
    the West
Yi

Himalaya

Numli-nyou

Hindu

Agni
Amrta
Asuras

Asvins
Baldev
Baruni
Brahma
Churning of the
    Ocean
Devas
Dharma
Gandharas
Garuda
Indra
Kadru
Mada
Madain
Mohini

Nagas
Pavarti
Rahu
Rhbus
Sarasvati
Siva
Soma
Sukanya
Sura
Trisiras
Tvastr
Vasuki
Vinata
Vishnu

India

Bhimo Raja
Boram Burha
Cadhyanc
Chandu
Cusna
Cyavana
Daspajka

Doini-Botte
Gadaba Brothers
Girl Nobody Loved
Kachra-Durwa
Kane-Timme
Kani
Kebo-Akbo
Kittung
Lita
Mahadeo
Mahalakshmi
Mahaprabhu
Mahua tree
Namuci
Nanga Baiga
Nirantali
Pandual
Parvati
Phan Ningsan
Piskisum
Rama
Samudra
Sing Bonga
Sukracarya

Sundimari Deota
Tallur Muttai
Vac
Varuna
Visvakarma
Vrtra

Japan

Drunkard Boy
Okuninushi
Shojo
Susa-no-no

Siberia

Bar Allei Toyon
Great Raven
Kezer-Tshingis-
   Kaira-Khan
Vahiyinin

Sikh

Bhanganath

CARRIBEAN

Arawak

Anura
Komatari

Haiti

Cohiba
Tabaca

Taino

Yaya

CENTRAL AMERICA

Aztec
Camaxtli
Cihuacoatl
God K
Lizard
Matlacihuatl

Mayahuel
Quetzacoatl
Tezcatlipoca
Tomiauhtecutli
Xochitl
Xolotl

Huichol

Deer Person
Elder Sister
Hikori
Kauyumari

Kieri Taweakame
Mother Peyote
Peyote
Tahuehuiakame
Tatewari
Wirikuta

Lacandon

Bol

Mayan

Acan
Acolhua
Aic-Ahau Quiche
Atlacoaya

Balams
Bolon Dzacab
Centzon Totochtin
Chimalpanecatl
Colhuatzincatl
Cuatapanqui
Cuextecatl
Four Hundred Rabbits
Ixcuina
Ixtlilton
Izquitecatl
Macuiltochtli
Macuilxochitl
Majajiagy
Omacatl

Ome Tochtli
Papaztec
Patecatl
Quatlapanqui
Siguamonta
Techalotl
Tepoztecatl
Tlaltecayohua
Tlazolteotl
Tlilhuatzin
Tzocaca
Yauhtecatl
Ytopul

Tarahumare

Uncle

EUROPE

Celtic and Welsh

Afagddu
Brew of Inspiration
Cauldron of Bran
Ceridwen
Gwion Bach

Christianity

Forbidden Fruit
Holy Grail
Talesin

Etruscan

Fulfluns

Finland

Osmo

Gaul

Bel

Germany

Lollus

Greece

Acetes
Admetus
Agathos daimon
Agave
Alphesiboe
Amalthea
Ambrosia
Amethyst
Ampelos
Amphictyon
Amphictyonis
Aphrodite

Ariadne
Aristaeus
Atropos
Aura
Autonoe
Bacchae
Bacchanalia
Bacchants
Bacchus
Bakkhai
Bakkhos
Butes
Calirrhoe
Centaur
Chariodotes
Charops
Cicones
Corybantes
Cronos
Delphi
Demeter

Dendrites
Deucalion
Dionysus
Elais
Eleusian Mysteries
Eleusis
Eleutherai
Erigone
Eurypylos
Fates
Ganymede
Hades
Hebe
Hera
Hypnos
Iacchus
Icarius
Ichor
Ino
Lycurgus
Maenads
Maron
Methe
Minyas's Daughters
Moirai
Morpheus
Myrrha
Nectar
Oedipus
Oeneus
Oeno
Oenopion
Oenotrus
Oinotrophoi
Orestheus
Orion
Pan
Pentheus
Persephone
Polymnus

Priapus
Pythia
Rhea
Satyr
Semele
Silenus
Staphylus
Tantalus
Thrita
Thyoneus
Thyrus
Titans
Triton
Zagreus

Ireland

Amen
Cauldron of Bran
Cauldron of
    Daghdha
Cluricaun
Dagda
Latis
Maeldun
Medb

Lithuania

Aitvaras
Ragutiene
Ragutis

*Scandinavia
(Norse)*

Aegir
Aesir
Alwiss
Asgard
Ask
Baugi

Berserks
Beyla
Bodn
Bolverk
Bragafull
Bragi
Byggvir
Byrgir
Donar/Thor
Einherjar
Fjalar
Freyja
Geirhild
Heidrun
Hrungnir
Hymir
Ivaldi
Kvasir
Mead of Poetry,
    Inspiration
Mimir
Mimir's Well
Odin
Yggdrasil

Rome

Bona Dea
Ceres
Comus
Fauna
Jupiter
Liber
Luxus
Somnus
Scotland
John Barleycorn
Slav
Nagyasszony
Svantovit

MIDDLE EAST

Egypt

Bes
Hathor
Osiris
Shesemu
Tenemet

Israel

Forbidden Fruit
Noah

Nabataea

Dusares

Persia

Duraosha
Frashmi
Haoma
Saura
Spenta Armaiti

Phrygia

Hyas

Sumer

Dumuzi
Enki
Geshtiananna
Gilgamesh
Im-dugud
Inanna
Ninkasi
Pa-gestin-dug
Siduri
Siris

NORTH AMERICA

Acoma

Corn Goddess
Hummingbird Man

Apache

Coyote
Ho

Ashluslay

Sitche

Blackfoot

Apikunni

Cherokee

Dagul'ku
Hummingbird

Chippewa

Four Manido

Chumash

Hukat
Momoy

Crow

No Vitals
Star Boy

Delaware

Grandfather
   Tobacco

Haida

Raven

Hitchiti

Tobacco Origin
   Story

Iroquois

False Faces
Hawenniyo
Skeleton Man

Joshua

Xowalaci

Kawaiisu

Coyote

Kickapoo

Kitzihiat

Kiowa

Peyote Woman

Menomini

Ma'nabush

Navajo

Sky Father

North America Native American

Gitche Manitou
Hukaht

Ojibway

Nanibozo
Okabewis

Papago

Elder Brother
Tobacco spirit

Penobscot

First Mother

Pima

Cactus Wine Origin Story
Siuuhu
Tobacco Spirit

Pueblo

Corn Goddess

Seneca

Awe-n-ha'i
Deagahgweoses
Hinon

Sioux

White Buffalo Woman
Wohpe

Susquehanna

Sky Maiden

Winnebago

Earthmaker

Yaqui

Tobacco Origin Story

Yokut

Pamashiut
Pichureyt
Tsukit
Ukat

Yuchi

Tobacco Origin Story

Yurok

Pulekukewerek

Zuni

A'neglakya

PACIFIC

Hawaii

Awa-iku
Ewa
Kanaloa
Kane
Makali'i
Maui
Oilikukaheana

Micronesia

Cherri-choulang

Papua

Bege
Ua-ogrere

Polynesia

Alofi
Lea
Lo'au
Miru
Mwatiktiki
Nan-capue
Pap-iea

Pava
Tanna

Samoa

Ava'ali'i
Suasamiavaava

Tagaloa

Tagaloa
Lefanoga

Tahiti	*Tonga*	*Yap*
Hiro	Pufafine	Tereteth
Pu'a		

SOUTH AMERICA

Amazon	*Chibcha*	*Uapes*
Mana	Huitaca	Jurupari

Acawaio	*Choroti*	*Warao*
Tobacco Spirit	Mohsek Eis	Kanabos
		Kurusiwari
Aymara	*Cuiva*	Mawari
Khunu	Namona	
	Yopo Woman	*Yanomamo*
Ayoreo		Hashoriwe
Kachui	*Desana*	Kinkajou
Puopie		Kuripowe
	Coadidop	Tomi-riwe
	Gahpi Mahso	
Cahuilla	Pamuri-gahsiru	*Yupa*
Mukat	Pamuri-mahse	
	Seme-peyaru-pora	Oseema
Cashinaua	Sibia-pora	Yupa
Tobacco Spirit		

References

Abel, Ernest L. *Alcohol Wordlore*. Buffalo: Prometheus Press, 1987.
_____. *Drugs and Behavior: A Primer on Neuropsychopharmacology*. New York: John Wiley & Sons, 1974.
_____. *Marihuana: The First Twelve Thousand Years*. New York: Plenum, 1980.
_____. "Was Fetal Alcohol Syndrome Recognized in the Ancient Near East?" *Alcohol and Alcoholism*, 1997, 32, 3–7.
Adkins, Lesley, and Roy A. Adkins. *Dictionary of Roman Religion*. New York: Facts on File, 1996.
Albert, Bruce, Hans Becher, Donald M. Borgman, Luis Cocco, Marcus E.M. Colchester, and Juan Finkers. *Folk Literature of the Yanomani Indians*. Los Angeles: University of California, 1990.
Albisetti, Cesar, Antonio Colbacchini, and Angel J. Venturelli. *Folk Literature of the Bororo Indians*. Los Angeles: University of California, 1983.
Albright, William F. "The Goddess of Life and Wisdom." *American Journal of Semitic Languages and Literature*, 1920, 36, 258–294.
Alexander, Hartley Burr. *The Mythology of All Races (Latin America)*. Boston: Marshall Jones, 1920, vol. 9.
Ananikian, Mardiros H. *The Mythology of All Races (Armenian)*. Boston: Marshall Jones, 1925.
Andersen, Johannes C. *Myths and Legends of the Polynesians*. New York: Farrar and Rinehart, 1928.
Anderson, Arthur J. O., and Charles E. Dibble. *General History of the Things of New Spain*. Salt Lake City: University of Utah Press, 1950–1982.
Anderson, Edward F. *Peyote: The Divine Cactus*. Tucson: University of Arizona Press, 1996.
Anesaki, Masaharu. *The Mythology of All Races (Japanese)*. Boston: Marshall Jones, 1928, vol. 8.
Arcand, Bernard, Walter Coppens, Isabel Kerr, and Ortiz Gomez Francisco. *Folk Literature of the Cuiva Indians*. Johannes Wilbert and Karin Simoneau (eds.). Los Angeles: University of California Latin American Center Publications, 1991.
Archer, John C. *The Sikhs in Relation to Hindus, Moslems, Christians, and Ahmadiyyas: A Study in Comparative Religion*. Princeton, NJ: Princeton University Press, 1946.

Arenas, Pastor, Jose A. Braunstein, Ana C. Dell'Arciprete, and Fernando P. Larray. *Folk Literature of the Makka Indians.* Johannes Wilbert and Karin Simoneau (eds.). Los Angeles: University of California Latin American Center Publications, 1991.

Armellada, Cesareo, Gustaf Bolinder, M. Candelier, Juan Caudmont, Chaves Melciades, et al. *Folk Literature of the Guajiro Indians.* Johannes Wilbert and Karin Simoneau (eds.). Los Angeles: University of California Latin American Center Publications, 1986.

Bachman, W. Bryant, and Gudmundur Erlingsson. *The Sagas of King Half and King Rolf.* Lanham, MD: University Press of America, 1991.

Bahr, Donald, Juan Smith, William Allison, and Julian Hayden. *Short Swift Time of Gods on Earth. The Hohokam Chronicles.* Berkeley: University of California Press, 1994.

Bancroft, Howard H. *The Works of Howard Howe Bancroft.* San Francisco: The History Company, 1886.

Barnard, Mary. "The God in the Flowerpot." *American Scholar,* 1963, 32, 578–586.

Barnouw, Victor. *Wisconsin Chippewa Myths and Tales and Their Relation to Chippewa Life.* Madison: University of Wisconsin Press.

Barthell, Edward E. *Gods and Goddesses of Ancient Greece.* Coral Gales, FL: University of Miami Press, 1971.

Bean, Lowell J., and Katherine S. Saubel. *Temalpakh. Cahuilla Indian Knowledge and Usage of Plants.* Banning, CA: Malki Museum, 1972.

Beck, Brenda E.F., P.J. Claus, P. Goswami, and J. Handoo. *Folktales of India.* Chicago: University of Chicago Press, 1987.

Beckwith, Martha. *Hawaiian Mythology.* Honolulu: University of Hawaii Press, 1976.

Belier, Wouter W. *Dead Gods: Origin and Development of Georges Dumézil's "Idéologie Tripartite."* Leiden: E.J. Brill, 1991.

Bell, Robert F. *Women of Classical Mythology. A Biographical Dictionary.* Santa Barbara: ABC-Clio, 1991.

Bhattacharji, Sukumari. *The Indian Theology: A Comparative Study of Indian Mythology from the Vegas to the Puranas, 1228–1229.* Cambridge: Cambridge University Press, 1970.

Blackburn, T. *December's Child. A Book Chumash Oral Narratives.* Berkley: University of California Press, 1975.

Bloomfield, Maurice. "Contributions to the Interpretation of the Veda: The Legend of Soma and the Eagle." *Journal of the American Oriental Society,* 1894, 16:1–24.

_____. "The Story of Indra and Namuci." *Journal of the American Oriental Society,* 1893, 15:143–188.

Bompas, Cecil H. *Folklore of the Santal Parganas.* London: David Nutt, 1909.

Bonefoy, Yves. *Mythologies.* Chicago: University of Chicago Press, 1991.

Boone, Elizabeth H. *The Codex Magliabechiano.* Berkley: University of California Press, 1983.

Booth, Martin. *Opium: A History.* New York: Simon & Schuster, 1996.

Bormida, Marcelo, Mario Califano, Ugo Casalegno, Celia O. Mashnshnek, and Luis M. Oefner. *Folk Literature of the Ayoreo Indians.* Johannes Wilbert and Karin Simoneau (eds.). Los Angeles: University of California Latin American Center Publications, 1972.

Bott, Elizabeth, and Edmund Leach. *The Significance of Kava in Tonga Myth and Ritual.* In: J. S. La Fonaine (ed.). *The Interpretation of Ritual.* London: Tavistock, 1972.

Boyce, M. *Haoma Priest of the Sacrifice.* In: W. B. Henning (ed.). *Zoroaster: Politician or Witch-Doctor?* London: Oxford University Press, 1970.

Briffault, Robert. *The Mothers: A Study of Origins and Institutions.* New York: Macmillan, 1927

Briggs, George W. *The Chamars.* London: Oxford University Press, 1920.

Brinton, Daniel G. *Myths of the New World.* New York: Leypold and Holt, 1968.

Brough, John. "Soma and Amanita Muscaria." *Bulletin of the School of Oriental and African Studies,* 1971, 34, 331–362.

Brown, W. Norman. "The Creation Myth of the Rig Veda." *Journal of the American Oriental Society* 1942, 62:85–98.

Budge, E. A. Wallis. *The Gods of the Egyptians.* New York: Dover, 1969.

Cahill, Suzanne E. *Transcendence and Divine Passion: The Queen Mother of the West in Medieval China.* Stanford, CA: Stanford University Press, 1993.

Campbell, J.M. "Note on the Religion of Hemp." Simla, India: Indian Hemp Drugs Commission Report, 1893.

Campbell, Joseph. *The Hero with a Thousand Faces.* Princeton: Princeton University Press, 1968.

Caso, A. *The Aztecs: People of the Sun.* Norman: University of Oklahoma Press, 1958.

Chase-Sardi, Miguel, Maria M. Costa, Celia O. Mashnshnek, Alejandra Sifredi, and Juan A. Tomasini. *Folk Literature of the Nivakle Indians.* Johannes Wilbert and Karin Simoneau (eds.). Los Angeles: University of California Latin American Center Publications, 1976.

Chevalier, Sonia R.B., Alberto V. Fric, Glyn Griffths, Lalervo Oberg, and D. Ribeiro. *Folk Literature of the Caduveo Indians.* Johannes Wilbert and Karin Simoneau (eds.). Los Angeles: University of California Latin American Center Publications, 1972.

Christian, F.W. *The Caroline Islands: Travel in the Sea of Little Islands.* London: Methuen, 1899.

Collocott, E. E. V. "Tales and Poems of Tonga." Honolulu: Bernice Pauahi Bishop Museum Bulletin, 1928.

Coomaraswamy, A. K. *Myths of the Hindus and Buddhists.* London: G. G. Harp, 1920.

Cordeau, Edgardo J. *Folk Literature of the Toba Indians.* Los Angeles: University of California Press, 1982.

Courlander, Harold. *Treasury of African Folklore: Tales of Yoruba Gods and Heroes.* New York: Crown, 1973.

Cox, Paul A. and Sandra A. Banack. *Islands, Plants, and Polynesians: An Introduction to Polynesian Ethnobotany.* Portland, Oregon: Dioscorides Press, 1991.

Craig, Robert D. *Dictionary of Polynesian Mythology.* Westport, CT: Greenwood Press, 1989.

Crooke, W. Ma, and Mal Paharia Male. In: *An Introduction to the Popular Religion and Folklore of Northern Indian.* Allahabad: Government Press, Northwestern Provinces and Oudh, 1894, vol. 8.

Dalby, Andrew. *Bacchus.* Los Angeles: Getty Publications. 2004.

Dange, Sadashiva A. *Myths from the Mahabharata.* 3 vols. New Delhi, India: Aryhan Books International, 1998.

Davidson, Hilda R. E. *Gods and Myths of Northern Europe.* London: Penguin Books, 1964.

_____. *Roles of the Northern Goddess.* New York: Routledge, Keegan Paul, 1998.

Davis, Frederick Hadland. *Japan.* Boston: David D. Nickerson and Co., 1923.

Day, Clarence Burton. *Chinese Peasant Cults: Being a Study of Chinese Paper Gods.* Shanghai, Singapore: Kelly and Walsh, 1940.

De Heusch, Luc. *The Drunken King or the Origin of the State.* Bloomington: Indiana University Press, 1982.

Del Campana, Domenico. *Folk Literature of the Mataco Indians.* Los Angeles: University of California Press, 1982.

DeMallie, Raymond J., and Elaine A. Jahner, (eds.). *Lakota Belief and Ritual.* Lincoln: University of Nebraska Press, 1980.

Dixon-Kennedy, M. *Encyclopedia of Russian and Slavic Myth and Legend.* Santa Barbara, CA: ABC-Clio, 1998.

Donotor, Tekla. *Hungarian Beliefs.* Bloomington: Indiana University Press, 1981.

Doolittle, J. *Social Life of the Chinese.* New York: Harper and Bros., 1865.

Dorson, Richard M. *African Folklore: Origin of Tobacco.* Garden City, NY: Anchor Books, 1972.

_____. *Folk Legends of Japan.* Rutland, VT: Charles E. Tuttle, 1962.

Dowson, John. *A Classical Dictionary of Hindu Mythology and Religion, Geography, History, and Literature.* London: Routledge, Kegan Paul, 1968.

DuBois, Thomas A. *Nordic Religions in the Viking Age.* Philadelphia: University of Pennsylvania Press, 1999.

Dumézil, Georges. *Archaic Roman Religion.* Chicago: University of Chicago Press, 1966.

_____. *Le Festin d'Immortalité. Etude de Mythologie Comparée Indo-Européenne.* Paris, 1924.

Elderkin, George W. "The Banquet-libations of the Greeks." *American Journal of Philology,* 1945, 66, 425–430.

Ellwood, Robert S. *The Feast of Kingship: Accession Ceremonies in Ancient Japan.* Tokyo: Sophia University, 1973.

Elwin, Verrier. *Myths of Middle India.* Delhi: Oxford University Press, 1991.

_____. *Myths of the North-East Frontier of India.* Shillong, India: North-East Frontier Agency, 1958.

_____. *Tribal Myths of Orissa.* Oxford: Oxford University Press, 1954.

Euripides. *The Bacchae.* New York: Farrar Strauss, 1990.

Farnell, Lewis R. *The Cults of the Greek States.* Oxford: Clarendon Press, 1909.

Farrand, Livingston, and Leo J. Frachenberg. "Shasta and Athapascan Myths from Oregon." *Journal of American Folklore*, 1915, 28:207–242.

Fee, Christopher R., and David A. Leeming. *Gods, Heroes, and Kings: The Battle for Mythic Britain.* Oxford: University Press, 2001.

Ferguson, John C. *The Mythology of All Races (China).* Boston: Marshall Jones Company, vol. 8, 1928.

Fernandez, J. W. *Bwiti: An Ethnography of the Religous Imagination in Africa.* Princeton: Princton University Press, 1982.

Firth, Raymond. *Rank and Religion in Tikopia.* London: George Allen and Unwin, 1970.

Fison, Lorimer. *Tales from Old Fiji.* Papakura, New Zealand: McMillan Press, 1924.

Ford, Patrick K. *The Mabinogi and Other Medieval Welsh Tales.* Berkeley: University of California Press, 1977.

Fowler, Murray. "The Role of Sura in the Myth of Namuci." *Journal of the American Oriental Society* 1942, 62:36–40.

Fox, William S. *The Mythology of All Races (Greek and Roman).* Boston: Marshall Jones Co., vol. 1, 1916.

Frey, Rodney. *The World of the Crow Indians.* Norman: Oklahoma University Press, 1987.

Fuller, Robert C. *Stairways to Heaven: Drugs in American Religious History.* Boulder, CO: Westview Press, 2000.

Furst, Peter T. *Flesh of the Gods.* New York: Praeger, 1972.

_____. "The 'Half-Bad' Kauyumari: Trickster-Culture Hero of the Huichols." *Journal of Latin American Lore,* 1977, 20:97–124.

_____. *Hallucinogens and Culture.* San Francisco: Chandler and Sharp, 1976.

_____. "Tobacco." In: Eliade, Mircea (ed.). *The Encyclopedia of Religion.* New York: Macmillan, 1995.

Gagliano, Joseph A. *Coca Prohibition in Peru.* Tucson: University of Arizona Press, 1994.

Gantz, Timothy. *Early Greek Myths: A Guide to Literary and Artistic Sources.* Baltimore: Johns Hopkins University Press, 1993.

Gayley, Charles M. *The Classic Myths in English Literature and in Art.* Boston: Ginn, 1911.

Gifford, Edward W. *Tongan Myths and Tales.* Honolulu: Bernice P. Bishop Museum Bulletin, 1924.

Gill, Samuel D., and Irene F. Sullivan. *Dictionary of Native American Mythology.* Santa Barbara, CA: ABC-Clio, 2002.

Ginsberg, Louis. *Legends of the Jews.* New York: Simon and Schuster, 1961.

Glendenning, Robert J. "The Archetypal Structure of Hymidqvida." *Folklore* (London), 91, 1980, 92–110.

Goodman, Felicitas. D. *Ecstasy, Ritual, and Alternative Reality.* Bloomington: Indiana University Press, 1988.

Gorer, Geoffrey. *Himalayan Village: An Account of the Lepchas of Sikkim.* London: Michael Joseph, 1938.

Grantham, Bill. *Creation Myths and Legends of the Creek Indians.* Gainesville: University of Florida Press, 2002.

Graulich, Michel. *Myths of Ancient Mexico*. Norman: University of Oklahoma, 1997, 106–107.

Graves, Robert. *The Greek Myths*. Middlesex, England: Penguin Books, 1992.

_____. *The White Goddess*. New York: Farrar, Straus and Giroux, 1966.

Green, Miranda. *The Gods of the Celts*. Totowa, NJ: Barnes and Noble, 1986.

Greimas, Algirdas J. *Of Gods and Men: Studies in Lithuanian Mythology*. Bloomington: Indiana University Press, 1992.

Grimal, Pierre. *The Dictionary of Classical Mythology*. New York: Blackwell Publishing, 1996.

Guerra, Francisco. *The Pre-Columbian Mind: A Study Into the Aberrant Nature of Sexual Drives, Drugs Affecting Behavior, and the Attitude Towards Life and Death with a Survey of Psychotherapy in Pre-Columbian America*. New York: Seminar Press, 1971.

Gupta, Shakti M. "Plant Myths and Traditions." In: O'Flaherity, W. (ed.). *Origin of Evil in India*. Leiden: E.J. Brill, 1971.

Guss, David M. *To Weave and Sing: Art, Symbol, and Narrative in the South American Rainforest*. Berkeley: University of California Press, 1989.

Guthrie, W. K. C. *The Greeks and Their Gods*. Boston: Beacon Press, 1955.

Hamblin, Dora J. *The First Cities: Emergence of Man*. New York: Time Life Books, 1983.

Hammon, N. G. L., and H. H. Scullard. *The Oxford Classical Dictionary*. Oxford: Clarendon Press, 1970.

Handy, E. S. C., and Elizabeth G. Handy. *Native Planters in Old Hawaii: Their Life, Lore, and Environment*. Honolulu: Bishop Museum Press, 1972.

Harner, Michael J. *The Jivaro. People of the Sacred Waterfalls*. Garden City, NY: Anchor Books, 1972.

_____. "The Role of Hallucinogenic Plants in European Witchcraft." In: Harner, M. J. (ed.). *Hallucinogens and Shamanism*. NY: Oxford University Press, 1973.

Henry, Teuri. *Ancient Tahiti*. New York: Krausse, 1971.

Herzfeld, Ernst. *Zoroaster and His World*. Princeton: University Press, 1947.

Hinnels, John R. *Persian Mythology*. London: Hamlyn, 1983.

Hoffman, W. J. "Mythology of the Menomoni Indians." *American Anthropologist*, 1890, 3:243–258.

Holmber, Uno. *The Mythology of All Races (Finno-Ugric, Siberian)*. Boston: Marshall Jones, vol. 4, 1927.

Hudson, Travis, and Ernest Underhay. *Crystals in the Sky: An Intellectual Odyssey Involving Chumash Astronomyu, Cosmology and Rock Art*. Santa Barbara: Ballena Press, 1978.

Hultkranz, Aku. *The Attraction of Peyote*. Stockholm: Almquist and Winksell, 1997.

Hunt, Eva. *The Transformation of the Hummingbird: Cultural Roots of a Zinacanecan Mythical Poem*. Ithaca: Cornell University Press, 1977.

Hyams, Edward. *Dionysus: A Social History of the Wine Vine*. New York: Macmillan, 1965.

Jacobsen, Thorkild. *The Treasures of Darkness*. New Haven, CT: Yale University Press, 1976.

Janson, H. W. *Apes and Ape Lore in the Middle Ages and the Renaissance*. London: University of London, 1952.

Jayne, Walter A. *The Healing Gods of Ancient Civilizations*. New York: University Books, 1962.

Jobes, Gertrude. *Dictionary of Mythology Folklore and Symbols*. New York: Scarecrow Press, 1961.

Jochelson, W. *The Yakut*. New York: American Museum of Natural History, 1933.

Johnston, Basil. *Ojibway Heritage*. Lincoln: University of Nebraska Press, 1990.

Josephsson, C. "Wine, Women and Men." In: Clare Josefsson (ed.). *Politics of Chaos Essays on Kuba Myth, Development and Death*. University of Gothenburg, Department of Social Anthropology, 1994, www.algonet.se/~claes4 /antro/claes8.htm.

Jones, George, and Thomas Jones. *Mabinogion*. London: Dent Everyman, 1984.

Karsten, Rafael. *The Civilization of the South American Indians*. New York: Alfred A. Knopf, 1926.

_____. *The Head-Hunters of Western Amazons: The Life and Culture of the Jibaro Indians of Eastern Ecuador and Peru*. Helsingfors, Germany: Adademische Buchhandlung, 1935.

_____. *Indian Tribes of the Argentine and Bolivian Chaco*. Helsingfors, Germany: Adademische Buchhandlung, 1931.

Keith, A. Berriedale. *The Mythology of All Races*. Boston: Marshall Jones, 1917, vol. 6.

Kelly, Walter K. *Curiosities of Indo-European Tradition and Folk-Lore*. Detroit: Singing Tree Press, 1969.

Kennedy, Joseph. *Coca Exotica*. Rutherford, NJ: Farleigh Dickenson University Press, 1985.

Kerenyi, Carl. *Dionysos Archetypal Image of Indestructible Life*. New Jersey: Princeton University Press, 1976.

Knapp, Bettina L. *Women in Myth*. Albany: State University of New York Press, 1997.

Knipe, David M. "The Heroic Theft: Myths from Rgveda IV and the Ancient Near East." *History of Religions*, 1967, 6, 328–360.

Kolata, Alan L. *Valley of the Spirits: A Journey into the Lost Realm of the Aymara*. New York: John Wiley & Sons, 1996.

Kroeber, A. L. *Yurok Myths*. Berkeley: University of California Press, 1976.

Landgon, Stephen H. *The Mythology of All Races (Semitic)*. Boston: Marshall Jones, vol. 5, 1931.

Latorre, Felipe A., and Dolores L. Latorre. *The Mexican Kickapoo Indians*. Austin: University of Texas Press, 1976.

Leach, Maria (ed.). *Funk and Wagnall's Standard Dictionary of Folklore, Mythology and Legend*. New York: Funk and Wagnall's, 1949.

Lebot, Vincent, Mark Merlin, and Lamont Linstrom. *Kava the Pacific Drug*. New Haven: Yale University Press, 1992.

Leeming, David, and Jake Page. *Goddess: Myths of the Female Divine*. New York: Oxford University Press, 1994.

Lemaistre, Denis. "The Deer That Is Peyote and the Deer That Is Maize. The Hunt in the Huichol 'Trinity.'" In: Stacy B. Schaeffer and Peter T. Furst (eds.). *People of the Peyote.* Albuquerque: University of New Mexico Press, 1996.

Lesko, L. H. "The Middle Kingdom." In: Lesko, B.S. (ed.). *Women's Earliest Records from Ancient Egypt and Western Asia.* Atlanta: Scholars Press, 1989.

Levi-Strauss, C. *From Honey to Ashes.* London: Cape, 1973.

Lindow, John. *Handbook of Norse Mythology.* Santa Barbara: ABC-Clio, 2001.

Littleton, C. Scott. "The Holy Grail, the Cauldron of Annwn, and the Nartyamonga: A Further Note on the Sarmatian Connection." *Journal of American Folklore*, 1979, 92, 326–333.

Lowie, Robert H. *The Crow Indians.* New York: Farrar & Rinehart, 1935.

Lumholtz, Carl. *New Trails in Mexico.* New York: Charles Scribner's Sons, 1912.

Lutz, H. *Viticulture and Brewing in the Ancient Orient.* New York: J. C. Heinricks, 1922.

MacCulloch, J. A. *The Religion of the Ancient Celts.* Folcroft Library Edition, 1977.

MacDonell, A. A. *Vedic Mythology.* New York: Gordon Press, 1974.

MacKenzie, Donald A. *Myths of Pre-Columbian America.* Boston: Longwood Press, 1978.

MacKillop, James. *Dictionary of Celtic Mythology.* New York: Oxford University Press, 1998.

Mahapatra, Sitakant. *The Realm of the Sacred: Verbal Symbolism and Ritual Structures.* Calcutta, India: Oxford University Press, 1992.

Mahony, William K. *The Artful Universe: An Introduction to the Vedic Religious Imagination.* Albany: State University of New York Press, 1998.

Mason, J. W. T. *The Meaning of Shinto.* New York: E. P. Dutton & Co., 1935.

_____. *The Meaning of Shinto: The Primaeval Foundation of Creative Spirit in Modern Japan.* Port Washington, New York: Kennkat Press, 1967.

Mayer, Fanny H. *The Yanagita Kunia Guide to the Japanese Folk Tale.* Bloomington: Indiana University Press, 1986.

McGee, R. Jon. *Life, Ritual, and Religion among the Lacandon Maya.* Belmont, CA: Wadsworth Publishing Co., 1990.

McLeish, Kenneth. *Myths and Legends of the World Explored.* New York: Facts on File, 1996.

Mercantante, Anthony S. *The Facts on File Encyclopedia of World Mythology and Legends.* New York: Facts on File, 1987.

Metzner, Ralph. *The Well of Remembrance: Rediscovering the Earth Wisdom Myths of Northern Europe.* Boston: Shambbala, 1994.

Meyerhoff, Barbara G. *The Peyote Hunt: The Sacred Journey of the Huichol Indians.* Ithaca: Cornell University Press, 1974.

Miller, Jeanine. *The Vision of Cosmic Order in the Vedas.* London: Routledge, Kegan Paul, 1998.

Miller, Mary, and Karl Taube. *The Gods and Symbols of Ancient Mexico and the Maya.* London: Thames & Hudson, 1993.

Miyahara, Kunie. "The Psychotropic Kieri in Huichol Culture." In: Stacy B. Schaefer and Peter T. Furst (eds.). *People of the Peyote: Huichol Indian History, Religion and Survival.* Albuquerque: University of New Mexico Press, 1996, 235–263.

Modi, Jivanji J. *Haoma.* In: Hastings, James (ed.). *Encyclopedia of Religion and Ethics.* New York: Charles Scribner & Sons, 1914, vol. 6, 506–510.

Moises, Rosalio, Jane H. Kelley and William Curry Holden. *The Tall Candle: The Personal Chronicle of a Yaqui Indian.* Lincoln: University of Nebraska Press, 1971.

Mooney, James. *Mythos of the Cherokees.* 1900. Repr. St. Claire Shores, Michigan: Scholarly Press, 1970.

Moore, Jerry D. "Pre-Hispanic Beer in Coastal Peru: Technology and Social Context of Prehistoric Production." *American Anthropologist* 1989, 91:682–695.

Morris, Edward Opler. *Myths and Tales of the Jicarilla Apache Indians.* New York: American Folklore Society, 1938.

Morse, Roger A. *Making Mead.* Cheshire, CT: Wisuas Press, 1998.

Muller, Max. *The Mythology of All Races.* Boston: Marshal Jones, 1918.

Nagar, Shantilal. *Indian Gods and Goddesses.* 2 vols. New Delhi, India: British Publishing Co. 1991.

Naranjo, Plutarco. "Hallucinogenic Plant Use and Related Indigenous Belief Systems in the Ecuadorian Amazon." *Journal of Ethnopharmacology* 1:121–145, 1979.

New Larousse Encyclopedia of Mythology. New York: Putnam Press, 1968.

Nicholson, Henry B. "The Octli Cult in Late Pre-Hispanic Central Mexico." In: David Carrasco (ed.). *To Change Places: Aztec Ceremonial Landscapes.* Niwot: University Press of Colorado, 1991.

Nicholson, Irene. *Mexican and Central American Mythology.* London: Hamlyn, 1967.

Nonnos. *The Epic of Dionysiaca.* Cambridge: Harvard University Press, 1940.

O'Meara, J. *The Voyage of Saint Brendan.* Atlantic Highlands, NJ: Humanities Press, 1976.

Oosten, Jarich G. *The War of the Gods.* London: Routledge, Kegan Paul, 1985.

Orchard, Andy. *Dictionary of Norse Myth and Legend.* London: Cassell, 1997.

Osborne, Harold. *South American Mythology.* New York: Peter Bedrick, 1983.

Parker, Arthur C. *Seneca Myths and Folk Tales.* New York: Buffalo Historical Society, 1923.

Parry, Hugh. *Visions of Enchantment.* Lanham, MD: University Press of America, 2001.

Pas, Julian F. *Historical Dictionary of Taoism.* Lanham, MD: Scarecrow Press, 1998.

Pausanias. *Descriptions of Greece.* London: Heinemann, 1918.

Penn, W. A. *The Soverane Herbe: A History of Tobacco.* London: Grant Richards, 1902.

Petrullo, Vincenzo. *The Diabolic Root: A Study of Peyotism, the New Indian Religion, Among the Delawares.* New York: Octagon Books, 1934.

Piankoff, A. *The Shrines of Tut-Ankh-Amon*. New York: Pantheon Books, 1955.

Plato. *Symposium*. Cambridge: Heffer, 1932.

Porphyry. "On the Homeric Cave of the Nymphs." In: *Selected Works of Porphyry*. Guildford: Promethus Trust, 1999.

Powell, Barry B. *Classical Myth*. Upper Saddle River, NJ: Prentice Hall, 2001.

Powell, J. W. *Myths of the Cherokee*. Smithsonian Institute Bureau of American Ethnology, 19th Annual Report, 1897–98. Washington, DC: Government Printing Office, 1900.

Price, Simon, and Emily Kearns. *The Oxford Dictionary of Classical Myth and Religion*. Oxford: Oxford University Press, 2003.

Probert Encyclopedia. www.probert-encyclopedia.co.uk.

Quinn, Vernon. *Leaves: Their Place in Life and Legend*. New York: Frederick A. Stokes, 1937.

Radin, Paul. *Indians of South America*. Garden City, NY: Doubleday, Doran, 1942.

_____. *The Trickster: A Study in American Indian Mythology*. New York: Schocken Books, 1972.

_____. *The Winnebago Tribe*. Lincoln: University of Nebraska Press, 1990.

Ratsch, Christian. *Dictionary of Sacred and Magical Plants*. Bridgeport, England: Prism Press, 1992.

Reed, Alma M. *The Ancient Past of Mexico*. New York: Crown Publishers, 1966.

Reichard, Gladys A. *Navaho Religion: A Study of Symbolism*. Tucson: University of Arizona Press, 1983.

Reichel-Dolmatoff, Gerardo. *Amazonian Cosmos: The Sexual and Religious Symbolism of the Tukano Indians*. Chicago: University of Chicago Press, 1971.

_____. *Beyond the Milky Way: Hallucinatory Imagery of the Tukano Indians*. Los Angeles: Latin American Center Publications, 1978.

_____. *Rainforest Shamans: Essays on the Tukano Indians of the Northwest Amazon*. Devon: Themis Books, 1997.

_____. *The Shaman and the Jaguar*. Philadelphia: Temple University Press, 1975.

Rhys, John. *Lectures on the Origin and Growth of Religion as Illustrated by Celtic Heathendom*. Oxford: Williams and Norgate, 1898.

Ripinsky-Naxon, Michael. *The Nature of Shamanism: Substance and Function of a Religious Metaphor*. Albany: State University of New York Press, 1993.

Robertson, Noel. "Athens' Festival of the New Wine." *Harvard Studies in Classical Philology*, 1993, 95, 197–250.

Robicsek, Francis. *The Smoking Gods: Tobacco in Maya Art, History, and Religion*. Norman: University of Oklahoma Press, 1978.

Rosenthal, F. *The Herb*. Leiden: E. J. Brill, 1971.

Ross, Anne. *Pagan Celtic Britain: Studies in Iconography and Tradition*. London: Routledge, Keegan Paul, 1967.

Ruck, Carl A. P., Jeremy Bigwood, Danny Staples, Jonathan Ott, and R. Gordon Wasson. "Entheogens." *Journal of Psychedelic Drugs*, 1979, 11:144–146.

Ruck, Carl A. P., Blaise D. Staples, and Clark Heinrich. *The Apples of Apollo: Pagan and Christian Mysteries of the Eucharist*. Durham: Carolina Academic Press, 2001.

Rudgley, Richard. *The Encyclopedia of Psychoactive Substances*. New York: St. Martin's Press, 1998.

Rydberg, Victor. *Teutonic Mythology: Gods and Goddesses of the Northland*. New York: Norroena Society, 1907.

Samorini, G. "The Bwiti Religion and the Psychoactive Plant Tabernanthe iboga (Equatorial Africa)." www.ibogaine.org/Samorini.html.

Sanders, Tao T. L. *Dragons, Gods and Spirits from Chinese Mythology*. New York: P. Bedrick Books, 1980.

Schaeffer, Stacy B., and Peter T. Furst (eds.). *People of the Peyote*. Albuquerque: University of New Mexico Press, 1996.

Schultes, Richard E., and Albert Hofmann. *Plants of the Gods: Their Sacred, Healing, and Hallucinogenic Powers*. Rochester, VT: Healing Arts Press, 1998.

Scott, J. L. *The Age of Fable*. Philadelphia: David Mackay, 1898.

Setchell, W. A. "Aboriginal Tobbacos." *American Anthropologist*, 1921, 23, 402.

Simek, Rudolf. *Dictionary of Northern Mythology*. Cambridge: D. S. Brewer, 1984.

Smart, Ninian. *Dimensions of the Sacred: An Anatomy of the World's Beliefs*. Berkeley: University of California Press, 1996.

Speck, Frank. *Ethnology of the Yuchi Indians*. Philadelphia: University of Pennsylvania Press, 1909.

Spence, Lewis. *The Civilization of Ancient Mexico*. Cambridge: Cambridge University Press, 1912.

_____. *Myths and Legends: Mexico and Peru*. New York: Dingwall-Rock Ltd., 1911.

Steubel, C., and B. Herman. *Tala o le Vavau: The Myths, Legends and Customs of Old Samoa*. Auckland, New Zealand: Polynesian Press, 1987.

Stevens-Arroyo, Antonio M. *Cave of the Jaqua: The Mythological World of the Tainos*. Albuquerque: University of New Mexico Press, 1988.

Stevenson, Matilda C. *Ethnobotany of the Zuni Indians*. Washington, DC: Bureau of American Ethnology, 1915.

Stewart, Omer C. *Peyote Religion: A History*. Norman: University of Oklahoma Press, 1987.

Stewart, R. J. *Celtic Gods and Celtic Goddesses*. London: Blandford, 1990.

Stutley, Margaret. *Shamanism: An Introduction*. London: Routledge, 2003.

Sullivan, Lawrence E. *Icanchu's Drum: An Orientation to Meaning in South American Religions*. New York: Macmillan, 1988

Swanton, John. *Myths and Tales of the Southeastern Indians*. Washington, DC: Government Printing Office, 1929.

Sykes, Egerton. *Who's Who in Non-Classical Mythology*. New York: Routledge, 1995.

Thompson, J., and A. Eric. *Maya History and Religion*. Norman: University of Oklahoma Press, 1970.

Titcomb, Margaret. "Kava in Hawaii." *Journal of the Polynesian Society* 1948, 57:105–169.

Torday, E. "Bushongo Mythology." *Folk-Lore* 1919, 22:41–47.

_____. *On the Trail of the Bushong*. London: Seeley, Service and Co., 1925.

Torrance, Robert M. *The Spiritual Quest: Transcendece in Myth, Religion, and Science*. Berkeley: University of Califronia Press, 1994.

Turville-Petre, E. O. G. *Myth and Religion of the North: The Religion of Ancient Scandinavia*. Westport, CT: Greenwood Press, 1964.

Underhill, Ruth M. *Papago Indian Religion*. New York: Columbia University Press, 1946.

Unwin, Tim. *Wine and the Vine: An Historical Geography of Viticulture and the Wine Trade*. London: Routledge, 1991.

Vaillant, George C. *Aztecs of Mexico*. New York: Doubleday, Doran, 1941.

Walker, Benjamin. *The Hindu World*. New York: Frederick A. Praeger, 1968.

Wasson, R. Gordon. *Soma, Divine Mushroom of Immortality*. New York: Harcourt Brace Jovanovich, 1971.

Wasson, R. Gordon, Albert Hofman, and Carl A.P. Ruck. *The Road to Eleusis: Unraveling the Secrets of the Mysteries*. New York: Harcourt Brace, 1978.

Weil, Andrew. *The Natural Mind*. Boston: Houghton Miffin, 1972.

Weiss, Gerald. *Campa Mythology: The World of a Forest Tribe in South America*. New York: American Museum of Natural History, 1925.

Werner, Edward T. C. *A Dictionary of Chinese Mythology*. Shanghai, Singapore: Kelly and Walsh, 1932.

Whitten, Norman E. "Ecological Imagery and Cultural Adaptability: The Canelos Quicha of Eater Ecuador." *American Anthropologist* 1978, 80:836–859.

Wilbert, Johannes. *Folk Literature of the Warao Indians*. Los Angeles: University of California, 1970.

_____. *Tobacco and Shamanism in South America*. New Haven: Yale University Press, 1987.

_____. *Yupa Folktales*. Los Angeles: University of California Press, 1974.

Williamson, Robert W. *Religious and Cosmic Beliefs of Central Polynesia*. Cambridge: Cambridge University Press, 1933.

Winter, Joseph C. (ed.). *Tobacco Use by Native North Americans: Sacred Smoke and Silent Killer*. Norman: University of Oklahoma Press, 2000.

Wolkstein, Dianne. *Inanna, Queen of Heaven and Earth*. New York: Harper and Row, 1983.

Worthen, Thomas D. *The Myth of Replacement*. Tucson: University of Arizona Press, 1991.

Wright, F. A. "The Food of the Gods." *Classical Review* 1917, 31: 4–6.

Yamamuro, Bufo. "Notes on Drinking in Japan." In: MacMarshall (ed.). *Beliefs, Behaviors, and Alcoholic Beverages: A Cross Cultural Survey*. Ann Arbor: University of Michigan Press, 1979, 270–288.

Younger, W. *Gods, Men and Wine*. London: Wine and Food Society, 1966.

Yu, Ronghe. "The Legend of the Historic Liquor 'Du Kang.'" *www.chinesefood.about.com/library/weekly/aa042800a*.

Zafiropulo, Jean. *Mead and Wine: A History of the Bronze Age in Greece*. London: Sidgwick and Jackson, 1966.

Zigmond, Maurice L. *Kawaiisu Mythology: An Oral Tradition of South-Central California*. Socorro, NM: Ballena Press, 1980.

Zimmer, Heinrich R. *Myths and Symbols in Indian Art and Civilization.* New York: Pantheon Books, 1963.

Znayenko, Myroslava T. *The Gods of the Ancient Slavs: Tatlishchev and the Beginnings of Slavic Mythology.* Columbus, OH: Slavica, 1980.

Index